n Studying N.T. I say.
1 Know what's in the Book
2. Leading Doctrines
3 Geography

Al. Pero

D1297230

Introduction

to the

Books of the Bible

By

CHRISTOPHER F. DREWES

ST. LOUIS, MO.
CONCORDIA PUBLISHING HOUSE
1929

PRINTED IN U. S. A.

FOREWORD.

Ever since God made a beginning of communicating His messages to man in writing by giving two tables of stone to Moses (Ex. 31, 18), Bible-reading has been a sacred privilege and duty of all believers. The Savior restated God's will that man should study His writings when He told both foes and friends to "search the Scriptures." John 5, 39. In the trying times of the Early Church many Christians paid for the privilege of reading the Word of God with their life-blood. The glory of the Reformation was the return of the open Bible into the hands and homes of the laity. To this day the Church of the Reformation sings: —

> A trusty weapon is Thy Word,
> Thy Church's buckler, shield, and sword;
> Lord, let us in this Word abide
> That we may seek no other guide.

The Bible is an outstanding book for its clearness, and every reader is able to learn from its pages God's plan of salvation. Yet the valuable information contained in this book will add greatly to intelligent Bible-reading in family worship, in schools and Bible classes, and in the private study of Scripture by Bible students. A knowledge of the language, composition, writer, authenticity, and outline of the various books of the Bible as given in this little volume will deepen the interest and add to the understanding of God's Book. The references to the wonderful preservation of God's Word through the ages as well as the simple directions on how to read God's Book will certainly meet with approval. At the end of the volume the reader will find a plan showing how the Bible can be read in one or three years.

The three classes of Bible-readers here mentioned will find this handbook of great practical value. The father or mother will find that the interest will be deepened in the reading of any book of the Bible in family worship after a brief review, as given in this handy volume, of the circumstances under which that Book was written. The answer to many questions directed by attentive children to their parents after the regular period of family devotion will be found here. The Bible readers in schools and Bible classes will find this book very helpful in their study of the Scriptures. In day-schools this book should serve very well to lead the pupils into the Bible itself. For the purpose of this book is not merely to add another volume to the many writings *about* the Bible, but to lead its readers into an intelligent study *of* the Bible. Bible classes in Sunday-schools will find this a valuable text-book for a one-year course of Bible study. Finally, all Bible students desiring to follow a well-planned method in their private study of the sacred Scriptures will find in this book a trusty guide.

We pray that this book may receive an even greater popular acclaim than did the *Concordia Bible Class* for the year 1919, in which the main parts contained in this book were originally published. The division into chapters found in the *Concordia Bible Class* has been retained. Many readers will welcome this.

May this volume become a blessing to many.

January 19, 1929. WM. H. LUKE.

Prayer.

Blessed Lord, who hast caused all the Holy Scriptures to be written for our learning, grant that we may in such wise hear them, read, mark, learn, and inwardly digest them, that by patience and comfort of Thy Holy Word we may embrace, and ever hold fast, the blessed hope of everlasting life which Thou hast given us in our Savior Jesus Christ. Amen.

CHAPTER 1.

The Holy Book.

Part I.

WHAT IS THE BIBLE? — The book which we are about to study is known as the *Bible*. This name is first found in Chrys'-os-tom, who lived from 347 to 407 after Christ. What is the Bible? The Bible is the written Word of God, or the collection of sacred writings from which we Christians get our religion. The name *Bible* is derived from the Greek language, in which *biblia* means *books*. So this name suggests that the Bible is really a collection of books, a divine library. As a matter of fact there are sixty-six (66) books in the Bible, written by many human authors.

OTHER NAMES OF THE BIBLE. — The Bible is also called the *Scriptures*, that is, the *Writings*, or *Writ*, because its sixty-six books were *written* by the prophets, e-van'-gel-ists, and apostles. Prior to the invention of the printing-press, in 1450, copies of the Sacred Volume had to be made by writing. The Latin Bible, called the Vul'-gate, was the first book printed by John Gutenberg, in 1455. It took him five years to print it. Here follow some of the passages in which the Bible is called the Scriptures: "Jesus saith unto them, Did ye never read in the *Scriptures?*" Matt. 21, 42. "Ye do err, not knowing the *Scriptures.*" Matt. 22, 29. "He opened to us the *Scriptures.*" Luke 24, 32. "Search the *Scriptures.*" John 5, 39. "They searched the *Scriptures* daily." Acts 17, 11. "Apollos, an eloquent man and mighty in the *Scriptures.*" Acts 18, 24.

Twice the Bible is called the *Holy* Scriptures, that is, the Sacred Writings. "Which He had promised afore by His prophets in the *Holy* Scriptures." Rom. 1, 2. "From a child [that is, from childhood] thou hast known the *Holy* Scriptures." 2 Tim. 3, 15. Translating this Latin title, we call the Bible *Holy Writ.* Can you mention a reason why the Bible is properly called *holy?* Here are several reasons:

1. God, who is the real Author of the Bible, is holy.
2. God used holy men in giving us His written Word.
3. The Bible contains holy and divine things.
4. God sanctifies men through the reading and study of His Book.

The Bible is also called *the Word of God.* Heb. 4, 12: "*The Word of God* is quick [living] and powerful." St. Paul calls the Scriptures the *oracles of God,* that is, the things spoken by God. He writes, Rom. 3, 2: "Unto them [to the Jews] were committed the *oracles of God.*" These names and titles mark out the Bible as being a book quite distinct from all the writings of men. They tell us that God is the Author of this holy Book, while all the other books in the world have human authors.

WHEN WAS THE BIBLE WRITTEN? — Moses was the first man whom God told to write the words which He spoke. We read Ex. 17, 14: "The Lord said unto Moses, Write this for a memorial in a book." Moses lived about 2,500 years after the beginning of the world. During those 2,500 years God frequently spoke to Adam, Noah, Abraham, and other holy men. Yet we do not read that any of these holy men were commanded by God to put the words which He spoke to them into a book. There was no urgent need of a Bible during those twenty-five centuries. Why not? Because the human family was relatively small and because men lived to a very great age and were thus able to hand down to their children and their children's children what God had spoken to them. The record shows, for instance, that Adam lived 56 years after the birth of La´-mech, who was his descendant in the eighth generation and the father of Noah. And Abraham was born 150 years before the death of Shem, Noah's son. But when men multiplied on earth and the span of human life grew short, God in His goodness determined that His Word should be committed to writing. God Himself made the beginning when He wrote the Ten Commandments on two tables of stone with His own finger. Ex. 31, 18.

However, the books of the Bible were not all written in the days of Moses. Moses lived about 1,500 years before Christ, but the last book of the Bible was written about 100 years after Christ. During these sixteen hundred years God from time to time moved various holy men to add to His Book. Altogether, about forty persons, in all stations of life, were engaged in the writing of the oracles of God.

Although the Bible was written during such a long period of time and by so many different men, this Book of the Lord nowhere contradicts itself. This perfect agreement of all its writers is a plain proof of the divine origin of the Bible.

THE LANGUAGES IN WHICH THE BIBLE WAS WRITTEN. The Bible was not written in English, but in Hebrew and Greek. The books of the Old Testament were written in Hebrew, the language of the Jews, while the books of the New Testament were all written in Greek. Greek was the language commonly spoken throughout the civilized world in the days of the holy apostles and e-van´-gel-ists. You may wish to know how Hebrew and Greek look. We shall print a sample of each. But remember that in reading Hebrew you begin at the right hand and read to the left.

בְּרֵאשִׁית בָּרָא אֱלֹהִים אֵת הַשָּׁמַיִם וְאֵת הָאָרֶץ

Gen. 1, 1, in Hebrew.

Οὕτως γὰρ ἠγάπησεν ὁ θεὸς τὸν κόσμον, ὥστε τὸν υἱὸν τὸν μονογενῆ ἔδωκεν, ἵνα πᾶς ὁ πιστεύων εἰς αὐτὸν μὴ ἀπόληται, ἀλλ᾽ ἔχῃ ζωὴν αἰώνιον.

John 3, 16, in Greek.

GENERAL DIVISION OF THE BIBLE. — The 66 books of the Bible were written in two distinct periods. Some (39) were written *before* the coming of Christ into the world and are called the books of the Old Testament, while the others (27) were written *after* the coming of Christ and are called the books of the New Testament. The numbers 39 and 27 may be remembered by the number of letters in the names Old Testament and New Testament: —

Old (3) Testament (9)   — 39
New (3) Testament (9) 3×9 = 27
————
66

SPECIAL DIVISIONS OF THE BIBLE. — The books of the Old Testament are usually arranged in *three* groups: 1. *Historical* books. These contain history. 2. *Poetical* books. These contain sacred poetry. 3. *Prophetical* books. These contain prophecy. The books of the New Testament admit of a similar arrangement into three groups: 1. *Historical* books. 2. *Doctrinal* books. These contain doctrine, or teaching. 3. One *prophetical* book. — The Bible student should, of course, commit to memory the names of the books of the Bible. By memorizing them by groups, he will more easily remember them. A classification of the books of the Bible is given on page 6.

THE TWO CHIEF DOCTRINES OF THE BIBLE. — There are many doctrines, or teachings, in the Scriptures. The main doctrines are two in number: the *Law* and the *Gospel.* Both agree in these points: 1. Both doctrines come from God. 2. Both doctrines are intended for all men. 3. Both doctrines will remain in force to the end of the world. Nevertheless the Law and the Gospel are two distinct and utterly diverse doctrines. Unless you are able to see the difference between both, you will be unable to understand the Bible; the Bible will remain a book sealed with seven seals.

What is the *Law?* The Law is that part of the Bible in which God tells us how we are to be and what we are to do or not to do. The Law is briefly summed up in the holy Ten Commandments. God has annexed both a threat and a promise to His Law. He threatens to punish all that transgress His commandments. But He promises every blessing to all that keep His commandments. Since we have all broken the divine Law and sinned, it condemns us all, calling down upon us God's wrath and displeasure, temporal death, and eternal damnation.

What is the *Gospel?* The Gospel is that part of the Bible in which God assures us that He is gracious to us, forgiving us all our sins and opening heaven to us for the sake of His Son, who suffered and died for our sins. So the Gospel is the most important teaching of the Bible. The Holy Book was written because of the Gospel and not because of the Law.

DIVISION INTO CHAPTERS AND VERSES. — The Bible is divided into 1,189 chapters and 31,175 verses. This division was not made by the holy writers. In the oldest copies of the Scriptures which have come down to us not even the words are divided. You will be able to see this at once when you look at the section taken from the oldest

THE BOOKS OF THE OLD TESTAMENT.

		Chapters
History	Genesis	50
	Exodus	40
	Leviticus	27
	Numbers	36
	Deuteronomy	34
	Joshua	24
	Judges	21
	Ruth	4
	I. Samuel	31
	II. Samuel	24
	I. Kings	22
	II. Kings	25
	I. Chronicles	29
	II. Chronicles	36
	Ezra	10
	Nehemiah	13
	Esther	10
Poetry	Job	42
	Psalms	150
	Proverbs	31
	Ecclesiastes	12
	Song of Solomon	8
Prophecy	Isaiah	66
	Jeremiah	52
	Lamentations	5
	Ezekiel	48
	Daniel	12
	Hosea	14
	Joel	3
	Amos	9
	Obadiah	1
	Jonah	4
	Micah	7
	Nahum	3
	Habakkuk	3
	Zephania	3
	Haggai	2
	Zechariah	14
	Malachi	4

		Chapters
History	Matthew	28
	Mark	16
	Luke	24
	John	21
	The Acts	28
Doctrine, or Teaching	Romans	16
	I. Corinthians	16
	II. Corinthians	13
	Galatians	6
	Ephesians	6
	Philippians	4
	Colossians	4
	I. Thessalonians	5
	II. Thessalonians	3
	I. Timothy	6
	II. Timothy	4
	Titus	3
	Philemon	1
	Hebrews	13
	James	5
	I. Peter	5
	II. Peter	3
	I. John	5
	II. John	1
	III. John	1
	Jude	1
Prophecy	Revelation	22

THE BOOKS OF THE NEW TESTAMENT.

Bible in the world written at least 1,500 years ago in Greek. The section is taken from the Bible found by Tischendorf in a monastery on Mount Sinai in 1844 and 1859.

The first division into chapters was made by one Cardinal Hugo in the Latin Bible about the year 1250. Others say Stephen Langton, archbishop of Canterbury, was the first to divide the Bible into chapters, about 1228.

The first English edition of the Scriptures which was divided into verses was the Bible published in Geneva, in 1560. This division into chapters and verses is convenient for reference.

The Geneva Bible was also the first Bible in which *italics* were used to indicate words which are not in the original Hebrew or Greek, but are required in English to

ΚΑΙΟΜΟΛΟΓΟΥΜε
ΝѠΟΜΕΓΑΕΟΤΙΝ
ΤΟΤΗΟΕΥΟΕΒΕΙΑϹ
ΜΥΟΤΗΡΙΟΝΟΟΕ
ΦΑΝΕΡѠΘΗΕΝϹΑΡ
ΚΙ· ΕΔΙΚΑΙѠΘΗΕΝ
ΠΝΙѠΦΘΗΑΤΤΕΛΟΙϹ
ΕΚΗΡΥΧΘΗΕΝΕ
ΘΝΕΟΙΝΕΠΙΟΤΕΥ
ΘΗΕΝΚΟΟΜѠ·
ΑΝΕΛΗΜΦΘΗΕΝ
ΔΟΞΗ

From "Dr. Schaff's Companion to the Greek Testament."
Published by Harper & Brothers.

Section from the Sinaitic Manuscript.

complete the sense. (The kind of type in which the word "italics" is printed in the foregoing sentence shows what is meant by *italics*.)

This may be the proper place in which to mention that the *summary of contents* prefixed to the several chapters is also of modern origin. Instead of this summary the Revised Version uses headings at the top of the page. These, too, are of recent origin. The same is true of the dates which are to be found in the margin of some editions. Those dates were fixed by Archbishop Ussher and published in 1660. These dates at the top of the page show when the events recorded on that page took place or when the page is supposed to have been written.

CHAPTER 2.

The Holy Book.

Part II. HOW WE GOT OUR BIBLE.

THE FALSE CLAIM OF THE MOHAMMEDANS. — The followers of the false prophet Mo-ham'-med (died 632) claim that the Ko-ran', which they think sacred, was written from the beginning in rays of light by the finger of God upon a gigantic tablet resting upon the throne of the Almighty and that He sent a copy of it straight down from heaven by the angel Gabriel. Of course, that is absolutely untrue. We make no such claim for our Bible. The Bible was written by *men* here on this earth. These men were God's penmen, or secretaries.

GOD'S PENMEN. — God wrote the Ten Commandments with His own finger on two tablets of stone. Ex. 31, 18. But this was the only writing of God. When He gave us the Scriptures, He used men as His secretaries: prophets, apostles, and e-van'-gel-ists, about forty in all. These did not write of their own accord. St. Peter writes: "No prophecy of the Scripture is of any private interpretation. For the prophecy came not in old time by the will of man, but holy men of God spake as they were moved by the Holy Ghost." 2 Pet. 1, 20. 21. "Holy men of God" is a name for the prophets. The same name may be applied to the apostles and evangelists. These holy men of God spoke in their writings. What was it that prompted them

to speak and write?   Was it their own will and inclination?
No. The prophecy of the Scripture did not come by the
will of man. Holy men of God spoke and wrote as they
were moved by the Holy Ghost. The Holy Ghost moved
them, that is to say, impelled them, urged them on. They
gladly obeyed this urging of the Holy Ghost and wrote
what He told them to write.

THE BIBLE IS GOD-BREATHED. — Not only did the
Holy Spirit give those holy men of God the impulse to
write, but He also gave them the words which He wanted
them to write. St. Paul says: "All Scripture is given by
inspiration of God." 2 Tim. 3, 16. The Greek word here
rendered "is given by inspiration of God" literally means
"is God-breathed" — "all Scripture is God-breathed." God
the Holy Spirit was in the holy writers and breathed into
their hearts and minds all the thoughts and words which
He wanted them to write down. Every word in the Bible
proceeded out of the mouth of God. Therefore the Bible
is God's Book.

VERBAL INSPIRATION. — By this is meant that the
words of the Bible were divinely inspired. There are those
who tell us that the thoughts were inspired, but that the
words were not inspired. They contend that the Holy
Spirit suggested to the minds of the holy writers only the
thoughts, leaving the writers free to choose the words in
which to express those thoughts. This claim is absurd.
The Bible is a book. A book consists of words. By saying
that the whole Bible is given by inspiration of God, St. Paul
says that all the *words* of the Bible are given by inspiration
of God.

Besides, it is plainly stated in the Bible that the
Holy Spirit taught and told His penmen the *words* which
He wanted them to write. St. Paul distinctly says of his
own and his fellow-apostles' words: "Which things also

we speak, not in the *words* which man's wisdom teacheth, but *which the Holy Ghost teacheth.*" 1 Cor. 2, 13. "The Lord said to Moses: Write thou these *words.*" Ex. 34, 27. "The word that came to Jeremiah from the Lord, saying, Write thee all the *words* that I have spoken to thee in a book." Jer. 30, 1. 2.

There are statements in the Bible which are not true, namely, words spoken by wicked men. Pharaoh, for instance, said: "Who is the Lord? I know not the Lord." The Pharisees said of Jesus: "This man blasphemeth." These words are in the Bible, but they are not true. But God told Moses and Matthew to write those words spoken by wicked people. Every word in the Bible was dictated by God.

PLENARY (FULL) INSPIRATION. — Many people say: "The Bible merely *contains* the Word of God." They wish to lead us to believe that the Holy Book contains parts that are *not* the inspired Word of God, but the word of man. Such an assumption immediately undermines all Christian faith. For the question at once arises: What parts are inspired, and what parts are not inspired? Who can tell? Such a theory leaves man in awful and fatal uncertainty. But St. Paul gives us the needed certainty when he says: "*All* Scripture is given by inspiration of God"; the whole Bible, in all its parts, comes from God. There is absolutely nothing in the Holy Scriptures that is not divinely inspired. In this country the Lutheran Church is almost alone in teaching the plenary inspiration of the Bible.

INERRANCY OF THE BIBLE. — Since all Scripture is given by inspiration of God, it is inerrant, wholly free from all error. For God, the real Author of this Book, is eternal Wisdom and eternal Truth. He cannot possibly be mistaken or in error, much less can He lie. His Word is

Truth. We may therefore with firm confidence trust in His Word in life and in death.

THE AUTOGRAPHS OF THE HOLY PENMEN. — An autograph is something written with one's own hand. The autographs of the prophets, apostles, and evangelists are the original writings which they penned with their own hand. As far as we know, none of these autographs are in existence. They have all disappeared long ago. But the loss of the autographs of the holy penmen need not alarm us. Before they disappeared, numerous copies of the books they wrote had been made. These copies are called *manuscripts*. Of these manuscripts other manuscripts were made. Of the latter approximately 4,000 copies are in existence to-day. Some contain the whole Bible, while others contain only parts of the Sacred Volume. One of the latter is a Hebrew text on papyrus from the second century. The text is Ex. 20, 2—17. This manuscript is probably 1,700 years old.

DISCOVERY OF THE SINAITIC MANUSCRIPT. — At the foot of Mount Sinai there is an old Greek-Catholic monastery called St. Catherine. This monastery was visited in 1844 by the German scholar Tischendorf, of Leipzig. Tischendorf was searching for old copies of the Bible. The monks of St. Catherine graciously showed him their ancient library. In glancing around, Tischendorf noticed in a basket, evidently a waste-paper basket, a number of leaves on which were written Greek inscriptions of a more ancient character than any he had ever seen. Examining these leaves, he discovered that they were parts of the Greek Bible. In this batch there were forty-three leaves. The librarian told him that two basketfuls of such leaves had already been used to kindle fire. Tischendorf was readily given permission to take the leaves with him, but was not permitted to see the book from which they had been taken.

In 1853 Tischendorf made a second trip to Mount Sinai, but without securing any further manuscripts. Six years later he was back once more. At first he met with the same kind of refusal that defeated him in 1853. A few days before his departure he had a talk with the steward of the monastery. In the steward's cell a bundle of loose leaves of parchment wrapped in a cloth was unfolded and set before Tischendorf. There was the treasure he had so long sought for! He was permitted to examine it in his own room that night. He said: "In the presence of the treasure thus found it was not possible for me to sleep." The leaves contained parts of the Old Testament and the New Testament entire. There were 346½ leaves of vellum, made from the finest and best quality of antelope skins. The leaves are 13½ inches wide by 14⅞ inches high. This manuscript was written about 340 A. D. and is close to 1,600 years old. (See cut on p. 8.) Besides this Sinaitic Manuscript there are several others of about the same age.

EARLY TRANSLATIONS OF THE SCRIPTURES. — About 300 years before Christ the Old Testament was translated into Greek. Alexander the Great had conquered the world, and Greek, the language of the conqueror, became the language of commerce and of culture. Alexander built Alexandria in Egypt and assigned a part of it to a colony of Jews. While these Jews thought and felt as Hebrews, yet to a great extent they spoke Greek, forgetting their mother tongue. This made it necessary to translate the Hebrew Old Testament into Greek. The translation is commonly called the *Sep'-tu-a-gint,* or Version of the Seventy, because it was commonly believed that this translation was prepared by seventy learned Jews in Alexandria.

From about 150 after Christ to about 400 after Christ the Scriptures were translated into the following languages: into Syriac about 150, into Latin about 200, into Coptic about 350, into Gothic about 350, into Ethiopic about 400, and into Armenian about 400. The Goths were a Germanic tribe. Bishop Ulfilas (310—383) translated the Bible into their language. The Lord's Prayer reads thus in Gothic: *Atta unsar, thu in himinam. veihnai namo thein. Quimai thiudinassus theins. vairthai vilja theins, sve in himina jah ana airthai. Hlaif unsarana thana sinteinan gif uns himma daga. Jah aflet uns thatei skulans sijaima, svasve jah veis afletam thaim skulam unsaraim. Jah ni briggais uns in fraistubnjai, ak lausei uns af thamma ubilin. Unte theina ist thiudangardi jah mahts jah vulthus in aivins. Amen.*

GERMAN VERSIONS. — There were German translations of the Bible before the days of Luther. However, these translations were quite defective. The great Reformer of the Church saw the need of a good German Bible and translated the New Testament. It was published September 21, 1522. In 1534 his complete German Bible appeared. It was hailed with delight. Thousands upon thousands eagerly read it. Although four hundred years have passed since the Luther Bible appeared, it is still the standard German Bible.

WYCLIF'S TRANSLATION. — The first English Bible was that of John Wyclif. Wyclif made his translation into English from the Latin Bible, the so-called Vul'-gate. Accordingly his was only a translation of a translation. The New Testament appeared in 1380, the Old Testament in 1382. Wyclif died in 1384. Forty years after his death the Roman Catholic authorities dug up his bones and burned them.

TYNDALE'S TRANSLATION. — William Tyndale of England became a follower of Luther. When a learned papist declared with some zeal to Tyndale: "We were better be without God's Law than the Pope's," Tyndale replied: "If God spare my life, ere many years, I will cause a plowboy to know more of the Scriptures than thou doest." Being compelled to leave England, he went to Germany and stayed with Luther for a while. In the spring of 1525 his New Testament appeared in print. Thousands of copies were secretly shipped to England. It was the first English version made directly from the Greek and the first English New Testament printed. "The version is vigorous, clear, and simple enough in style for the 'plowboy' to under-

William Tyndale.

stand." Tyndale also translated various portions of the Old Testament. But he was not able to finish the Old Testament. The Catholics strangled him and then burned his body at the stake, in 1536.

OTHER ENGLISH TRANSLATIONS. — October 4, 1535, there appeared *Biblia. The Bible, that is, the Holy Scriptures of the Olde and New Testament, faithfully and truly translated out of Douche and Latyn into Englishe.* Miles Coverdale, bishop of Exeter and later pastor of a Lutheran

Luther, with the Aid of Friends, Translating the
Old Testament.

church in Germany, was the author of this translation.
It was the first complete English Bible in print. In April,
1539, the *"Great Bible"* appeared. It was so called because
of its size. The Geneva Bible, which appeared in 1560,

has already been mentioned. It is probably best known as the *Breeches Bible,* because it translated Gen. 3, 7: "They sewed fig-leaves together and made themselves *breeches.*" In 1569 the *Bishops' Bible* was published. It had been revised and brought out by a committee of bishops.

King James I.

KING JAMES'S BIBLE. — In 1604 King James I of England appointed forty-four learned men for translating the Bible. They began their work in 1607, finishing it four years later, in 1611. It is advisable to read the preface of the translators. This King James's Bible is also called the

Authorized Version. It has been in use now for more than 300 years. The beauty of its style is admirable.

In the Authorized Version the *marginal references* from one passage to another, so helpful to Bible students, were adopted.

REVISED VERSION. — Since the Authorized Version was made, 319 years ago, some of its words have grown obsolete, some have even completely changed their meaning. Take the word "sometime," which used to mean "once," referring to past time. Eph. 2, 13: "Ye, who sometime were far off, are made nigh by the blood of Christ." Here the word "sometime" does not mean "occasionally" or "now and then." The meaning is: "Ye that *once* were far off," that is, *formerly*. Another word is "conversation." "Ye have heard of my *conversation* in time past in the Jews' religion." Gal. 1, 13. In King James's time it meant our whole conduct or manner of life. To-day the word "conversation" usually means *talking*. "Prevent" used to mean "go before." 1 Thess. 4, 15: "We which are alive and remain unto the coming of the Lord shall not *prevent* them which are asleep." Now "prevent" has come to mean "hinder." For this reason and also for further reasons a revision of the Authorized Version was deemed desirable.

In 1871, a considerable number of British and American scholars began the work of revision. In 1881 the revised New Testament appeared, in 1885 the entire Bible. The American scholars were not fully satisfied with all the changes and published their own revision in 1901. While the Revised Version renders some parts of the Scriptures more faithfully into English, it is nevertheless far from perfect and contains some very unfortunate renderings and unnecessary alterations. Therefore most English Protestant Christians prefer the good old King James's Bible.

NUMEROUS TRANSLATIONS. — There is no other book

in the world that has been translated into so many different languages and dialects as the Holy Bible. The number of languages and dialects into which the whole Book or parts of it have been translated is not less than 830. Every year new translations appear. Would you like to hear how

The
Bible con-
tains 3,566,480
letters.   810,697
words. 31,175 verses.
1,189 chapters and 66
books. The longest chap-
ter is the 119th Psalm, the
shortest and middle chapter
the 117th Psalm.   The middle
verse is the eighth of 118th Psalm.
The longest name is in the eighth
chapter of Isaiah.   The word "and"
occurs 46,657 times, the word "Lord"
1,855 times.   The thirty-seventh chapter of
Isaiah and the nineteenth chapter of the
second Book of Kings are alike.   The longest
verse is the ninth of the eighth chapter
of Esther.   The shortest verse is the
thirty-fifth of the eleventh chapter of John.   In the twenty-
first verse of the
seventh
chapter
of Ezra is
all the alphabet
but "J."   The name
of our God is not men-
tioned once in the Book of
Esther.   It contains Knowledge,
Wisdom, Holiness and Love.

The Tree of Life.

John 3, 16 sounds in the Chinese Bible? *"Dshang-ti ngai si ren sen tzi chaing ta ti to sen tzi t'ze ch'i ta men chiau fan hsin fu ta ti pu chi mie wang fan yo yuen sen."*

THE PURPOSE OF THE BIBLE. — We must not close this chapter without pointing out the purpose for which God gave us His holy Book. St. Paul writes to Timothy: "And that from a child thou hast known the Holy Scriptures, which are able to make thee wise unto salvation through faith which is in Christ Jesus. All Scripture is given by inspiration of God and is profitable for doctrine [teaching], for reproof [that is, for refuting false teachers], for correction [that is, for amendment], for instruction in righteousness, that the man of God may be perfect, throughly furnished unto all good works." 2 Tim. 3, 15—17. Again, St. Paul says: "Whatsoever things were written aforetime were written for our learning that we through patience and comfort of the Scriptures might have hope." Rom. 15, 4. The one great purpose for which God gave us His written Word is to teach us the way to heaven. This way is faith in Jesus Christ. St. John writes in his gospel: "These are written that ye might believe that Jesus is the Christ [the promised Messiah], the Son of God, and that, believing, ye might have life through His name." John 20, 31. The Savior Himself says: "Search the Scriptures [that is, study them diligently], for in them ye think ye have eternal life; and they are they which testify of Me." John 5, 39.

CHAPTER 3.

The Holy Book.

Part III. HOW TO READ THE BIBLE.

READ IT WITH REVERENCE. — The Bible is the written Word of the Lord of lords and King of kings. Therefore we should regard and treat it with respect and reverence. God says: "But to this man will I look, even to him that is poor and of a contrite spirit and trembleth at My Word." Is. 66, 2.

READ THE BIBLE WITH INTEREST. — Of course, you read the Bible. But do you enjoy it? Some people read the Bible simply because it is their duty so to do. They do not care for it and are glad when the reading is done. Jesus wants us to read the Bible with interest and close attention. We heard him say: "*Search* the Scriptures." "When Christ referred the Jews to the Scriptures, He sent them not to a mere reading, but to a careful and considerate search. He said not, 'read,' but, 'search.'" (*Chrysostom.*) We should follow the example of the Be-re´-ans. "They *searched* the Scriptures daily." Acts 17, 11.

Be Ready to Follow the Word. — "Be ye doers of the Word and not hearers only, deceiving your own selves." Jas. 1, 22. Miles Coverdale has these pertinent words in his preface of his *Biblia* (1535): "Go to now, most dear reader, and sit thee down at the Lord's feet, and read His words, and, as Moses teacheth the Jews, take them into thine heart. And, above all things, fashion thy life and conversation according to the doctrine of the Holy Ghost therein that thou mayest be partaker of the good promises of God in the Bible and be heir of His blessings in Christ; in whom, if thou put thy trust, and be an unfeigned reader or hearer of His Word with thy heart, thou shalt find sweetness therein and spy wondrous things to thy understanding, to the avoiding of all seditious sects, to the abhorring of thy old sinful life, and to the stablishing of thy godly conversation."

Read It with Prayer. — The writer of Ps. 119 repeatedly prays to God, asking Him to cause him to understand His Word. "Blessed art Thou, O Lord; teach me Thy statutes." Verses 12. 26. 68. "Open Thou mine eyes that I may behold wondrous things out of Thy Law." V. 18. "Make me to understand the way of Thy precepts; so shall I talk of Thy wondrous works." V. 27. "Teach me, O Lord, the way of Thy statutes, and I shall keep it unto the end." V. 33. "Give me understanding, and I shall keep Thy Law." V. 34.

HELPS. — Every Bible student should have at least a *reference Bible.* The parallel passages to which such a Bible refers on the margin are a great aid. They help us in getting the proper meaning and in broadening our knowledge of the passage. Take an example. Matt. 2, 1 we read: "Now, when Jesus was born in Bethlehem of Judea, in the days of Herod the king," etc. Here a reference Bible will point to Luke 2, 4. 6. 7. There you will find another and fuller account of the birth of Jesus in Bethlehem. — A *concordance* is also a help. A concordance is an alphabetical index of words showing the places in the Bible where each principal word may be found. — A *Bible dictionary* is another help. All these helps are found in the *Concordia Home and Teachers' Bible.* (Cloth edition, $2.50.)

THE OLD TESTAMENT.

CHAPTER 4.

The Historical Books.

The Pentateuch in General.

ITS NAME. — The first five books of the Bible, written by Moses, are called *The Five Books of Moses.* Another name by which they are designated is *The Pen'-ta-teuch.* This Greek name signifies that the writings of Moses are contained in a *book of five volumes,* for *Pentateuch* means *the five-volume book.*

In the Scriptures the Pentateuch is often referred to as *The Book of the Law,* as in Deut. 31, 26, or briefly as *The Law, Thora,* as in Neh. 8, 2, or as *The Law of Moses,* as in Luke 2, 22, because legislation forms so large a part of the Pentateuch.

ITS AUTHOR. — In late years the so-called higher critics have tried to show that the Pentateuch was not written by Moses. They have succeeded only too well in spreading doubt and unbelief in many quarters. But we would rather believe Christ and His holy apostles, who ascribe this magnificent work to the God-appointed leader of Israel. Christ says: "These are the words which I spake unto you that all things must be fulfilled which were written in the *Law of Moses,* and in the Prophets, and in the Psalms, concerning Me." Luke 24, 44. He said to the Jews: "Had ye believed *Moses,* ye would have believed Me; for he wrote of Me. But if ye believe not *his writings,* how shall ye believe My words?" John 5, 46. 47. Read also Acts 13, 39; 15, 5; 1 Cor. 9, 9. It is clear that our Lord Jesus Christ looked upon Moses as the writer of the five books ascribed to him.

ITS PURPOSE. — The Five Books of Moses tell us how the *theocracy* and its *Code of Law* were established among the people of Israel. Theocracy means "government by God" and denotes that form of government in which God is the recognized King of the state and controls all civic affairs by His laws and institutions. To establish it in Israel, God not only renewed the revelation of the Moral Law on Mount Sinai and gave His people a complete system of religious forms, but He also added all statutes necessary for their civil and social intercourse. This pure theocracy came to an end when the children of Israel later demanded, and were given, a king as a visible head and ruler of their state. 1 Sam. 8.

"If we turn over the pages of the Pentateuch, from Genesis to Deuteronomy, we shall see a great *variety of contents.* The book of *Genesis* begins with the Creation and primeval times and passes on to patriarchal life in the land of Canaan. In *Exodus* we are told of the hard

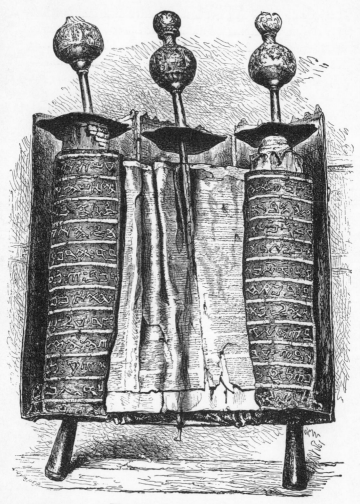

The Samaritan Pentateuch.

This very ancient scroll is in the synagog of Nablus (Shechem). It is written in Hebrew on ram-skins about 15×25 inches, which are much worn and patched in many places. The text is written in gold, which still preserves its luster. It is kept in a cylindrical silver case, opening on two sets of hinges. The roll is exhibited to the congregation once a year, on the Day of Atonement, when it is devoutly kissed. Another roll is ordinarily used.

bondage of Israel in Egypt, their deliverance under Moses and Aaron, the giving of the Law at Sinai, and the setting up of the Tabernacle. *Leviticus* is full of laws, referring, for the most part, to worship and ceremonial. *Numbers* tells of the wanderings in the desert, and *Deuteronomy* contains the farewell addresses of Moses to the people as they were about to enter the Promised Land. The time covered by the Pentateuch thus extends from the Creation to the death of Moses. Under all this variety of contents we recognize two *main elements* of which the Pentateuch is made up. The first is *History*. The Pentateuch is not by any means a universal history, though it begins with the whole human race and speaks of the countries over which the race is spread. Nor does it even carry into detail many of the subjects which it takes up. Yet the main stream of the narrative is never interrupted; and even when we lose sight of it for a time under other interests, it comes up again and flows on to the end. Nations and families are enumerated and then dismissed without further notice, the attention being made to concentrate upon *one family* — that of *Abraham*. This family is represented as set apart in a peculiar manner from the beginning for a great purpose. It is plainly the nation of Israel that is in view throughout, and that nation is under special divine training; and the Pentateuch exhibits the first stage of the history and the first steps of the training, up to the point when the people are ready to enter the land of Canaan, which was assigned to them as their dwelling-place. The other element is *Law*, and this feature is so prominent in the books that it has given its name to the whole Pentateuch. One of the books (Leviticus) is entirely composed of laws, others (Exodus and Numbers) have laws mixed up with the history, and another (Deuteronomy) has laws incorporated in long addresses."

CHAPTER 5.

Genesis.

THE BEAUTY OF THIS BOOK. — Luther says: "In all Scripture there is nothing more beautiful than the whole of Genesis." He began his lectures on this beloved book June 3, 1535, and completed them only shortly before his death, which occurred February 18, 1546.

ITS NAME. — The name *Genesis* is a Greek word, signifying *origin,* or *beginning.* It is the book of the beginning of things. Its purpose is to trace the beginnings of history. Genesis records —

1. *The Origin of the World.* "In the beginning God created the heaven and the earth."

2. *The Origin of the Human Race.* Gen. 1, 26. 27; 2, 7.

3. *The Origin of the Sabbath.* Gen. 2, 3.

4. *The Institution of Marriage.* Gen. 2, 18 f.

5. *The Origin of Sin.* Gen. 3. Read Rom. 5, 19.

6. *The First Preaching of the Gospel.* Gen. 3, 15. Compare with John 3, 16.

7. *The Beginning of Sacrifices.* Gen. 4, 3. 4.

8. *The Beginning of Poetry, of Cities, of Music,* etc. Gen. 4, 17—24.

9. *The First Judgment of God upon a Sinful World.* Gen. 6—8.

10. *The Beginning of the Chosen Race of Israel.* Gen. 12.

DIVISION. — The Book of Genesis may be divided into two chief parts. *Part I,* Gen. 1 to 11, records the beginnings of all history to the confusion of tongues. *Part II,* Gen. 12 to 50, shows how God paved the way for the establishment of a theocracy. It contains the history of Abraham and his family to the death of Joseph.

THE PERIOD. — The first period of human history, beginning with the creation of man and ending with the Flood, comprises about 1,700 years. The period of the *Patriarchs* begins with the deliverance of Noah from the ark and ends with the death of Joseph, covering a space of about 600 years. At its close the *family* of Abraham had multiplied and become a numerous *people*.

CHRONOLOGY. — The figures of the gen-e-al'-o-gies in Gen. 5 and 11 (see also Gen. 21, 5 and 25, 7) may be tabulated and dates derived from them as follows: —

	Age at Son's Birth	Remainder of Life	Total Life	Year of Birth	Year of Death
Adam	130	800	930	1	930
Seth	105	807	912	130	1042
E'-nos	90	815	905	235	1140
Ca-i'-nan	70	840	910	325	1235
Ma-ha'-la-le-el	65	830	895	395	1290
Ja'-red	162	800	962	460	1422
E'-noch	65	300	365	622	987
Me-thu'-se-lah	187	782	969	687	1656
La'-mech	182	595	777	874	1651
No'-ah	500	450	950	1056	2006
Date of Flood	...	...	...	....	1656
Shem	100	500	600	1556	2156
Ar-phax'-ad	35	403	438	1656	2093
Sa'-lah	30	403	433	1691	2124
E'-ber	34	430	464	1721	2185
Pe'-leg	30	209	239	1755	1994
Re'-u	32	207	239	1785	2024
Se'-rug	30	200	230	1817	2047
Na'-hor	29	119	148	1847	1995
Te'-rah	70	135	205	1876	2081
A'-bram	100	75	175	2006	2181

PROPHECY OF GENESIS. — Besides the remarkable prophecy of Noah, Gen. 9, 25—27, which revealed a definite plan of God covering the future of all mankind, Genesis contains several distinct *Messianic promises* of God.

The first, couched in very general terms, designates the Savior as the *Seed of the Woman* and as the future Conqueror of the Serpent. Chap. 3, 15. This is rightly called the *Pro-te-van-gel'-i-um, i. e.,* the first Gospel. As far as we know, this one promise sufficed to sustain the people of God in the saving faith throughout the long period preceding the Flood. To the Patriarchs the promise regarding the Redeemer was made more definite; for God declared that the Savior should come from the posterity of Abraham, Isaac, and Jacob. To Abraham, God said: "In thy seed shall all the nations of the earth be blessed." Gen. 22, 18. This promise was repeated to Isaac, Gen. 26, 4; to Jacob, Gen. 28, 14. In this form the Gospel comforted these holy men until to Jacob was granted the further knowledge that the Promised One should spring from the tribe of Judah. (Gen. 49, 10—12; *Shiloh* = the Man of Peace, Prince of Peace.)

TYPES OF CHRIST IN GENESIS. — "Search the Scriptures, for in them ye think ye have eternal life; and they are they *which testify of Me.*" John 5, 39. "To *Him* give *all* the prophets witness." Acts 10, 43. Christ is the sum and center of all the Scriptures. Not only is Christ found in the Book of Genesis, in the *prophecies* referred to in the preceding paragraph, but also in many *types.* The word *type* means image, picture. A type is a divinely purposed picture, or illustration, of some truth. It may be (1) a person, (2) an event, (3) a thing, (4) an institution, or (5) a ceremonial. Some of the most notable types of Christ are: —

Mel-chiz'-e-dek, Gen. 14, 18. Melchizedek = King of Righteousness; King of Salem = King of Peace. Melchizedek is a priest. In Jesus, the Prince of Peace, the offices of King and Priest are united. Heb. 7.

Isaac, Gen. 22. The offering of Isaac is one of the most perfect pictures in the Scriptures of the great sacrifice Jesus, the Lamb of God, offered on Mount Calvary.

Joseph, Gen. 37. Joseph sold by his brothers at the price of a slave; condemned, etc.

Judah, Gen. 44, 32—34. Judah is a type of Christ, our Substitute.

The Ark, Gen. 6—8. The Ark is a type of the salvation, the refuge God has provided for us in Christ.

SUMMARY OF CONTENTS. — *I. The Beginnings of History.* Chaps. 1 to 11.

1. Creation. The fall of man. The first promise of a Savior. The expulsion of Adam and Eve from Paradise. The birth of Cain and Abel. The crime of Cain. Chaps. 1 to 4.

2. Genealogy of the Patriarchs before the Flood. Chap. 5.

3. Noah and the Flood. Chaps. 6 to 9.

4. The Patriarchs from Noah to Abraham. Chaps. 10 and 11.

II. History of the Patriarchs. Chaps. 12 to 50.

1. *Abraham.* Chaps. 12, 1—25, 10. God calls Abraham. Abraham obeys and departs for Canaan. During a famine he went down to Egypt. His return to Canaan and his peaceful separation from his nephew Lot. The battle of the kings. (The first battle mentioned in the Bible.) Abraham rescues Lot. Mel-chiz´-e-dek blesses Abraham. Abraham's belief in God's promise that He will give him a son. The birth of Ish´-ma-el. Circumcision is instituted by God. Isaac is promised to Abraham. Destruction of Sodom. Abraham removes to Gerar and deceives A-bim´-e-lech, king of Gerar. The miraculous birth of Isaac. Ishmael is sent away. Trial of Abraham's faith when he is asked by God to offer his only son. Death and burial of Sarah. Marriage of Isaac. Second marriage of Abraham. His death at the age of 175 years.

2. *Isaac.* Chaps. 24 to 35. He marries Rebekah. Birth of Esau and Jacob. Esau sells Jacob his birthright. Isaac goes to Gerar because of famine. God appears to him and repeats the promise that He will give the land of Canaan to him and to his seed. Isaac dissembles. Covenant with Abimelech. Isaac grows rich. Esau marries two Hittite women. Blessing of Jacob and

Esau. Jacob flees from Esau to Mesopotamia. (See Map 1.)
After Jacob's return, Isaac dies at the age of 180 years.

3. *Jacob and His Sons.* Chaps. 25 to 50. Jacob the twin
brother of Esau. Deceiving Isaac, he obtained the first blessing.
His flight to Mesopotamia. The vision of Jacob's ladder. The
promises continued to him. He meets Rachel. Service and marriage in Mesopotamia. His family and wealth. Returning to
Canaan, he is pursued by Laban. Their covenant. Jacob's vision
of Ma-ha-na'-im. He wrestles with the Angel. Is reconciled to
Esau. Slaughter of Shechemites. Jacob purges his household of
idols. The promises renewed to him. Rachel bears Benjamin and
dies. Joseph's two dreams. Envy of his brothers. Sold into
slavery. Sin of Judah. Joseph advanced, tempted, falsely accused, and imprisoned. He interprets dreams and is exalted.
Seven years of famine. His brothers come to buy grain. He
makes himself known to them; sends for his father. Jacob and
his family arrive in Egypt; settle in Goshen. (Map 1.) Jacob
blesses his sons (poetry); prophesies concerning Christ; dies 147
years old; is buried in Canaan. Joseph shows kindness to his
brothers; dies at the age of 110 years, after charging his brothers
to carry his bones up to Canaan the day when his people would
return to the Promised Land.

CHAPTER 6.

Exodus.

NAME AND PURPOSE OF THE BOOK. — Genesis ends
with the death of Joseph. Exodus, however, does not
begin where Genesis stopped, but a long interval is now
passed over without record. The *family* of Jacob had now
increased into a large *nation,* numbering 600,000 men, besides women, children, and old men. Exodus begins with
the story of the departure of the children of Israel from
the land of bondage and of their journey into the Promised
Land.

Exodus is a Latin word, indicating the most striking
event recorded in this book, namely, the *departure* of the

Israelites from Egypt. Exodus means *going out, departure*. This remarkable occurrence had been foretold by God many times as a promise (read Gen. 15, 13—16; 35, 11 f.), to the fulfilment of which the children of God looked forward in firm faith (read Gen. 48, 21 f.; 50, 25). *The chief purpose of the book* is to relate how the theocracy was established among the people of Israel by the solemn giving of the Law on Mount Sinai. Thus was that covenant made and confirmed which God had graciously planned for

Mount Si'-na-i.

His people. The Book of Exodus falls into two parts, the first containing *History,* the second *Legislation.*

THE MOSAIC LAW. — The laws which God gave to the children of Israel through Moses at Mount Sinai are of three distinct kinds: the Moral Law, the Ceremonial Law, and the Civil Law.

1. The *Moral Law.* This law relates to our morals, to our conduct, or behavior. It points out what is sinful and wrong and also what is right and pleasing to God. The Moral Law is also called the *Natural Law* because it is

known to all men by nature, without special revelation. Rom. 2, 12—15. The Moral Law is briefly summed up in the Ten Commandments. It is binding not only upon the Jews, but upon all men. It is binding upon all men not only for a time, but perpetually. God wrote the Ten Commandments on two tablets of *stone*. And Christ says: "Verily I say unto you, Till heaven and earth pass, one jot or one tittle shall in no wise pass from the Law till all be fulfilled." Matt. 5, 18.

2. The *Ceremonial Law*. This law prescribes all the ceremonies which God wanted the Jews to observe when they worshiped Him. The Ceremonial Law included all rules and regulations regarding the Sabbath and other holy days, regarding the place of worship, the priesthood, and the sacrifices. While the Moral Law is binding upon all men at all times, the Ceremonial Law was binding upon the Jews only, and that only during the centuries before the coming of Christ. With the coming of Christ the Ceremonial Law was abolished, or set aside. It is no longer binding on the people of God. Eph. 2, 15; Col. 2, 16 f.; Heb. 9; 10, 1—22.

3. The *Civil Law*. This included all rules and regulations given by God for the government of the Jews as a nation. The Civil Law became null and void when the Jews were scattered over the whole earth.

REMEMBER: The Law of Moses was not meant to instruct us how to earn salvation through works, or deeds, as it was sadly misunderstood by the Jews in later days. Righteousness before God and life cannot be attained by the works of the Law. "By the works of the Law shall no flesh be justified." Gal. 2, 16.

MESSIANIC PROPHECY AND TYPES. — The Book of Exodus contains no direct promises concerning Christ. Yet the book is replete with Messianic prophecy in that it describes manifold *types* of which Christ is the *antitype* and the fulfilment. (*Antitype* = that of which the type is the figure or representation.) Paul calls these types the shadow of things to come (Col. 2, 17), the shadowgraphs disappearing when the body came. The most notable types in Exodus are: —

The Burning Bush. — Chap. 3. The Angel of the Lord (the Son of God) appeared to Moses in the burning bush. The bush was burning, but it was not consumed. A little thorn-bush of the desert ablaze with God! A picture of the Incarnation. God manifesting Himself in a visible form.

The Passover Lamb. — Chap. 12. The Passover Lamb is a type of Christ and His redemption. "Christ, our Passover, is sacrificed for us." 1 Cor. 5, 7. 8. The first-born of the children of Israel in Egypt were saved from death by the Lamb without blemish, whose blood was shed in their stead. "Ye were redeemed with the precious blood of Christ, as of a Lamb without blemish and without spot." 1 Pet. 1, 18. 19.

The Manna. — Chap. 16. The bread which the Lord rained from heaven is a type which Jesus applied to Himself in John 6, 48—51, saying: "I am that Bread of Life. Your fathers did eat manna in the wilderness and are dead. . . . I am the Living Bread which came down from heaven; if any man eat of this Bread, he shall live forever; and the Bread that I will give is My flesh, which I will give for the life of the world."

The Smitten Rock. — Chap. 17. Compare 1 Cor. 10, 4: "They drank of that spiritual Rock that followed them; and that Rock was Christ." And John 4, 13. 14: "Whosoever drinketh of the water that I shall give him shall never thirst; but the water that I shall give him shall be in him a well of water springing up into everlasting life."

Moses. — The central personage of Exodus is Moses. Moses is a type of Christ in many respects. 1. Moses saw God face to face. Ex. 33, 11. 2. He was chosen by God to lead His people out of bondage. Acts 7, 25. 3. Moses interceded for his people. Ex. 32, 31—35; Heb. 7, 25; 1 John 2, 1. 2.

Aaron. — The high priest Aaron was a type of our great High Priest. Aaron was the mediator, or go-between, between God and the people. The Epistle to the Hebrews points out to us how Jesus is the perfect Mediator and High Priest who was prefigured by Aaron. See especially Heb. 4, 14—5, 5.

The Tabernacle. — Chaps. 25. 26. The Tabernacle was built according to a design furnished by God Himself and afterward became the pattern for the Temple of Solomon. It consisted of three chief sections, the *Court,* the *Holy,* and the *Holy of Holies,* which were placed in this order from east to west. The people were admitted only to the Court; the priests entered the Holy; but the high priest alone was permitted to enter the Holy of Holies, and he but once a year. In the Court stood the great altar of burnt offerings, with the perpetual fire. In the Holy were placed the table with the showbread, the altar of incense, and the candlestick with seven arms. The mysterious darkness of the Holy of Holies concealed the Ark of the Covenant. In Heb. 8, 5 we are distinctly told that the Tabernacle was a shadow of heavenly things. It was the outward sign of God's presence, God's tent in the midst of the tents of the children of Israel, the meeting-place between God and man.

SUMMARY OF CONTENTS. — *I. Preparations for the Exodus.* Chaps. 1, 1—12, 28: Increase and oppression of the Israelites. Birth and education of Moses, the deliverer; his patriotism, flight to Mid'-i-a-n (Map 1), his call, and equipment. Moses and Aaron speak to Pharaoh. Aaron's rod turned into a serpent (the first miracle in the Old Testament). The ten plagues. The institution of the Passover. — *II. Journey of Israel from Egypt to Sinai.* Chap. 12, 29—19, 13: The Exodus; passage of the Red Sea; destruction of Pharaoh and his host; song of Moses and of Miriam (poetry); the bitter waters of Mar'-ah made sweet; the quails; manna; water from the rock; battle with Am'-a-lek; Jeth'-ro's advice; preparations for the giving of the Law. — *III. The Solemn Legislation.* Chaps. 19 to 40: The Ten Commandments and the fundamental ordinances of the people; building of the Tabernacle ordered; Aaron and the people sin (the Golden Calf), but are restored to grace upon the intercession of Moses. The Tabernacle is built.

CHAPTER 7.

Leviticus.

NAME AND PURPOSE. — This book received the name by which we quote it because it pertains chiefly to the duties of the Levites and priests. It contains detailed ordinances describing the Levitic worship as it was to be observed in the Tabernacle and afterward in the Temple. The laws in Leviticus, mostly of a ceremonial character, constitute a manual, a handbook, to the priests in the performance of their functions and duties. Certain supplements to this Levitic law were added in the Book of Numbers.

LEVITIC SACRIFICES. — God prescribed two kinds of sacrifices, bloody and unbloody sacrifices. The idea of the bloody sacrifices was that of substitution. By transgressing the Law of God, the Israelite forfeited his life and deserved to die. The sacrificial victim became his substitute and died in the sinner's stead. Thus his sin was covered and blotted out with the blood of the sacrifice. His life was saved because the sacrificial animal died for him. — All animals thus offered were required to be altogether without fault or blemish. Cattle, sheep, and goats, together with turtledoves and young doves, comprise the list of sacrificial animals. — The *bloodless* sacrifices were of two kinds, meat-offerings and drink-offerings. The gifts here consisted of meal, cakes, grain, oil, incense, salt, or wine, according to circumstances. A portion of the offering was burned; what remained belonged to the priests.

THE SACRIFICES WERE TYPES OF CHRIST. — The New Testament, particularly the Epistle to the Hebrews, shows conclusively that the entire system of sacrifices in the Old Testament was nothing less than a typical representation of the vicarious sacrifice of Jesus Christ, which was foreshadowed by every bloody offering in the Temple. We all had sinned. Jesus Christ became our Substitute, taking our sins on Himself and dying for them in our stead. For His sake there is now remission of sins, life, and salvation.

REVIEW OF JEWISH FESTIVALS. — Chaps. 23 to 25 of Leviticus contain ordinances concerning the Jewish festivals. The *Sabbath,* the seventh day of every week, was to be observed as a day of rest, in memory of the Sabbath of the Lord which followed the work of creation. Gen. 2, 3. It foreshadowed the rest of the children of Israel in Canaan and the further rest of paradise, the heavenly Canaan. — The *Passover* was to preserve the memory of the divine deliverance from Egypt. It typified the future deliverance of the spiritual Israel from the bondage of sin. The Passover was observed on the fourteenth day of the first month, called A'-bib, or Ni'-san (corresponding to the latter half of our month of March and the first half of April). The Feast of the Passover introduced the *Feast of Unleavened Bread,* which lasted seven days. — The *Harvest Festival* was set for the fiftieth day after the Passover; hence it was later called *Pentecost, i. e.,* the fiftieth day. On this occasion the first-fruits of the harvest were offered to the Lord. — *New Year's Day* of the Jews (*rosh ha-shannah* in Hebrew) was the first day of the seventh month, Tisri, or

Ethanim (September—October). — The *Great Day of Atonement* was observed on the tenth day of the month of Tisri, in the early part of October. It was a day of penance, on which the people were to mortify their bodies by fasting. The *Feast of Tabernacles* began on the fifteenth day of Tisri and continued for seven days. It was to remind the Jews that their fathers dwelt in tents during their sojourn in the wilderness. "Boughs of goodly trees, branches of palm-trees, and the boughs of thick trees, and willows of the brook" were to be used for decorations. Lev. 23, 40. — Besides these feasts, which were to be observed with sacrifices and religious worship, the Lord also ordained that the land should not be put to seed in every seventh year (*the Sabbatical Year*) and that every *fiftieth* year should be a *Year of Jubilee.* Lev. 25, 8 ff. The beginning of the jubilee was announced by the sounding of trumpets on the first day of Tisri. During such a year the land rested, the same as during the Sabbatical Year. Every Jewish servant was restored to liberty, and every parcel of land which had been sold was returned to its original owner, in order that every family might retain the inheritance belonging to it.

SUMMARY OF CONTENTS. — *I. Sacrifices.* Chaps. 1 to 7. — *II. Consecration.* The consecration of Aaron and his sons as priests. Aaron offers sacrifices for himself and the people. The sin of Na'-dab and A-bi'-hu. The priests' duties and portions. Chaps. 8 to 10. — *III. Their Food.* Distinction of clean and unclean animals. Chap. 11 — *IV. Personal and Ceremonial Purifications.* Chaps. 12 to 15. — *V. The Great Day of Atonement.* Chap. 16. — *VI. Laws concerning the Slaughter of Beasts.* Blood not to be eaten. Chap. 17. — *VII. Unlawful Marriages.* Chap. 18. *VIII. Sundry Laws.* Chap. 19. — *IX. Molech-worship* and other sins forbidden. Laws against unchastity. Chap. 20. — *X. Ordinances regarding Priests.* Chaps. 21 and 22. — *XI. Laws concerning Religious Festivals.* Chaps. 23 to 25. — *XII. Warnings and Promises.* Chap. 26. — *XIII. Laws regarding Vows and Tithes.* Chap. 27.

CHAPTER 8.

Numbers.

NAME AND CONTENTS. — This book received its name from the fact that its first chapter tells of the numbering of the people. According to chap. 26 the numbering was repeated at a later period. The book is a brief record of the history of the chosen nation from the second year after leaving Egypt to its arrival at the borders of Canaan in the fortieth year of its pilgrimage. God's object in bringing the children of Israel out of Egypt was to bring them into the Promised Land. In the Book of Numbers we have an account of their *failure* to occupy it. — Interspersed between the various parts of the narrative we find additional legislation, most of the laws referring to the civil life of the people, together with some further instructions concerning the religious ceremonial.

MESSIANIC PROPHECY. — A notable prophecy, out of the mouth of Balaam, is recorded chap. 24, 17. 19: "There shall come a Star out of Jacob, and a Scepter shall rise out of Israel. Out of Jacob shall come He that shall have dominion." (Poetry.) The Star out of Jacob is Jesus, the Babe of Bethlehem. He is the "bright and morning star."

The Brazen Serpent. — Chap. 21, 5—9: "And the people spake against God and against Moses, Wherefore have ye brought us up out of Egypt to die in the wilderness? For there is no bread, neither is there any water; and our soul loatheth this light bread. And the Lord sent fiery serpents among the people, and they bit the people; and much people of Israel died. Therefore the people came to Moses and said, We have sinned, for we have spoken against the Lord and against thee; pray unto the Lord that He take away the serpents from us. And Moses prayed for the people. And the Lord said unto Moses, Make thee a fiery serpent and set it upon a pole; and it shall come to pass that every one that is bitten, when he looketh upon it, shall live. And Moses made a serpent of brass and put it upon a pole. And it came to pass that, if a serpent had bitten any man, when he beheld the serpent of brass, he lived." This story is of peculiar interest. Our Lord Himself claimed it as a picture of the salvation which men were to find in Him; for John 3, 14. 15 we read: "As Moses lifted up the serpent in the wilderness, even so must the Son of Man be lifted up, that whosoever believeth in Him should not perish, but have eternal life." The power to save did not lie in the serpent of brass. Wherein did it lie? There is no answer to that question till we come to the cross of Calvary. The Son of Man, who is also the Son of God, hung there for us. There is life for a look at the Crucified One. The divinely appointed remedy was a serpent of brass lifted up, harmless, but bearing the image of that which wrought the woe. "For He hath made Him to be sin for us who knew no sin, that we might be made the righteousness of God in Him." 2 Cor. 5, 21. "Every bitten Israelite that looked, *lived;* every child of Adam, dead in trespasses and sins, who has looked to Jesus as His Savior has received eternal life from Him."

SUMMARY OF CONTENTS. — *I. Preparations for the Departure from Mount Sinai.* Chaps. 1 to 10: Numbering and reviewing of the tribes. The order of the tribes in their tents. The Levites. The unclean are removed out of the camp. Restitution in trespasses. The trial of jealousy. The law of the Naz'-a-rites. The Aaronic blessing — the first public prayer in the Old Testament. The offerings of the princes at the dedication of the altar. Consecration of the Levites. The Passover commanded and ordinances concerning its observance. Use of the silver trumpets. *II. Journey of the People up to the Beginning of the Fortieth Year.* Chaps. 10 to 19: The Israelites remove from Sinai to Par'-an. What happened at Tab'-e-rah and Ha-ze'-roth. The twelve spies. The people murmur and are excluded from enter-

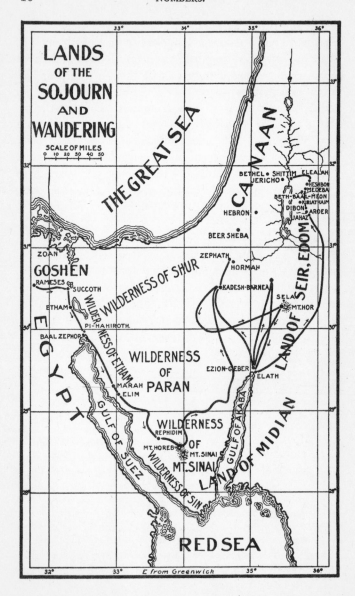

ing the Promised Land. Laws concerning divers offerings. The Sabbath-breaker is stoned. The rebellion of Kor'-ah and his band. Aaron's priesthood confirmed. Portions of the priests and Levites. Purification of the unclean with the ashes of a red heifer. — *III. The First Ten Months of the Fortieth Year.* Chaps. 20 to 36: Miriam dies at Ka'-desh. Moses smites the rock and brings forth water. E'-dom refuses peaceful passage to Israel. The death of Aaron on Mount Hor. The fiery serpents. Journey from Hor to Pis'-gah. Si'-hon and Og are defeated. Balaam and his prophecies. The people practise idolatry, and 24,000 are slain. The second numbering of Israel. Ordinances concerning inheritances. Moses told of his approaching death. Joshua to be his successor. Offerings to be observed. Law concerning vows. Victory over the Mid'-i-an-ites. Reu'-ben, Gad, and the half tribe of Ma-nas'-seh settle in Gil'-e-ad, on the east side of Jordan. Record of Israel's journeys. Directions concerning the conquest and division of Canaan.

CHAPTER 9.

Deuteronomy.

ITS NAME AND PURPOSE. — The Latin name *Deu-te-ro-no'-mium* (Second Law), from which the English name is derived, may be translated "the second giving of the Law." It describes the book as essentially a restatement of all the commandments and statutes which the Lord had given to His people. — The book contains the last discourses of Moses, the man of God, addressed to the children of Israel. Before taking leave from this earth, the venerable leader once more reminds them of all the mercies, ordinances, and promises of God. The time is the beginning of the eleventh month of the fortieth year after the exodus from Egypt to the seventh day of the twelfth month in the same year; the place is the encampment of Israel east of the Jordan and opposite Jericho, in the land of Moab. Here the great prophet makes his closing appeal to those whom he had led and formed into a nation, asking them to keep inviolate the covenant of the Lord and to walk in His ways. He eagerly desires the happiness of his people. "Oh, that there were such an heart in them that they would fear Me and keep all My commandments always, that it might be well with them and with their children forever!" Chap. 5, 29. The last three sections of the book, which contain the announcement of the death of Moses, his last blessing, and the narrative of his death, may have been added to Deuteronomy by the inspired author of the Book of Joshua.

"The forty years of wandering are at an end. The children of Israel are in sight of the Promised Land. Moses recognizes the fact that his leadership is about to end, but that the covenant is to abide. A crisis has come in the affairs of the nation, and a review of Israel's history and a restatement of God's laws must be made. A new generation had grown up, which had not heard the original promulgation of the Law at Sinai. A new country was before the nation. This country was devoted to an idolatrous worship of the most seductive kind. On every high hill and in every grove this worship was carried on. An unflinching devotion to God was necessary to resist this alluring worship, which was more to be dreaded than an armed resistance. Moses endeavors to impress his hearers with the advantages of obedience and the disadvantages of disobedience to God's Law."

Among the last utterances of Moses we find a great *Messianic prophecy* concerning the prophetic office of Christ. It reads: "The Lord, thy God, will raise up unto thee a Prophet from the midst of thee, of thy brethren, like unto me; unto Him ye shall hearken." Chap. 18, 15; compare Acts 3, 22; 7, 37; Matt. 17, 5; Heb. 1, 1. 2; John 1, 45; 6, 14. Luther says: "This is the noblest passage and indeed the kernel of the entire Old Testament."

Summary of Contents. — *I. Three Discourses of Moses,* addressed to Israel. Chaps. 1 to 30. The *first* discourse is a brief review of the journey through the desert and warns against apostasy. In the *second* discourse the laws and ordinances of God are summarized, with some explanations and many urgent, fatherly admonitions to keep the Law. In the *third* discourse Moses declares most impressively both the blessing and the curse of the Law. — *II. Moses Delivers the Book of the Law to the Levites and Sings a Song of Praise.* Chaps. 31—32, 47. — *III. Three Supplements.* Chaps. 32, 48—34: Announcement of Moses' death; the last blessing of Moses; narrative of his death and burial on Nebo.

CHAPTER 10.

The Book of Joshua.

The Book. — The Book of Josh'-u-a is so named from its principal character, Joshua, the new leader of the children of Israel, and contains their history under his leadership. The book covers a period of about twenty-five years, 1450 to 1425 B. C. Deuteronomy ended with the account of the death of Moses, the servant of God, who had brought the people to the borders of the Promised Land. The Book of Joshua takes up the thread where Deuteronomy dropped it and continues the history of the children of Israel, telling how they conquered Canaan and took possession of it.

The Purpose of the Book. — The main object of the Book of Joshua is to show that God is faithful and true, fulfilling the promises made to the Patriarchs that He would give the land of Canaan to His chosen people. Accordingly, the book relates how the Lord helped Joshua and Israel conquer and occupy Canaan. — The author also takes pains to point out that Joshua was faithful and true to the Lord and that he never wearied of urging the people also to remain faithful and true. They obeyed his words;

"Israel served the Lord all the days of Joshua." Chap. 24, 31.

THE AUTHOR. — While the book bears Joshua's name, it was probably not written by him. For it records several incidents which happened after his death. For example, chap. 15, 13—19 relates how Ca´-leb took possession of his inheritance at He´-bron; but the conquest of He´-bron by Ca´-leb was not completed until after the death of Joshua, as appears from Judg. 1, 10—15. But while this book was probably not written by Joshua himself, the writer was evidently a person who passed over the Jordan with him, for he writes: "Until *we* were passed over." Chap. 5, 1.

JOSHUA A TYPE OF JESUS. — The name Joshua is the contracted form of Je-hosh´-u-a. See Num. 13, 16. Je-hoshua signifies "Jehovah's Salvation," or, "Jehovah Saves." In the New Testament, Joshua is twice called Jesus. Acts 7, 45, and Heb. 4, 8. Jesus is the Greek form of the name. In Joshua's life may be found many points of resemblance to that of our Lord Jesus, the Captain of our salvation: 1) Both were called and commissioned by God to lead His chosen people. 2) Both saved God's people from their enemies. 3) Joshua, the son of Nun, brought God's chosen people into the Promised Land and gave them rest and a home in it; Jesus brings the elect of God into the heavenly Canaan, into eternal life in heaven, and gives them true and eternal rest. Eph. 1, 11. 14; Heb. 3 and 4.

THE CITIES OF REFUGE, to any of which the manslayer who had killed a person unawares and unwittingly might flee, so that he need not die by the hand of the avenger of blood, may also be regarded as a type of Christ, to whom, by faith, we flee for refuge against the avenging Law of God. Chap. 20.

Summary of Contents. — *I. The Conquest of Canaan.*
Chaps. 1 to 12: God commissions Joshua to lead the people and
promises to assist him at all times. Joshua prepares the people
to pass over the Jordan. Chap. 1. — Joshua sends two young men
to spy out Jericho. Ra'-hab hides them. Heb. 11, 31; Jas. 2, 25.
The spies return in safety. Chap. 2. — The people cross the
Jordan on dry ground, in commemoration of which twelve stones
are erected in Gil'-gal. Chaps. 3 and 4. — Circumcision is renewed. The Passover is kept (for the first time in forty years).
The manna ceases. The Captain of the host of the Lord appears
to Joshua, encouraging him. Chap. 5. — By faith the walls of

The Jordan near Jericho.

Jericho fall down; Israel takes the city and burns it. Rahab is
saved. Chap. 6. — The Israelites are repulsed at A'-i because
covetous A'-chan has stolen things devoted to God. Achan is put
to death for his sacrilege. Israel now takes and burns A'-i.
Chap. 7. — The Law recorded and read at E'-bal and Ger'-i-zim.
Chap. 8. — Having heard that God had commanded Israel to
destroy all the Canaanites, the inhabitants of Gib'-e-on by fraud
secure a solemn promise from the Israelites that they will let
them live. Chap. 9. — The Southern Canaanites combine against
Joshua and are defeated at Beth-ho'-ron; God causes a destructive
hail to fall on the fleeing enemy; at Joshua's prayer the sun and
the moon stand still while Israel pursues and utterly destroys the

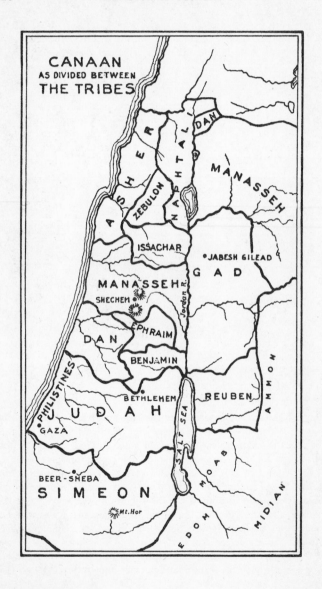

CANAAN
AS DIVIDED BETWEEN
THE TRIBES

enemy. Chap. 10. — The Northern Canaanites unite against Joshua and are overwhelmed at the waters of Me'-rom. Ha'-zor is captured and burned. All the country is taken by Joshua. Chap. 11. — List of 31 kings and their people defeated and driven out by the children of Israel. Chap. 12. — *II. The Distribution of the Land.* Chaps. 13 to 22. Indicating the boundaries of the land to be divided. Chap. 13. — How the land was apportioned: Nine and a half tribes have their inheritance on the west side of Jordan, and two and a half tribes on the east. Chaps. 14 to 17. (Map.) — The Tabernacle is set up at Shi'-loh; continued division of the land. Chaps. 18 and 19. — Six cities of refuge are designated. Chap. 20. — The tribe of Levi receives 48 cities. Chap. 21. — The soldiers of the two and one half tribes who had helped their brethren conquer the land return to their homes beyond Jordan and build an altar of testimony during their journey. Chap. 22. — *III. Last Days of Joshua.* Chaps. 23 and 24. The last grand assembly of the tribes presided over by Joshua. His farewell address. His death and burial. Joseph's bones are buried.

CHAPTER 11.

The Book of Judges. — The Book of Ruth.

JUDGES.

NAME. — The book is named from the heroes who appear as leaders and deliverers of Israel in the period succeeding Joshua and ending with the rise of Samuel. The exploits of these leaders and deliverers form the central and principal part of the book. They are called *Judges,* principally because they *judged* Israel in the sense of defending it against its enemies and delivering it from oppression. For this reason they are called "saviors" in Neh. 9, 27. Thirteen Judges are named in the book.

CHRONOLOGY. — The length of the period covered by the Book of Judges cannot be established with certainty. Chap. 11, 26, however, gives us a certain basis to figure on: When Jeph'-thah became judge, 300 years had passed since

Israel came to Canaan. Subtract 25 years for the period under Joshua. Jeph´-thah judged 6 years; Elon, 10; Abdon, 8 — total, 24 years. Then followed 40 years of oppression under the Phi-lis´-tines (chap. 13, 1), from which Samson began to deliver the Israelites. This makes the time of the Judges approximately 350 years (from about 1425 to about 1100 B. C.).

CHARACTER OF THE PERIOD. — In his farewell address, Joshua had earnestly warned the people against idolatry and solemnly exhorted them to remain faithful to Jehovah, the God of their fathers. They gave their solemn promise. But when this God-fearing generation had passed away, "there arose another generation after them which knew not the Lord nor yet the works which He had done for Israel. And they forsook the Lord God of their fathers, which brought them out of the land of Egypt, and followed other gods, of the gods of the people that were round about them, and bowed themselves unto them, and provoked the Lord to anger." Chap. 2, 10—12. Therefore the Lord punished them and "delivered them into the hands of spoilers that spoiled them, and He sold them into the hands of their enemies round about, so that they could not any longer stand before their enemies. Withersoever they went out, the hand of the Lord was against them for evil, as the Lord had said, and as the Lord had sworn unto them; and they were greatly distressed." Chap. 2, 14. 15. All in all, the years of foreign oppression were 111. Time and again the Lord showed that He is long-suffering and merciful. Whenever the people cried to Him in their affliction and repented of their idolatry, the Lord took pity on them and raised up a judge, or heroic leader, and by the hand of the judge delivered them out of the hand of the enemies who oppressed them and vexed them. However, after the death of the judge the people quickly relapsed into idolatry, and thus sin, punishment, repentance, and deliverance followed in succession through those three and a half centuries.

THE AUTHOR. — Regarding the authorship of the Book of Judges nothing can be stated with positive certainty. Most scholars ascribe the book to Samuel, the great prophet, who forms the connecting link between the time of the Judges and of the kings.

SUMMARY OF CONTENTS. — *I. Introduction.* Chap. 1, 1—2, 9. This section is retrospective, giving an account of the extent to which Canaan had been subdued after the death of Joshua. — *II. The Deeds of the Judges.* This is the main part of the book. Chap. 2, 10—16, 31. This is preceded by an introduction of its own, chap. 2, 10—3, 6, which is prospective, giving a summary of the whole period to be treated of. Then follow the exploits of the Judges. — *III. Two Detached Episodes,* placed at the end of the book. These episodes evidently belong to the earlier period of the Judges. The one is the story of Mi'-cah, his idols and his priest. This priest was a grandson of Moses. This story shows how the worship of God was soon corrupted and illustrates the rough spirit of those dark ages in the early history of Israel. Chap. 17 and 18. The horrible story of the Levite in Gib'-e-ah. The outrage in Gibeah precipitates the ruinous war against the tribe of Benjamin. Chaps. 19 to 21.

SCHEME OF JUDGES.

Judge	Tribe	Enemy	Years of Rule
1. Othniel	Judah	Mesopotamians, 8 years	40
2. Ehud	Benjamin	Moabites, 18 years ⎫	80
3. Shamgar	Judah?	Philistines ⎭	
4. ⎰Deborah ⎱Barak	Ephraim ⎫ Naphtali ⎭	Jabin, 20 years	40
5. Gideon	Manasseh (West)	Midianites, 7 years	40
6. Abimelech	Manasseh (West)	. . . .	3
7. Tola	Issachar	. . . .	23
8. Jair	Manasseh (East)	. . . .	22
9. Jephthah	Gad	Ammonites, 18 years	6
10. Ibzahn	Judah?	. . . .	7
11. Elon	Zebulun	. . . .	10
12. Abdon	Ephraim	. . . .	8
13. Samson	Dan	Philistines, 40 years	20

The foregoing "Scheme of Judges" names the thirteen Judges, the tribe to which the individual judge probably belonged, the enemies who oppressed Israel, together with the years of oppression, also the number of years which each judge ruled in Israel.

RUTH.

PURPOSE. — This short book tells the charming story of Ruth the Mo-ab-it´-ess, who lived "in the days when the Judges ruled" (chap. 1, 1), probably during the latter part of the rule of the Judges. It is one of the sweetest stories

Bethlehem.

in the Bible. Here we see that even in the darkest period God had men and women who served Him in holiness of life. In Na-o´-mi we have a specimen of a good woman, who is highly esteemed. In Ruth we have an example of modesty and patience, coupled with a remarkable belief in the true God. In Boaz we have the model rich man of his age, a man of fine spirit and of strict integrity. One of the objects of the writer of the book is to show how goodness is rewarded. The chief purpose, however, is to trace the genealogy of King David to the Moabitess Ruth. Chap. 4, 17—23. "This information gains in significance if we remember that the genealogy of David is at the same time that of our Savior."

DATE. — At the outset the writer says that the things recorded in the book took place when the Judges ruled in Israel — an intimation that in the days of the writer the Judges had ceased to rule. Again, as the genealogy here recorded ends with David's name, it appears probable that the book was not written before David had become a person of influence and renown.

AUTHOR. — The author remains unknown to us; but it has been suggested that David himself might well have written this account of an important event in his family history.

SUMMARY OF CONTENTS. — *I. Sojourn in Moab* for about ten years, during which time Naomi's husband and two married sons die. Chap. 1, 1—5. — *II. Return of Naomi with Ruth to Bethlehem.* Chap. 1, 6—22. — *III. Ruth Gleans in the Field of Boaz.* — *IV. Bold Act of Ruth:* She asks Boaz to do the part of a near kinsman. Lev. 25, 25. — *V. Boaz's Redemption of Naomi's Property and Marriage of Ruth.* Ruth, the former heathen, becomes an ancestress of Christ. Chap. 4.

CHAPTER 12.

The Books of Samuel.

NAME. — The two books of Samuel were originally one in the Hebrew Bible. The Septuagint (see chapter 2, p. 13) divided the book into two. The Latin translation of the Bible, the Vul'-gate, called both the "Books of Kings." Accordingly, the Authorized Version describes the First Book of Samuel as "otherwise called the First Book of the Kings."

PURPOSE. — "Beginning with a biographical sketch of Samuel's life before he became the last judge of Israel, the author takes up the thread of history at the point where the Book of Judges drops it after relating the end of Samson and carries it forward to the close of David's reign." In the Book of Judges we have read again and again: "In those days there was no king in Israel." When Samuel, the last judge, was old, he made his sons judges. Their ill government furnished the elders of Israel an occasion to come to Samuel with the demand: "Now make us a king to judge us like all the nations." 1 Sam. 8. This demand grieved Samuel; but he was ordered by God to accede to the people's wishes; reluctant at first, he finally yielded and anointed Saul king of Israel. While Saul was the *first* king, his successor David became the *greatest* king of Israel. Samuel, Saul, and David are the three great characters of these two books. "But the books were not merely written to be a record of the lives of three great men whom God gave to His people, although their story is full of human interest. The Christian reader will retain the proper point of view that this story sets forth the providential control which God exercised over the affairs of His people, achieving His purposes without fail."

DATE OF WRITING. — The fact that these two books bear the name of Samuel must not lead us to assume that they were written by him. 1 Sam. 25, 1 records the death of this famous and faithful man of God; hence all that follows must have been written by some other man. Certain evidences which are found in passages preceding chap. 25, 1 make it clear that the first 24 chapters of the first book also were written after Samuel's death. Such an evidence is the antiquarian remark 1 Sam. 9, 9: "He that is now called a prophet was beforetime called a seer." Again, the author mentions Israel and Judah separately and also specifies "kings of Judah." 1 Sam. 11, 8; 15, 4; 27, 6. This makes it fairly certain that the writer lived after the division of the kingdom, which took place after the death of Solomon.

MESSIANIC PROPHECY. — 2 Sam. 7, 12 ff. The first promise of the Messiah was given to Adam and Eve in Paradise. The second promise pointed out the Patriarch Abraham as a progenitor of the Messiah. The third promise stated that He was to come out of the tribe of Judah. The prophecy before us points out that the Messiah should spring from the royal house and lineage of David. Read Acts 13, 23; Rom. 1, 3. Note that our Savior is called "Son of David."

SCHOOLS OF PROPHETS. — Samuel established schools of prophets. There had been prophets, or seers, before his time. But during the dark days of the judgeship of Eli, prophecy had almost ceased. 1 Sam. 3, 1. But when Samuel grew up, "all Israel, from Dan to Be-er-she'-ba, knew that Samuel was established to be a prophet of the Lord." 1 Sam. 3, 19—21. Samuel founded a school of prophets at Ra'-mah. About a century later there were such schools at Bethel, Jericho, and Gilgal. 1 Sam. 19, 20; 2 Kings 2, 3. 5; 4, 38. Under the superintendence of an elderly prophet, styled "father" or "master" (1 Sam. 10, 10—12; 2 Kings 2, 3), promising young men were gathered into these schools and instructed in the interpretation of the Law, in music, and in sacred poetry. 1 Sam. 10, 5. After their graduation they discharged the office of religious teachers among the people.

SUMMARY OF CONTENTS. — *I. Samuel, the Last Judge in Israel.* 1 Sam. 1 to 12: Samuel's birth and dedication to God. The wicked sons of Eli. Samuel's vision and call as prophet. Loss of the Ark of the Covenant. Death of Eli. Return of the Ark. Samuel made judge. His victory over the Philistines through God's help. The people ask for a king. Samuel anoints Saul. Samuel formally lays down his office as judge. — *II. Saul's Reign till His Rejection by God.* 1 Sam. 13 to 15: His first military campaign against the Philistines and the victory of his son Jon'-a-than. Other wars and successes of Saul. His disobedience to God in the war against Am'-a-lek. His rejection. — *III. History of Saul from His Rejection to His Death.* 1 Sam. 16 to 31: David is secretly anointed by Samuel; becomes musician to Saul; his victory over Go-li'-ath; persecuted by jealous Saul, he flees from place to place. The Philistines make war against Saul. Saul consults the witch at Endor. David is obliged to leave the army of the Philistines. He recovers the spoil taken by the Am'-a-lek-ites. The Philistines defeat Saul's army, his sons are killed, and he commits suicide. — *IV. David as King.* 2 Sam. 1 to 4: David mourning for Saul and Jonathan. His return to the land of Israel. He is made king at He'-bron over Judah, where he reigns seven and a half years, while Saul's son Ish-bo'-sheth is made king over Israel (the northern tribes). A two-year struggle between the house of Saul and David. David wins in the end and is made king over all Israel. — *V. Increasing Greatness and Glory of David.* 2 Sam. 5 to 9: David takes Jerusalem and makes it his capital. He twice defeats the Philistines. He brings the Ark to Zion in Jerusalem and, while not allowed to build the Temple, gathers materials for it. He enlarges the kingdom by conquests over the Philistines, Moabites, Edomites, and Syrians, extending its boundaries from the Mediterranean to the River Eu-phra'-tes. (Map 1.) David shows kindness to the lame son of his faithful friend Jonathan. — *VI. Adverse Experiences of the Great King David.* 2 Sam. 10 to 20: His great sin with Bath-she'-ba and his repentance. Ammon's incest. Rebellion of Absolom. The revolt of Sheba. — *VII. End of David's Reign.* 2 Sam. 21 to 24: Three years of famine. Four battles against the Philistines. David's psalm of thanksgiving and his last words. The names of his mighty men. The numbering of the people, followed by the plague.

CHAPTER 13.

The Books of the Kings.

THEIR NAME AND PURPOSE. — Like the Books of Samuel the Books of the Kings formed but one book in the Hebrew original. The division into two parts was made by the seventy learned Jews who translated the Old Testament into Greek in the third century before Christ (Septuagint). Our Authorized Version has these titles: "The First Book of the Kings, commonly called the Third Book of the Kings," and: "The Second Book of the Kings, commonly called the Fourth Book of the Kings." These two books get their name from their contents: they contain a history of the kings of the Jews, beginning with Solomon and ending with the captive king Je-hoí'-a-chin — 1015 to 560 B. C. However, these books do not give us a history of kings such as human histories furnish. They give us history with a moral. "Like all historical books of the Bible they are not intended merely as a source of historical information, but were written chiefly for religious purposes." The writer points out again and again how God fulfilled His promise to David, His servant, that He would always keep a man from his house and lineage on the royal throne. (1 Kings 2, 4; 8, 20; 11, 12. 13. 34—39; 15, 4. 5; 2 Kings 8, 19, and other passages.) Again, the writer tells us in a well-nigh stereotyped formula whether the reign of a king was good or evil "in the eyes of the Lord." And again, he describes in great detail the labors of the prophets of the Lord, particularly the labors of the great prophets Elijah and Elisha in the Northern Kingdom of Israel. And, finally, the fact that the author wrote from a religious standpoint appears also from the fact that he shows the division of the kingdom, the overthrow of Israel (the Northern Kingdom of the ten tribes), and the Babylonian Captivity of Judah (the Southern Kingdom of the tribes of Judah and Benjamin) to have been the proper consequence and condign punishment of the sins of the people; and thus his history shows the ruin to which sin inevitably leads if not repented of, but persisted in. See 2 Kings 17, 7—23.

Sources. — The author repeatedly refers to historical records where the interested reader might find a fuller account of the particular subjects in hand. These records are three in number: 1. "The Book of the Acts of Solomon" (mentioned once, 1 Kings 11, 41). 2. "The Book of the

Chronicles of the Kings of Israel" (mentioned seventeen times; see 1 Kings 14, 19, etc.). 3. "The Book of the Chronicles of the Kings of Judah" (fourteen times; see 1 Kings 14, 29, etc.). These three books were not written by so-called "court historians," but by various members of the schools of the prophets spoken of in the foregoing chapter. The contents of these three prophetic books were known to the writer of the Books of Kings, and under the guidance of the Spirit of God he chose from these documents such material as suited his purpose.

THE AUTHOR. — From 2 Kings 25, 27 it appears that the author wrote his history after Je-hoi'-a-chin, king of Judah, had been in the Babylonian Captivity about thirty-seven years. That brings us down to the year 561 B. C. This was also the first of the two years in which E'-vil-me-ro'-dach was king of Babylon, and in this first year he advanced the captive king Je-hoi'-a-chin. Now, E'-vil-me-ro'-dach reigned two years only. As the writer does not mention the end of his reign, it is probable that he wrote his work about 560 B. C. The unknown author seems to have lived among the captive Jews in Babylon. Suffice it to say that he was a holy man of God, who wrote as he was moved by the Holy Ghost.

SOLOMON A TYPE OF CHRIST. — Of the 22 chapters in the First Book of Kings 11 chapters are devoted to the history of King Solomon, the son and successor of David. He is in many respects a type of "great David's greater Son," of Christ, our King. Solomon's name signifies "Peaceful": Christ is the true "Prince of Peace." Is. 9, 6. 7; Rom. 5, 1. 10. Solomon built the magnificent Temple at Jerusalem: Christ is the Builder of the great spiritual temple, the Church. Eph. 2, 20; 1 Pet. 2, 5. Solomon excelled all men of his time in wisdom (1 Kings 4, 30): Christ is the Possessor of "all the treasures of wisdom and

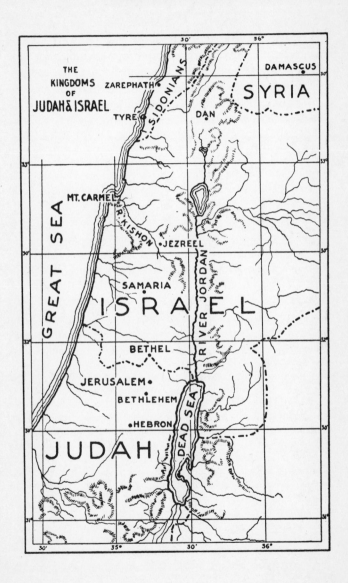

knowledge" (Col. 2, 3). Solomon's kingdom was one of great glory (1 Kings 4, 20—25): the glory of Christ's Kingdom of Grace here on earth, though invisible, is greater than that of Solomon's kingdom, and eye hath not seen nor ear heard, neither hath entered into the heart of man the great glory of His kingdom in heaven.

SUMMARY OF CONTENTS. — I. *The Reign of Solomon.* 1 Kings 1 to 11: Solomon is anointed king. The death of David. Solomon marries Pharaoh's daughter. His officers, power, wealth, and wisdom. He builds the Temple and his royal palace. Dedication of the Temple, 1005 B.C. Solomon's navy fetches gold from O'-phir. The Queen of Sheba's visit. Solomon's polygamy and idolatry. Solomon's death after a reign of forty years, 1015 to 975 B.C. — II. *The Division of the Kingdom* and the Story of the Two Kingdoms. 1 Kings 12 to 2 Kings 17: Under Re-ho-bo'-am, Solomon's son, ten of the twelve tribes revolt, and the splendid kingdom is split in two: the Kingdom of Israel, in the North, and the Kingdom of Judah, in the South. Continual hostility between both kingdoms. King Ahab of Israel and his wife Jez'-e-bel establish the worship of the sun-god Baal, calling forth the flaming witness of Elijah and Elisha, the prophets. Je-hosh'-a-phat, king of Judah, and Ahab of Israel form an alliance and become involved in fateful troubles with the Syrians. Death of Ahab and his wicked wife Jez'-e-bel. Elijah ascends to heaven. Miracles of Elisha. Je'-hu slays A-ha-zi'-ah of Judah and Je-ho'-ram of Israel. Renewed hostility between the two kingdoms, until the Kingdom of Israel is overthrown by the king of As-syr'-i-a and Israel carried away out of its own land to Assyria, about 722 B.C., and the ten tribes disappear from history. The king of Assyria sent heathen colonists to settle their country. (Map 1.) — III. *The Kingdom of Judah till the Babylonian Captivity.* 2 Kings 18 to 25: Under eight successive kings the Kingdom of Judah survives the Kingdom of Israel about 130 years. Sen-nach'-e-rib of Assyria invades Judah; his general's defiant speech before Jerusalem; the good King Hez-e-ki'-ah is comforted by the prophet Isaiah and prays; God destroys the Assyrian army during the night. Hez-e-ki'-ah's illness, restoration to health, and sinful ambition; Isaiah foretells the Babylonian Captivity. The wicked reign of Ma-nas'-seh and of A'-mon. Jo-si'-ah, the good king, institutes a general religious reformation after the finding of the Book of the Law. His son Je-ho'-a-haz is deposed by the king of Egypt, who makes Je-hoi'-a-kim king. Neb-u-chad-nez'-zar, king of Babylon, besieges and takes Jerusalem (606 B. C. beginning of the Seventy Years' Captivity); Je-hoi'-a-kim rebels against the king of Babylon after three years and procures his own ruin. Je-hoi'-a-chin's evil reign. Jerusalem captured, and Je-hoi'-a-chin and his royal family carried away to Babylon into captivity, about 599 B. C. Zed-e-ki'-ah made king. He rebels against the king of Babylon; Jerusalem is laid waste, the Temple destroyed, about 588 B. C. All but the poor of the land are carried away to Babylon.

BAB'-Y-LON. The name comes from Bab-y-lo'-ni-a, the Greek form of Ba'-bel (Gate of God). Babylon was a city situated on both banks of the Eu-phra'-tes River, about 250 miles above its junction with the Ti'-gris. It gave its name to the province of which it was the capital. The most ancient name of the country was Shi'-nar. Gen. 10, 10. Babylonia was an extensive plain, extending about 400 miles northwest and southeast along the Tigris and the Euphrates, and about 100 miles wide, interrupted by no hill or mountain. — The Babylonian Empire was founded about 2,000 B. C. After about 700 years the Assyrians, whose country adjoined Babylonia, conquered the Babylonians and held their country till 625 B. C. In this year the Chal-de'-ans, who occupied the southern part of Babylonia on the Persian Gulf, made themselves masters of all Babylonia. The second Chaldean king was Neb-u-chad-nez'-zar, one of the greatest rulers of all history. He founded the New Babylonian Empire, which Jeremiah called "the praise of the whole earth." Jer. 51, 41. He brought the Jews into the Babylonian Captivity. Under Bel-shaz'-zar, his grandson, Babylon was besieged and taken by Cyrus, the Persian, in 538 B. C. Cyrus made Susa the capital of his kingdom. (Map 1.)

CHAPTER 14.

The Books of the Chronicles.

THE NAME. — These two books, which were written as one volume, bear a name in the Hebrew Old Testament which literally signifies "Words of Days," but which in a free translation means "Annals," "History." The English title "Chronicles" (Narratives of Events) is the equivalent of the Latin name suggested by Jerome (born 331, died 422), the reviser of the ancient Latin version, who described these books as "a chronicle of the whole of sacred history." As a matter of fact the two Books of Chronicles cover a period of almost 3,500 years, from Adam to the grandsons of Ze-rub´-ba-bel.

CONTENTS. — Chronicles contain: 1. genealogical tables, together with historical notes and geographical lists; 2. the history of David; 3. the history of Solomon; 4. the history of the Kingdom of Judah down to the Babylonian Captivity.

Several of the genealogical lists are peculiar to Chronicles, being found in no other books of the Bible. In the history of David, Solomon, and the Kings of Judah the Books of Chronicles have upwards of 40 sections agreeing very closely with the Books of Samuel and the Books of the Kings, occasionally showing a different arrangement and in a number of instances furnishing supplemental information, and, while omitting some events mentioned in Samuel and Kings, adding other matters not found in these books, the latter being particularly true with reference to matters pertaining to the worship of the true God. Again, while the Books of the Kings give us the history of both the kings of Israel and of Judah, the Books of Chronicles deal with the history of Judah only, the Northern Kingdom of Israel being alluded to only when its affairs touch those of the Southern Kingdom. In all these points the author follows a purposeful plan.

THE PURPOSE. — The purpose of Chronicles is not, in the main, to give a general history of David down to the Babylonian Exile, but rather to point out from this history —

1. How the Lord fulfilled the promises given to David, His servant;

2. How the true worship of God was preserved throughout those centuries, what was the attitude of king and people toward this worship, and how the preservation of this worship brought peace and prosperity, while its neglect resulted in ruin. See 2 Chron. 15, 2.

THE DATE AND THE AUTHOR. — Chronicles close with the statement that King Cyrus of Persia issued a written proclamation throughout all his kingdom permitting the Jews to return to Jerusalem. 2 Chron. 36, 22. 23. He made this proclamation in the first year of his reign, which was about 536 B. C. Accordingly, these books must have been written after this date, after the return of the Jews to the land of their fathers. On the other hand, the work must not be dated much later, for the author speaks of *darics* (1 Chron. 29, 7, *R. V.*), which were Persian gold coins bearing on one side the image of Darius; the Jews used these Persian coins only while under the Persian rule. — If you read the last two verses in Chronicles and the first two verses in Ezra, you will perceive that both are almost identical. This circumstance gives rise to the thought that Ezra, a learned and pious scribe, who was one of those who returned to Jerusalem, wrote the Books of Chronicles as well as the book bearing his name. The Jewish Talmud unhesitatingly ascribes the work to Ezra, the gifted and good scribe who was endowed with the spirit of prophecy.

MESSIANIC PROPHECY. — 1 Chron. 17, 11—15. See the Messianic prophecy in chapter 12, p. 53.

SUPPLEMENTARY READING. — Read Ps. 137 in connection with the history of the Babylonian Exile.

SUMMARY OF CONTENTS. — *I. Genealogy from Adam to the Grandsons of Ze-rub'-ba-bel,* together with some historial notes and geographical lists. 1 Chron. 1 to 10. — *II. The History of*

David's Reign. 1 Chron. 11 to 30: Detailed information concerning David's plans for the Temple and his last decrees. — *III. The History of Solomon and the Kings of Judah down to the Babylonian Captivity.* 2 Chron. 1 to 36: Building and dedication of the Temple. The Queen of Sheba visits Solomon. Outstanding and characteristic deeds and experiences of various kings of Judah, many of which are not mentioned in the Books of the Kings. The proclamation of Cyrus.

TABLE OF THE KINGS.

Kings of the Whole Nation.

Saul	1095—1055
David	1055—1015
Solomon	1015— 975

Kings of Judah.	Kings of Israel.
Re-ho-bo'-am ....975—957	Jer-o-bo'-am I ...975—953
A-bi'-jah ....957—955	
Asa ....955—914	Na'-dab ....953—952
	Ba'-a-sha ....952—930
	E'-lah ....930—929
	Zim'-ri 929
	Om'-ri ....929—918
Je-hosh'-a-phat. . .914—889	A'-hab ....918—897
	A-ha-zi'-ah .....897—896
Je-ho'-ram ......889—884	Jo'-ram ....896—883
A-ha-zi'-ah .....884—883	Je'-hu ....883—856
Ath-a-li'-ah .....883—877	
Jo'-ash ....877—838	Je-ho'-a-haz .....856—840
A-ma-zi'-ah .....838—810	Je-ho'-ash ......840—824
Uz-zi'-ah ......810—758	Jer-o-bo'-am II ...824—783
	Anarchy ....783—772
	Zach-a-ri'-ah 772
	Shallum ....772—771
	Men'-a-hem .....771—760
	Pek-a-hi'-ah .....760—759
Jo'tham ....758—742	Pe'kah ....759—739
A'-haz ....742—727	Anarchy ....739—730
Hez-e-ki'-ah .....727—698	Ho-she'-a ....730—722
Ma-nas'-seh .....698—643	End of kingdom . . 722
A'-mon ....643—641	
Jo-si'-ah ....641—610	
Je-ho'-a-haz 610	
Je-hoi'-a-kim ....610—599	
Je-hoi'-a-chin 599	
Zed-e-ki'-ah .....599—588	
End of kingdom . . 588 B. C.	

CHAPTER 15.

The Books of Ezra, Nehemiah, and Esther.

EZRA.

THE AUTHOR. — The Book of Ezra was written by the famous priest and scribe whose name it bears. Ezra was born in the Babylonian Captivity of the Jews and seems to have been held in high regard at the Persian court, as appears from the gracious and important commission given him by King Ar-tax-erx'-es (Ar-taks-urks'-ees). Chap. 7, 11 f. He wrote his book between 450 and 444 B. C.

THE PERIOD. — The Book of Ezra covers a period of about 80 years (about 538—458 B. C.). During this period the following six kings of Persia reigned over the Jews: —

1. Cyrus the Great, who captured Babylon 538 B. C. and died 529 B. C. 2. Cambyses (Kam-bi'-sees), his son, 529—522 B. C. 3. Smerdis, who reigned only seven months, 521 B. C. 4. Darius I, son of Hystaspes (Hys-tas'-pees), 521—485 B. C. 5. Xerxes I (A-has-u-e'-rus), 485—465 B. C. 6. Artaxerxes Longimanus (Lon-gi-ma'-nus), 465 to 424 B. C.

God had predicted and promised that at the end of seventy years He would bring His people back to Palestine. Jer. 29, 10. Ezra records the accomplishment of this word of the Lord. Chap. 1, 1. Having in 538 B. C. given the victory to Cyrus, king of Persia, over the Babylonians, who held Israel captive, He stirred up the spirit of Cyrus, so that he made a proclamation concerning the rebuilding of the Temple and the return of the Jews to their own country. 42,360 Jews availed themselves of the opportunity, returning under the leadership of Zerubbabel (Ze-rub'-ba-bel = born in Babel), the prince of Judah, who was made governor of the returned exiles. They found the Temple

of Solomon in ruins and immediately took steps to rebuild it. Owing to the bitter opposition of the foreign
and half-pagan colonists who had been settled around Jerusalem and whose offer to assist in rebuilding the house
of God was declined, the Temple was not finished till 516
B. C. Then (between chaps. 6 and 7) follows a gap of
about 58 years in the history of the returned Jews. In
458 B. C. Ezra was commissioned by Artaxerxes to visit the
Holy City. Under Ezra's leadership the second band of
Jewish exiles returned to the land of their fathers. Ezra
found that during the 80 years which had passed since the
arrival of the first colony many had contracted mixed marriages, that is, they had married heathen, idolatrous wives,
contrary to the Law of Moses. This evil Ezra reformed,
bringing the people back to the true worship of God.

POINTS TO BE NOTED. — 1. The returned exiles now
begin to be called *Jews,* the shortened form of Judeans.
Chap. 4, 12. 2. The returned Jews did not form a free and
independent nation; their country was a province of Persia
(chap. 2, 1) and remained such till the fall of the Persian
Empire, 331 B. C. 3. After the Babylonian Captivity we
hear little or nothing of idols and idolatry among the Jews.
The exile cured them of this sin.

SUMMARY OF CONTENTS. — *I. Return of the First Colony of
Exiles under Zerubbabel.* Chaps. 1—6: Decree of Cyrus; the
number and names of those who returned from Babylon; the
altar set up and the foundation of the second Temple laid; ad-
versaries stop the building of the Temple; the prophets Haggai
and Zechariah urge the renewal of building operations; the
Temple is finished and dedicated. An interval of about 58 years.
II. Return of the Second Colony under Ezra. Chaps. 7—10: Artaxerxes gives Ezra permission to go to Jerusalem; a considerable
company of Jews goes with him; they are laden with gifts for
the Temple; having arrived in the Holy City, Ezra promptly
causes the people to put away their heathen wives.

NEHEMIAH.

THE AUTHOR. — The Book of Ne-he-mi´-ah opens with the statement: "The words [history] of Nehemiah." This initial sentence plainly points out Nehemiah as the writer of this book. Nehemiah was in Shushan (Lily), or Susa, the palace. (Map 1.) Shushan was the chief of the three capitals of the Persian Empire. Here Nehemiah held the important and lucrative post of cupbearer to King Artaxerxes Longimanus (Long-handed). In 445 B. C. the king gave him leave of absence and appointed him Governor of Judah. This position he held for about fourteen years. He penned his "words," or history, about 431 B. C., in the time of Malachi.

THE CONTENTS. — Nehemiah relates his own history, which is closely interwoven with that of his people. His book is a sequel to the Book of Ezra. It covers a period of about fourteen years. The principal object of the writer is to describe the circumstances attending the rebuilding of the wall of Jerusalem and its dedication. Through his brother Hanani, who had recently visited Jerusalem, Nehemiah heard that the Jews in the Holy Land were in great affliction and reproach, that the wall of Jerusalem was still broken down and the population, therefore, without protection against hostile attacks. His heart was touched by the account of this sad condition. In his grief he prayed to God and then asked and obtained permission of the king to go to Jerusalem and to rebuild the wall of the city. Entrusted with full powers as governor, he proceeded to Palestine in 445 B. C. and, despite great opposition on the part of the neighboring heathen, had the wall of Jerusalem rebuilt within fifty-two days. He introduced many reforms among the people, abolishing usury, reviving the knowledge of the Law, restoring the strict observance of the Sabbath, enforcing the payment of religious dues, and compelling those who had married foreign, idolatrous wives to divorce them.

IMPORTANCE. — The Book of Nehemiah contains the last of the divinely inspired records of Jewish history we possess. The Book of Esther, although placed after the Book of Nehemiah, relates an incident which took place under King Xerxes, in the days of Ezra and Nehemiah, and was evidently written before the Book of Nehemiah. The Books of the Maccabees, which continue the history of the Jews, were not given by inspiration of God; they are human books. Thus the Book of Nehemiah brings to a close the canonical history of God's people in the Old Testament.

SUMMARY OF CONTENTS. — *I. Efforts of Nehemiah for the Good of Jerusalem.* Chaps. 1—7: His prayer for the Holy City; arrival in Jerusalem; rebuilding of the wall; open opposition offered to this work by the angry heathen neighbors, whose cooperation was refused; Nehemiah relieves the poor Jews oppressed by usury; his own generosity; he returns to Persia for a time; after his return to Jerusalem he finds a list of those who first returned from Babylon; money given for the Temple. — *II. The Solemn Restoration of Divine Worship.* Chaps. 8—10: The public reading of the Law of Moses for the instruction of the people; joyful observance of the Feast of Tabernacles; repentance of the people; public confession of God's past goodness; the people enter into a voluntary covenant with God; terms of the covenant. — *III. Various Lists; Remaining Labors of Nehemiah.* Chaps. 11—13: List of those who dwelled at Jerusalem and in the country towns; the priests and Levites who came with Zerubbabel; dedication of the wall with great pomp and ceremony; Nehemiah reforms various abuses.

ESTHER.

ESTHER. — This book takes its name from the fair and patriotic Jewish maiden Esther (Star), who is the principal character in the episode of Jewish history which it relates. This episode occurred principally in the Persian palace at Susa, after the first exiles had returned to Palestine with Zerubbabel. Not all the Jews took advantage of the opportunity given them by Cyrus, in 536; on the contrary, many remained in the land of captivity, where they were prospering. One of these was Mordecai, the cousin of Esther. When her parents died, he adopted her as his own daughter. In process of time God made her queen of the great Persian King A-has-u-e´-rus (Xerxes) and used her as His instrument to save His people from extermination, which was planned and plotted by the prime minister of the king, wicked Haman.

PURPOSE. — The Book of Esther was written not only to show how God wonderfully protected and saved His chosen people, from whom the Messiah was to come, but chiefly to explain how the Feast of Purim (Feast of Lots) came to be observed. Chap. 3, 7; 9, 20—26.

PECULIARITY OF THE BOOK. — The careful reader will notice that the name of God is nowhere found in this book. But while the divine name is nowhere mentioned, God Himself is in every chapter. "In no other book of the Bible is His providence more conspicuous."

DATE OF THE STORY. — It is generally believed that Ahasuerus was the Xerxes of secular history, who reigned from 485 to 465 B. C. and was defeated by the Greeks at Thermopylae (Ther-mop´-e-le) and Sal´-a-mis in 480 B. C. The *author* of this book is unknown; some ascribe the work to Ezra, others to Mordecai.

SUMMARY OF CONTENTS. — *I. Esther is Chosen Queen.* Chaps. 1 and 2: Great feast of Ahasuerus; Queen Vashti refuses to appear and is deposed; the choice of Esther to be queen; Mordecai discovers a plot against the king's life. — *II. Rise of Haman and His Murderous Plan against the Jews.* Chaps. 3—5: Mordecai, being a Jew, refuses to prostrate himself before Haman, and Haman, in revenge, resolves to destroy the entire nation of the Jews; Mordecai reports this plot to Esther and persuades her to risk going uncalled to the king and petitioning him in behalf of her people; she devises a plan to prevent the massacre. — *III. Deliverance of the Jews.* Chaps. 6—10: Ahasuerus finds that

Mordecai has received no reward for having saved his life and deputes Haman to confer high honor and dignity on Mordecai; Esther sues for her people's lives and denounces Haman to the king; Haman is hanged on the gallows he has prepared for Mordecai, while Mordecai is advanced in the kingdom; the king issues a second decree, permitting the Jews to resist those who should attack them, and to kill them in their own defense; the memorial Feast of Purim is instituted; Mordecai prime minister.

CHAPTER 16.

The Poetical Books.

BIBLICAL POETRY. — The contents of the five books immediately following the Book of Esther are poetical. This does not mean that they are the productions of the imagination of men. "*All* Scripture is given by inspiration of God"; that includes also the poetical books of the Bible. They are God's Word. "The term 'poetical' is not to be taken as implying fancifulness or unreality, but as relating to form only." We have met with examples of poetry in our reading of the historical books. Can you point out some of these examples? There is poetry also in the prophetical writings, particularly in the Lamentations of Jeremiah. However, the *Book of Job,* the *Book of Psalms, Proverbs, Ec-cle-si-as'-tes,* and the *Song of Solomon* are the five poetical books.

PECULIARITIES OF BIBLICAL POETRY. — Hebrew poetry makes use of neither rhyme nor meter (meter = measure, the regular change of short and long syllables). Yet it is true poetry. The essence of poetry lies not in rhyme and metric rhythm, but in the nature and adornment of the thoughts expressed. The thoughts of Biblical poetry are lofty and elevated, and these thoughts are expressed in the most appropriate language and adorned with many and beautiful figures of speech. As regards the mechanical character of Hebrew poetry, *parallelism,* or repetition of ideas, is its most prominent feature. The fundamental principle of this parallelism is that every verse must consist of at least two corresponding parts or members. For example: —

> Show me Thy ways, O Lord;
> Teach me Thy paths. Ps. 25, 4.

Here we have two corresponding, or parallel, sentences. The second line repeats the thought of the first line in different, but closely corresponding words. This is called *synonymous* parallelism. The thought is identical. *Antithetic* parallelism presents in the second line a contrast to the thought expressed in the first line. Example: —

> A soft answer turneth away wrath;
> But grievous words stir up anger. Prov. 15, 1.

Synthetic parallelism carries the thought of the first line forward in the second line with some addition. The thought is developed or enriched by the parallel. Example:

> The Law of the Lord is perfect, converting the soul;
> The Testimony of the Lord is sure, making wise the
> simple. Ps. 19, 7.

The Revised Version divides the poetic books of the Bible into lines, thus marking the contents as poetry. In the Authorized Version this feature is missing.

As to its nature and purpose Hebrew poetry is 1. devotional, 2. didactic (intended to teach).

THE BOOK OF JOB.

AUTHOR AND DATE. — The name of the writer of this book is not known. Some ascribe the book to Moses, others to Job himself, others to Solomon (thus Luther), and still others to various other persons. Luther says: "It is possible, even presumable, that Solomon composed and wrote this book; for his style of speaking in this book of Job is about the same as in his other books. Moreover, this history of Job was old and very familiar and well known to everybody in the days of Solomon."

POETIC STRUCTURE. — All expositors unite in declaring that the Book of Job is one of the grandest productions of Hebrew poetry. Some call it the greatest poem in the world's great literatures. It is full of sublime sentiments and bold and striking images.

A DIFFICULT BOOK. — It presents difficulties both in point of diction and of subject-matter. Regarding the difficulty of translating, Luther wrote to a friend in 1524: "In the translation of Job we have had hard work on account of the loftiness of the singularly magnificent style, so that he [Job] seems to be far more impatient with our translation than with the comfort of his friends. This circumstance is delaying the printing of the third part of the Bible."

HISTORICAL VALUE. — Though the book is a poem, it is founded on historical fact. Both Ezekiel (chap. 14, 14. 20) and James (chap. 5, 11) refer to Job as a real person, who really lived. The land of Uz in which he lived is generally thought to have been a region east of Palestine in Northern Arabia and west of the Arabian Desert, extending to Chaldea. (See Map 1.) There are numerous indications in the book which support the inference that he lived in the patriarchal age, probably just prior to the deliverance of Israel out of the bondage of Egypt. Ussher places the trial of Job about thirty years before the Exodus, 1521 B. C.

ITS PURPOSE. — This book, which bears a name that has become a synonym for patience under suffering, discusses the great and perplexing problem: "Why does a righteous God inflict suffering on a good man?" Luther says in his excellent introduction to this book: "The Book of Job treats this question — whether God causes also the pious to suffer adversity. Here Job stands fast and maintains that God afflicts also the pious without cause [without their having committed some special sin], solely to His praise, as Christ John 9, 3 also testifies of the man born blind." Job was a good man. God Himself bears witness to his piety. Despite his piety one calamity after another befalls him. His three friends who visit him in his great calamities express the opinion that suffering is always punishment for sin, that is, for some particularly great sin. This thought they repeat over and over in varying forms. Finally El´-i-phaz bluntly says to Job: "Is not thy wickedness great and thine iniquities infinite? For thou hast taken a pledge from thy brother for naught and stripped the naked of their clothing. Thou hast not given water to the weary to drink, and thou hast withholden bread from the hungry. Thou hast sent widows away empty, and the arms of the fatherless have been broken. Therefore snares are round about thee." Chap. 22, 5—10. Believing that the great evils which have come upon Job are his punishment for having committed some great sin, his three friends advise him to confess and repent, which will lead to restored communion with God and renewed prosperity. Job resents these stinging insinuations and charges that he must have committed some extraordinary sin to produce such extraordinary suffering. God Himself takes his part against his three friends. Hence it follows that suffering is not always punishment for sin. When Job had silenced his three friends, E-li´-hu, a young friend, takes up the word, rebuking both the three friends and Job, vindicating the justice of God. He sets forth that God punishes the transgressor, but delivers the godly after he has been proved and purified and has endured the suffering imposed upon him for this purpose. By showing that the object of affliction is the good of the sufferer, Elihu brings the problem of suffering nearer to a solution and prepares the way for the discourse of God. Chaps. 38—42. In terms both magnificent and majestic God calls Job's attention to the wonders of the entire animate and inanimate creation, and by questions which time and again He puts to the sufferer, He teaches him to realize that he does not even understand the thoughts of God in nature, much less those in human life, and that therefore he had wrongfully questioned the justice of divine Providence. Job now humbly confesses his folly and repents in dust and ashes.

The afflictions of Job were intended to be a *test,* or *trial.* Chaps. 1 and 2. His faith in God and his patience were severely tried, but his sufferings did not lead him to forsake God or godliness. Perplexed and in great pain, he utters some hard things against God, saying that God is arbitrary, and thus sins with his lips. But though his faith is seemingly extinct, it rises again and again and at last gains the victory. God owns him as His beloved child, shows kindness to him, and restores him to more than his former wealth and position. Satan, who said at the outset that Job was serving God only for what he got and that his piety was only a refined sort of selfishness, did not succeed in causing Job to forsake and curse God. And thus the trial of Job redounded to the discredit of Satan and to the honor of God. (See also the *Apology of the Augsburg Confession,* Art. VI, §§ 55. 56.)

JOB'S MESSIANIC HOPE. — In the certain prospect of his immediate dissolution the great sufferer beautifully and eloquently expresses his belief in the resurrection of the body and the life everlasting, saying: "I know that my Redeemer liveth and that He shall stand at the Latter Day upon the earth; and though after my skin worms destroy this body, yet in my flesh shall I see God; whom I shall see for myself and mine eyes shall behold, and not another." Chap. 19, 25—27.

SUMMARY OF CONTENTS. — *I. Historical Prolog* (Introduction; written in prose): Job's prosperous and happy condition; his affliction and his conduct in suffering. Chaps. 1 to 3. — *II. Dispute between Job and His Three Friends* regarding the cause of his calamities. Chaps. 4 to 31. — *III. Elihu's Discourse.* Chaps. 32 to 37: He vindicates the justice of God's government of the world. — *IV. The Lord's Discourse.* Chaps. 38 to 41: God himself intervenes and ends the discussion. — *V. Historical Epilog* (Conclusion; in prose): Job confesses his folly; he is restored to more than his former wealth and position. Chap. 42.

CHAPTER 17.
The Book of Psalms.

TITLES OF THE BOOK AND GENERAL CHARACTER. — The usual Hebrew title of the Book of Psalms is *Tehillim* = Praises. This title expresses well the general character of the 150 sacred poems contained in the book; they are poems of praise to God, or they at least end in praise. Praise is the prevailing tone; it makes up the bulk of the book and breathes in almost every psalm. Another Hebrew name for the book is *Tephilloth* (Tef-fil-lote') = Prayers. See Ps. 72, 20. This is perhaps the most appropriate title. The individual psalms are prayers of one kind or another. Here in this great, divinely inspired prayer-book are prayers for all states and conditions of life. Luther says: "The Psalter is the prayer-book of all saints, and every one, no matter what his case may be, can find psalms and words in it that suit his case and fit him so well, just as if they had been written thus for his sake alone, so that he himself could neither write nor find them better himself nor would want to wish them better." Hence the Psalter has been peculiarly dear to the people of God in all ages. The pious preacher-poet Herberger counted that day lost on which he had not read a psalm. The name *psalm* has come to us from the Septuagint, the Greek translation of the Old Testament. The Greek word *psalmos* means a poem to be sung to a stringed instrument. As the poems of the Psalter were sung with musical accompaniment in the Jewish worship, the name Psalms appeared appropriate and was adopted by the writers of the New Testament. See Luke 20, 42.

DATE OF COLLECTION. — The Book of Psalms is obviously a collection. 150 separate sacred poems, the production of different persons and belonging to different periods covering more than a thousand years, have here been brought together and united in one volume. We are not told by whom this was done. It is evidently the work of an enlightened man, who was learned in the Scriptures. Tradition says it was Ezra, the celebrated priest and scribe. He must have completed the collection after the Babylonian Captivity, for Ps. 137 was manifestly written after the return from Babylon. See also Psalms 74, 79, 126.

ARRANGEMENT. — The Psalter is divided into five sections, or books. The collectors probably had in mind the division of the Law of Moses into five books (Pentateuch). The Talmudic exposition of Ps. 1 says: "Moses gave to the Israelites the five books of the Law, and as a counterpart to these David gave them the Psalms, which consist of five books." Each of the five books closes with a doxology. See Ps. 41, 13; 72, 18. 19; 89, 52; 106, 48; 150, the whole of which is a doxology in itself.

AUTHORSHIP. — Of the 150 psalms 100 have headings, or titles, bearing the author's name; the remaining 50 are anonymous; the Talmud calls them orphan psalms. These headings "are integral parts of the sacred songs, added by the authors. It is quite in keeping with the practise of Hebrew and Arabic writers for an author to place his name over a poem, instead of under it, as is the custom with us." The name of David is written over 73 psalms. From other sources we learn that David, "the sweet psalmist of Israel," wrote other psalms besides these 73. Asaph, a Levite and one of the three heads of David's choir at Jerusalem, wrote 12; the sons of Korah, a celebrated family of singers and poets in the days of David, composed 11; Solomon, 2; Moses, 1; Heman, a chief musician for the Temple in David's days, 1; and Ethan, one of the three masters of the Temple-music, 1.

MESSIANIC PSALMS. — Our Lord Himself testified that there are things written concerning Him in the Psalms. Luke 24, 44. We find seventeen Messianic psalms. Psalms 2, 8, 16, 22, 23, 24, 40, 45, 47, 68, 69, 72, 89, 93, 97, 110, 118 are properly Messianic psalms; they refer to the Messiah, the promised Redeemer. We have portrayed in these psalms Christ's person and work, His birth, betrayal, agony, death, triumph over death, His ascension into heaven and enthronement at the right hand of God the Father Almighty.

VARIOUS NOTES. — The headings, or superscriptions, which many psalms have are of value not only as regards the authorship of about 100 psalms, but also in other respects. Fourteen titles furnish information of great interest regarding the historical circumstances under which the particular poems were written. (See the titles to Psalms 3, 7, 18, 30, 34, 51, 52, 54, 56, 57, 59, 60, 63, and 142.) Others tell of the purpose of the poem (see Ps. 38, etc.), others of the "chief musician," the leader of the Temple-choir, or of the instrument to be used for the accompaniment (see Psalms 4, 6, 54, 67, etc.). "Certain expressions found in some superscriptions are extremely puzzling and have exercised the imagination of older commentators. . . . The English translators simply retained the

Hebrew words (as in Ps. 9: *muth-labben;* Ps. 45: *shoshan-nim;* Ps. 46: *alamoth,* etc.), prefixing the preposition 'upon.' Most probably all these expressions referred to melodies, or tunes, according to which the psalms were to be sung."

Psalms 120 to 134 bear the title "Songs of Degrees." Of this title different explanations are given. Some regard the degrees as "steps" and accept a rabbinical explanation, *viz.,* that the particular psalms were written for chanting on fifteen steps, which led from the Court of the Women in the Temple to the Court of the Men. But there is no sufficient evidence of the existence of these steps. Others, translating the Hebrew word for degrees by "ascents," or "goings up," view these psalms as having been written for the pilgrims who annually "went up" to Jerusalem at the three great festivals, to chant on their journeys. This seems to be the most acceptable explanation.

The difficult word *selah,* which occurs 71 times, also is explained in various ways. It is generally believed to have been a musical direction for a pause in the singing of a psalm, during which perhaps there was an instrumental interlude.

CHAPTER 18.

The Proverbs of Solomon.

GENERAL CHARACTER OF THE BOOK. — This book contains a great variety of proverbs in poetic form. A *proverb* is a sentence which briefly and forcibly expresses some practical truth, a wise maxim. Being short, sharp, impressive, the proverb attracts attention and imprints itself on the memory. The scope of the wise sayings in our book is to direct us so to order our life and conduct as to please God and promote our own welfare. It is essentially a book of good works, particularly for young people, who are repeatedly addressed therein. (See chaps. 1, 4; 4, 1, etc.)

THE AUTHOR. — "He [Solomon] spoke three thousand proverbs." 1 Kings 4, 32. Some of these 3,000 Solomonic proverbs have been gathered together in the Book of Proverbs. This book opens with the words: "The proverbs of Solomon, the son of David, king of Israel." The section beginning chap. 10 and ending with chap. 24 bears the heading "The Proverbs of Solomon." Chap. 25 opens with the remark: "These also are proverbs of Solomon, which the men of Hezekiah, king of Judah, copied out." Chap. 30 is inscribed: "The words of Agur, the son of Ja´-keh, even the prophecy." And chap. 31 contains "the words of King Lem´-u-el, the prophecy that his mother taught him." It is clear that Solomon *spoke* the proverbs in chaps. 1—29, but it is not so clear that he also *wrote* them. The text plainly states that chaps. 25—29 were copied out by the men of the good king Hez-e-ki´-ah, who lived and reigned about 300 years after Solomon. These holy men probably also added chaps. 30 and 31. Who Agur, the son of Jakeh, and King Lemuel were is a question that cannot be determined with any degree of certainty.

ARRANGEMENT OF CONTENTS. — *The Introduction.* Chap. 1, 2—6: The purpose and use of this collection of proverbs. — *I. To Sons.* Chaps. 1 to 9. The first section consists of 15 admonitory discourses, addressed to the youth, exhibiting the benefits and greatness of wisdom, encouraging the ardent pursuit thereof, and dissuading from folly, that is, sin and vice, which are opposed to wisdom. — *II. The Folly of Sin.* Chaps. 10 to 19. While the proverbs in the first section are somewhat connected, those in the two succeeding sections (chaps. 10 to 19 and 20 to 29) are loosely strung together, although evidently gathered together according to topics. — *III. Warnings and Instructions.* Chaps. 20 to 29. — Chap. 31, 10—31 we have "the praise and properties of a good wife."

CHAPTER 19.

Ec-cle-si-as´-tes.

NAME AND AUTHOR. — The name Ec-cle-si-as´-tes is derived from the Greek and means the Preacher; hence the full name and title given in our Bible reads, "Ecclesiastes, or the Preacher." In Luther's translation of the Bible our book bears this title, "The Preacher Solomon." This title is correct; for in the opening sentence we read: "The words of the Preacher, the son of David, king in Jerusalem." This description applies only to Solomon, for no other son of David was king in Jerusalem. The universal consent of antiquity attributed the authorship of Ecclesiastes to Solomon. The book seems to have been written by Solomon in his old age, probably in the year 977.

THE PURPOSE. — Luther says: "This book is one of the most difficult books in the entire Bible, which no one has so far fully understood. The reason, however, why this book has been very dark to many is twofold. One of these reasons is that they have not seen the object and scope of the writer. Therefore our first endeavor must be to seize the probable scope of the book: what the writer aims at and what he has in mind; for if one does not know this, it is impossible to understand the style." The aim of the writer is to teach. "Because the preacher was wise, he still taught the people knowledge; yea, he gave good heed and sought out, and set in order, many proverbs. The Preacher sought to find out acceptable words; and that which was written was upright, even words of truth." Chap. 12, 9. 10. His theme is: "Vanity of vanities, saith the Preacher, vanity of vanities; all is vanity." Chap. 1, 2. "Vanity" here does not mean empty pride, conceit. The word in the original is "breath." Breath is a picture of vanity, emptiness, want of substance to satisfy desire. Solomon relates how, in his wanderings through a long life, he vainly sought satisfaction and gratification in preferment and pleasure, in power and honor, in human labor and riches. These things are mingled with toil, worry, and vexation of spirit. The Preacher's position is not a pessimism or a creed of despair. On the contrary, he writes: "Rejoice, O young man, in thy youth and let thy heart cheer thee in the days of thy youth." Chap. 11, 9. While exhorting his hearers not to set their affections on the vain pleasures and possessions of this life, he exhorts them cheerfully to enjoy the gifts of God in His fear and with contentment. Chaps. 2, 24; 3, 12. 14. 22; 5, 7. 18—20; 8, 12. 15; 9, 7—10; 11, 1—6. He sums up: "Let us hear the conclusion of the whole matter: Fear God and keep His commandments; for this is the whole duty of man." Chap. 12, 13.

SUMMARY OF CONTENTS. — *I. The Theme:* All is vanity. Chap. 1, 1—3. — *II. The Theme Proved.* Chap. 1, 4—3, 22. — *III. The Theme Unfolded.* Chap. 4, 1—10, 20. — *IV. The Fear of God and Good Works Bring Real Satisfaction.* Chaps. 11 and 12.

THE SONG OF SOLOMON.

ITS CHARACTER AND PURPOSE. — The opening verse calls this book the "Song of Songs," that is, the most excellent song, and ascribes it to Solomon. It is not an anthology, or collection, of love-songs; if it were, it would not have been placed in the canon, in the collection of sacred books. The book must not be taken literally, but allegorically; it consists of an allegory. An *allegory* is a narrative describing real or supposed facts only for the purpose of representing certain higher truths or principles than the narrative, in its literal aspect, could possibly have taught; it is "a figurative sentence or discourse, in which the principal subject is described by another subject resembling it in its properties and circumstances. The real subject is thus kept out of view, and we are left to collect the intentions of the speaker or writer by the resemblance of

the secondary to the primary subject." The Song of Songs
depicts, under the allegory of the bridal love of Solomon
and Shu'-la-mite, the mutual love of the Lord and His
Church. This is a favorite allegory, or figure, in the Bible.
Ps. 45; Hos. 2, 19. 20; Matt. 9, 15; John 3, 29; 2 Cor. 11,
1—4; Eph. 5, 25 ff.; Rev. 19, 6—8, and other passages
represent the Lord as the heavenly Bridegroom and His
Church as His bride. Whoever does not understand God's
revealed plan of salvation and has not experienced the love
of Christ or love to Christ, to him this book will remain a
sealed book, "while the saintliest men and women of the
ages have found it a source of pure and exquisite delight."

The beautiful hymn "Draw Us to Thee," written by
F. Fabricius in 1668, is based on chap. 1, 4.

SUMMARY OF CONTENTS.—*I. Title of the Book.* Chap. 1, 1.—
II. The Mutual Affection of the Lovers. Chap. 1, 2—2, 7: The
Bride praises the Bridegroom and His love and longs for Him.
Chap. 1, 2—7. The Bridegroom praises her beauty. Chap. 1,
8—11. She praises the Bridegroom. Chap. 1, 12—2, 7. — *III. The
Mutual Seeking and Finding of the Lovers.* Chap. 2, 8—3, 5. —
IV. The Fetching of the Bride to the Marriage. Chap. 3, 6—5, 1:
The words of a chorus of the daughter of Zion. Chap. 3, 6—11.
The beauty of the Bride is praised. Her longing. Chap. 4. —
V. Love Scorned, but Won Again. Chap. 5, 2—6, 8: A tem-
porary separation because of her lack of zeal. She seeks Him
with great lamenting and regains Him with eternal joy. —
VI. Shu'-la-mite, the Attractively Fair, but Humble Princess.
Chap. 6, 10—8, 4. — *VII. Unbroken Communion.* Chap. 8,
5—14.

CHAPTER 20.

The Prophetical Books.

WHAT IS A PROPHET? — We have now come to the
third and last division of the Old Testament, to the prophetical books. They are 17 in number and were written
by 16 prophets. What is a prophet? A prophet is an of-

ficial spokesman of God. As the priest spoke for men to God, so the prophet spoke for God to men. God told and taught the prophet what to say. The divine communications at times referred to future events; hence has arisen the popular idea that the prophet was simply an inspired foreteller of things to come. However, this definition is incomplete. The office of the prophet was not simply to *fore*tell, but in general to *forth*tell, to utter what God had revealed to him, whether this pertained to past, present, or future. — Why did God send His prophets? Read 2 Chron. 36, 15. 16.

Not all prophets were moved by God to commit their messages from Him to writing for the purpose of having them embodied in the Bible. Only 16 were so-called writing-prophets. Of these 16 the first 4 (Isaiah, Jeremiah, Ezekiel, Daniel) are called major ("greater") prophets, while the remaining 12 are called minor ("lesser") prophets. The terms major and minor refer not to their comparative importance, but solely to the volume, or length, of their books. — The period during which they prophesied was approximately 400 years. The order in which their books are given in the Bible is not the chronological order. Isaiah, for example, whose book occupies the first place, lived and prophesied later than Obadiah, Joel, Jonah, Amos, and Hosea. The following table gives approximately the year in which the individual prophet entered on his prophetic career.

CHRONOLOGICAL TABLE OF THE PROPHETS.

O-ba-di'-ah	880	Ha-bak'-kuk	640
Jo'-el	850	Jer-e-mi'-ah	628
Jo'nah	810	Zeph-a-ni'-ah	624
A'-mos	787	Dan'-iel	606
Ho-se'-a	785	E-ze'-ki-el	595
I-sa'-iah	760	Hag'-ga-i	520
Mi'-cah	750	Zech-a-ri'-ah	520
Na'-hum	710	Mal'-a-chi	440

ISAIAH.

THE PROPHET. — The name borne by this great prophet — Isaiah — signifies "Jehovah's Salvation." Isaiah calls himself the son of Amoz (not Amos); but who Amoz was is not recorded. Jerusalem was the home of Isaiah and the scene of his labors. He received his prophecies "in the days of Uz-zi′-ah, Jotham, Ahaz, and Hezekiah, kings of Judah" (chap. 1, 1), that is, from about 760 to about 710 B. C. Micah and Nahum were his contemporaries.

RANK AMONG THE PROPHETS. — Isaiah is properly placed at the head of the list of Old Testament writing-prophets, for he is the greatest of them all, the prince of prophets. Not only the volume of his prophecies, but the great variety, beauty, and force of his style and also the fulness of his predictions respecting the Messiah give this highly gifted person preeminence among the Hebrew prophets. Isaiah is called the Evangelist of the Old Testament. His book is quoted 120 times in the New Testament.

MESSIANIC PROMISES. — Christ declares that the Scriptures of the Old Testament testify of Him and exhorts us to search for Him there. John 5, 39. Particularly do the Old Testament *prophets* testify of the Savior. St. Peter writes: "Of which salvation the prophets have inquired and searched diligently, who prophesied of the grace that should come unto you; searching what or what manner of time the Spirit of Christ which was in them did signify when it [He] testified beforehand the sufferings of Christ and the glory that should follow." 1 Pet. 1, 10. 11. Of all these prophets no one spoke so fully and so clearly of Christ and His work of redemption as did Isaiah. He portrays the Messiah's wonderful person, describing Him as both divine and human and calling Him Immanuel, that is, God with us, God in our flesh. He says that His name shall be called The Mighty God (chap. 9, 6), that He should be born of a virgin (chap. 7, 14), and that He should be a descendant of David (chap. 11, 1). He graphically describes Christ's states of humiliation and exaltation, His sufferings, and the glory that should follow (chap. 53). He plainly points out that Christ's sufferings and death were to be vi-ca´-ri-ous (that He would suffer in our stead; chap. 53, 5), for the purpose of saving us from the guilt and punishment of sin. He predicts the growth and extension of Christ's kingdom or of the Christian Church. All these things regarding the Messiah and His kingdom, Isaiah describes so vividly and graphically that an uninformed person might be led to think that he lived in the New Testament and had seen them with his own eyes. Chap. 53 is the most beautiful pearl in his crown of Messianic prophecies. Acts 8, 26—40.

THE PERIOD. — As stated before, Isaiah prophesied between 760 and 710 B. C. The history of Israel during these fifty years is recorded 2 Kings 14—20 and 2 Chron. 26—32. This history should be read again; it is essential to a correct understanding of our book. The period of Israel's history under consideration was, in the main, a period of national prosperity; the land was full of silver and gold; neither was there any end of their treasures. Chap. 2, 7. At the same time the land was also full of idolatry, immorality, and evils of all kinds. Chap. 2, 6—9. Isaiah calls the Jews a sinful nation, a people laden with iniquity, a seed of evil-doers, children that are corrupters; they have forsaken the Lord, they have provoked the Holy One of Israel to anger, they are gone away backward. Chap. 1, 4. While they still attend the Temple services, bring offerings, and observe other religious rites and ceremonies, they do so only outwardly, being a hypocritical nation. Chap. 10, 6; 29, 13 ff. The mass of the people are confirmed in their apostasy and unbelief, and it is the task of the prophet, by no means a pleasant one, to preach to them of the coming judgment. Only a small number, a remnant, has remained true to God; and it is Isaiah's evident delight to comfort this small residue of faithful children with divine promises of help and salvation.

AUTHENTICITY. — When we speak of the authenticity, or genuineness, of the Book of Isaiah, we mean to say that Isaiah wrote every one of the 66 chapters contained in this book. Rationalistic critics deny this statement, but their denial is based on very flimsy arguments.

SUMMARY OF CONTENTS. — I. *Prophecies about Judah and Israel and Various Foreign Nations:* Assyria, Babylon, Moab, Syria, Egypt, Tyre, etc. The main enemy at this time is Assyria. Chaps. 1 to 39. — II. *"The Book of Consolations."* The restoration of the remnant of Israel. The Servant of Jehovah as the Messianic King. The final glory of the New Testament Church. The main enemy is Babylon. Chaps. 40 to 66.

CHAPTER 21.

Jeremiah.

THE PROPHET. — Nearly a hundred years lie between Isaiah and Jeremiah. When Jeremiah was still very young, — he called himself a "child," chap. 1, 6, — God commissioned him to become His prophet. This was in the thirteenth year of King Josiah of Judah, or about 628 B. C. He belonged to a priestly family and was born at An'-a-thoth, a little village about four miles north of Jerusalem. He seems to have remained unmarried for prophetic reasons. Chap. 16, 2. Most of his prophetic messages were delivered in Jerusalem. He lived to see the utter destruction of the Holy City and the Temple by the Babylonians, or Chaldeans, in 588 B. C., but was not carried away captive to

Babylon; on the contrary, the Babylonian king Neb-u-chad-nez´-zar showed him special favors. The king's captain released him from the prison in which the Jews had put him in Jerusalem and offered him a home in Babylon; but with the captain's consent Jeremiah chose to remain with the remnant of poor Jews whom the Babylonians left in Judea. Chaps. 39, 11—14; 40, 1—6. Shortly thereafter, however, a prominent Jew named Ishmael killed his countryman Ged-a-li´-ah, whom Nebuchadnezzar had made governor; and fearing the vengeance of the Babylonians, the Jews who remained in Palestine determined to go down into Egypt to live there. Jeremiah endeavored to dissuade them from going there, but they would not listen to him and even took him along with them to Egypt, where we last hear of him, still protesting against the idolatry of his people. Chap. 41 ff. Tradition tells us that he was stoned by the Jews in Egypt.

THE PERIOD. — 2 Kings 22 to 25 and 2 Chron. 34 to 36 give us the history of Judah during this period. It was a most critical period of the nation's history. Judah and Jerusalem had forfeited their day of grace by shameful sinning and contempt of the Word of God and were hastening to their doom. Of the five kings under whom Jeremiah prophesied only the first one, Josiah, was a pious ruler. He commanded the Law of Moses to be read to the people, repaired the Temple, reestablished the true worship of the true God, and abolished the heathen abominations which had been introduced under previous kings. But his successors, Je-ho´-a-haz (who reigned three months), Je-hoi´-a-kim (who reigned eleven years), Je-hoi´-a-chin (who reigned three months), and Zed-e-ki´-ah (who reigned eleven years), were all wicked kings, and under their reign the people relapsed into gross paganism and immoral practises. Idolatry was openly practised by old and young (chaps. 1, 16; 7, 18); even human sacrifices were offered to Moloch (chaps. 19, 5; 32, 35). Covetousness, dishonesty, murder, adultery, stealing, false swearing, and other sins were rampant. Chaps. 2, 34; 5, 27—29; 6, 7; 7, 9, etc. The moral corruption tainted even prophet and priest. Chaps. 6, 13; 8, 10; 23, 11—15. Judah had become a "degenerate plant" (chap. 2, 21) and was ready to be pulled out by the roots. To save His people from impending destruction, the Lord, in His mercy and compassion, sent them His prophets, among them Jeremiah, to plead with them, warn them, and call them to repentance, promising that He would not carry out His threat regarding their punishment if they would repent. Chaps. 4, 14; 5, 15—17; 6, 21; 18, 8, etc. Year after year Jeremiah came to them with messages from God; but they would not hearken and obey. Chaps 25, 3; 35, 15, etc. His townsmen at Anathoth threatened to kill him because he prophesied in the name of the Lord. Chap. 11, 18—21. Every one cursed him. Chap. 15, 10. 15. They said, "Come and let us smite him with the tongue!" They preferred to listen to the false prophets, who were predicting peace and prosperity. Chaps. 23, 27. 29. All mocked Jeremiah, the prophet of evil. Chap. 20, 7. The priests and the prophets and all the people in Jerusalem took him, saying, "Thou shalt surely die! Why hast thou prophesied in the name of the Lord, saying, 'This city shall be desolate without an inhabitant'?" Chap. 26, 8—11. Je-hoi´-a-kim murdered the faithful prophet U-ri´-jah and dishonored his corpse. Chap. 26, 20 ff. When Ba´-ruch, Jeremiah's penman, had written the latter's prophecies into a book, Je-hoi´-a-kim had the book brought to him, contemptuously tore it in pieces, and cast it into the fire. Chap. 36. During his reign the Babylonian Captivity of Judah began. Neb-u-chad-nez´-zar, king of Babylon, captured Jerusalem and pillaged the Temple (606 B. C.).

First Je-hoi'-a-chin and then Zed-e-ki'-ah was made king of the remaining Jews. Although Zedekiah and his people saw how God had begun to carry out His threats, they refused to heed Jeremiah's words. They captured him as a deserter, the princes smote him, and put him in prison many days. With the king's permission they took him and lowered him into a miry subterranean dungeon, where he was to die of hunger; one of the king's servants succeeded in getting him out of the dungeon and putting him back in the court of the prison, where he stayed till Nebuchadnezzar took the city and freed him. Chaps. 37 to 40. Despite all these trying experiences Jeremiah, though naturally mild, sensitive, and retiring, remained faithful to his task as a prophet. He ever found comfort and strength in the promise the Lord gave him at the beginning: "Be not afraid of their faces; for I am with thee to deliver thee.... They shall fight against thee; but they shall not prevail against thee." Chaps. 1, 8. 18; 15, 20; 20, 11.

CHARACTER OF JEREMIAH'S PROPHECY.—The character of his prophecies is indicated by his name, which signifies "Jehovah throws down," and also in the Lord's words of instruction: "See, I have set thee over the nations and over the kingdoms to root out and to pull down and to destroy and to throw down, to build and to plant." Chap. 1, 10. Accordingly, he not only pronounces woes against the wicked, but also utters promises of divine grace and deliverance for the benefit of the few who remained true to God. Amid the thunder of approaching doom are heard the sweet strains of promise.

MESSIANIC PROMISES. — Among the promises referred to are Jeremiah's prophecies regarding the Messiah. See chap. 23, 5. 6; 30, 9; 33. The prophecy of the New Covenant refers to the days of the New Testament, which began with the coming of Christ. Chap. 31, 31—34.

ARRANGEMENT. — The Book of Jeremiah, in the chronological order of its several predictions and divine messages, is somewhat difficult of arrangement; but we may divide it into the following four groups: —

I. Jeremiah is Called. He Denounces Judah. He sets forth Judah's sins, calls to repentance, appeals to the covenant, and predicts the captivity of the Jews and the restoration of the faithful remnant. Chaps. 1 to 35. — *II. The Prophet's Personal History during and after the Siege of Jerusalem;* his sojourn and work in Egypt. Chaps. 36 to 45. — *III. Prophecies Concerning Foreign Nations,* particularly concerning the Babylonians. Chaps. 46 to 51. — *IV. Historical Conclusion.* Detailed account of the capture of Jerusalem by the Babylonians and the exile of its inhabitants. Chap. 52.

THE LAMENTATIONS OF JEREMIAH.

The Septuagint version prefixes the following statement to the Lamentations: "And it came to pass, after Israel was led into captivity and Jerusalem laid waste, that Jeremiah sat weeping, and lamented with this lamentation over Jerusalem, and said. . . ." The book consists of five poems, or songs, each of which is an elegy, or lamentation, occupying a chapter. The general theme of these poems is one, the destruction of Jerusalem. The *purpose* of the poems is to call the impenitent people to repentance and to comfort the penitent with the promise of God. Agreeably to the subject, the style of the Lamentations is lively, tender, pathetic, and affecting. — Date: 588 B. C.

SUMMARY OF CONTENTS. — *First Song:* Jerusalem is desolate and empty, for the Babylonians have carried her inhabitants away captive; this calamity has justly come upon her by reason of her many and grievous sins. — *Second Song:* The Lord has brought this great misery on Jerusalem according to His word; the city has provoked Him to anger and made Him her enemy. — *Third Song:* The Prophet bewails his own calamities; God's unending mercy nourishes the hope of relief; the people are exhorted to repent; Jeremiah's experience in the dungeon. — *Fourth Song:* The destruction of the Temple, the distress of the siege of Jerusalem; all is deserved; the capture of Zed-e-ki'-ah and those who tried to escape from the besieged city; Edom, which rejoices at the fate of Jerusalem, is threatened with a like fate. — *Fifth Song:* Prayer to God that He would not forget the pitiful condition of His stricken people, an appeal to His pity.

CHAPTER 22.

E-ze'-ki-el.

THE PROPHET. — Among the ten thousand prominent people of Jerusalem whom Neb-u-chad-nez'-zar, king of Babylon carried into captivity from Jerusalem to Babylon in 599 B. C., together with King Jehoiachin (2 Kings 24, 11—16), was Ezekiel, a priest, the son of Buzi. In the fifth year of this captivity (595 B. C.) Ezekiel was called by God to be a prophet, and he labored in this capacity for at least twenty-two years among the exiled Jews. He lived in the northern part of Mesopotamia, at Tel-a-bib', by the river Che'-bar (Ke'-bar). There he owned a house (chap. 8, 1) and was married (chap. 24, 18). Ezekiel seems to have enjoyed the esteem of the captive Jews, for their elders frequently resorted to him for advice and guidance (chaps. 8, 1; 14, 1; 20, 1; 33, 31); yet he shared the lot of other true prophets in that most of his hearers did not hearken to him nor do his words, chaps. 3, 7; 33, 30—32. The last date given in his book is the twenty-seventh year of his captivity (about 573 B. C.; chap. 29, 17). But how long he lived after this date it is impossible to tell.

THE SITUATION. — In 599 B. C. Nebuchadnezzar, king of Babylon, had taken Je-hoi'-a-chin and 10,000 of the chief Jews to Babylon, leaving the poorest and commonest people in Judah and Jerusalem and making Zed-e-ki'-ah their king. Jeremiah prophesied in the name of the Lord that Zedekiah and his people would ere long have to follow their brethren into captivity. False prophets and prophetesses in Judah and Jerusalem, however, denied the truth of this message. They claimed to have visions from God and flattered the people by saying there was no danger threatening them. Chaps. 12, 24; 13, 23; 22, 25. 28. Thus the people were seduced; the false and foolish hope was raised in their hearts that Jeremiah's prophecy of impending doom and destruction would fail (chap. 12, 22—24), that they would forever remain in their native land, and that those who had been taken to Babylon would soon return (chaps. 11, 15; 33, 24). Now, in 595, God called and commissioned Ezekiel in Babylon to corroborate Jeremiah's prophecy. Ezekiel told them again and again: Judah and Jerusalem have justly deserved punishment; their heart does not fear and love the Lord, but is wholly given to idolatry of every kind — on every high hill, in all the tops of the mountains, under every green tree, and under every thick oak they burn incense to all their idols; they worship the sun: they even offer their own children to Moloch. Chap. 5, 11; 8, 16, etc. Prophets, priests, princes, and people are corrupt; they have filled the land with violence and all manner of vice. Chap. 22, etc. Therefore the enemy shall besiege Jerusalem. Chap. 4. A third part of the inhabitants shall die with pestilence and famine, a third part shall fall by the sword, and the Lord will scatter a third part into all the winds. Chaps. 5, 12; 11, 9; 14, 22. 23. God will make Jerusalem waste and the land desolate. Chaps. 5, 14; 6, 14. The final desolation is surely coming, and it is coming soon. Chaps. 7, 1—15; 12, 27. 28. The very day on which Nebuchadnezzar began the siege of Jerusalem, Ezekiel received a revelation from God, saying, "The king of Babylon set himself against Jerusalem this same day." Chap. 24, 2. Eighteen months later, when the city had fallen into the hands of the Babylonians, one that had escaped out of Jerusalem came to Ezekiel in Babylon, saying, "The city is smitten!" Chap. 33, 21. Thus God fulfilled every word He had spoken by the mouth of His holy prophet.

CHARACTER OF EZEKIEL'S PROPHECY. — The roll of his prophecy which the Lord handed to Ezekiel "was written within and without; and there was written therein lamentations and mourning and woe." Chap. 2, 9. 10. To deliver such heavy prophecy to a rebellious nation that had rebelled against God was not an easy and pleasant task; but the Lord comforted His prophet, saying, "Be not afraid of their words nor be dismayed at their looks, though they be a rebellious house." Chap. 2, 6. — The *purpose* of the heavy message was to warn Judah and Jerusalem, to lead them to repentance, and to save them from impending destruction. "Cast away from you all your transgressions whereby ye have transgressed and make you a new heart and a new spirit; for why will ye die, O house of Israel? For I have no pleasure in the death of him that dieth, saith the Lord God, wherefore turn yourselves and live ye." Chap. 18, 31. 32; see also chap. 33, 11. Mingled with the messages of divine wrath and punishment are sweet promises to the effect that God will not utterly destroy the entire nation, but preserve a remnant of His people and at the end of seventy years bring them back to Palestine and bless and defend them. This was the chief part of Ezekiel's prophetic work. Its purpose was to sustain the faith of the believing remnant. Chap. 11, 17—20; 20, 40—44; 28, 24—26; 34, 11—16; 36, 8—15. 25—38; 37. Beginning with chap. 40, Ezekiel records a series of sublime visions referring to the restoration of Jerusalem and the Temple; but everything is on so vast a scale that the description is evidently not intended to be taken literally, but symbolically; it is a symbol of the Church of the New Testament.

MESSIANIC PROPHECIES. — The highest branch of the cedar which God promised to set up (chap. 17, 22 ff.), the Shepherd whom He promised to set up over His redeemed people (chap. 34, 11—23), and the promised King (chap. 37, 24), all refer to Christ.

DIFFICULTY. — Ezekiel largely delivered his messages by means of symbolical actions, riddles, and parables the meaning of which was not clear to the people; they were obliged to ask for an explanation. These explanations are given in the book for our benefit. However, there are no explanations to be found here of the magnificent allegories and bewildering similitudes with which the last nine chapters particularly abound. "Luther, who had found the true Gospel-key leading to the understanding of the wonderful visions of this prophet, nevertheless expresses the opinion that their full understanding would hardly be achieved by any one in this life." Yet some misguided people, who think they have the "light" and "know it all," claim to have found the full meaning. However, the meaning is not in the text, but in their mind and is utterly at variance with other clear passages of Scripture. Their meaning spells "millennium," and that is a dream. *Millenarianism* = the expectation of a universal blooming time and glory for the Church this side of heaven; the notion that before the end of the world all nations will be converted to Christ; that the saints will visibly rule with Christ over the wicked and enjoy peaceful and blissful security and prosperity on earth. Christ's Kingdom of Glory is in heaven. (See chapter 51, p. 218.) Beware of the unscriptural idea of a "millennium"!

SUMMARY OF CONTENTS. — *I. Prophecies Relating to the Final Destruction of Jerusalem.* Chaps. 1 to 24. — *II. Prophecies against Heathen Nations,* the enemies of God's people. Chaps. 25 to 39. — *III. Prophecies Telling of the Restoration of Israel and the Future Glory of Christ's Kingdom.* Chaps. 40 to 48.

CHAPTER 23.

Daniel.

THE PROPHET. — In the third year of the reign of Je-hoi´-a-kim, king of Judah (about 606 B. C.), Neb-u-chad-nez´-zar, king of Babylon, came to Jerusalem and besieged it; and the Lord gave Jehoiakim into his hands, and he deported a number of young men from distinguished Jewish families to Babylon. (Map 1.)   Among these was Daniel ("God my Judge"), one of the few who remained loyal to God. He was a youth "in whom was no blemish, but well-favored [handsome], and skilful in all wisdom and cunning in knowledge and understanding science." Chap. 1, 4. Because of these gifts of body and mind he was chosen by Neb-u-chad-nez´-zar's chief officer in charge of the household, together with three of his friends, to be taught the learning and the language of the Chaldeans and thus to be prepared for the high position of standing in the king's palace as a personal adviser. Chap. 1, 4. The language referred to was Syriac, or Ar-a-ma´-ic (the Hebrew name of Syria is Aram). *Aramaic* was a dialect akin to Hebrew; during and after the exile it gradually became the spoken tongue of the Jews. Daniel wrote a large part of his book in Aramaic. Chap. 2, 4—7, 28. Daniel and his three friends showed themselves very proficient advisers to the king. "In all matters of wisdom and understanding that the king inquired of them he found them ten times better than all the magicians and astrologers that were in all his realm." Chap. 1, 20. The wise men of the East, who about 600 years later came to worship the Christ-child at Bethlehem, belonged to this caste of "magicians," magi, or wise men of Babylon. In the second year of his reign (603 B. C.) Neb-u-chad-nez´-zar had a dream which he forgot before morning, and none of all the wise men were able to tell the dream or to show its meaning. The king became angry and gave orders to have all the wise men killed. In answer to prayer God made known to Daniel the king's dream and its meaning. The king was delighted and promoted Daniel, making him a great man and master of all the magicians. Chap. 2, 48; 4, 9. During the life of Nebuchadnezzar, Daniel remained a man of great influence at court, and it was due to him that the king made private and public acknowledgment of the greatness and glory of Israel's God. Chaps. 2, 47; 4. Nebuchadnezzar is supposed to have died about 563 B. C.

Under the following kings Daniel seems to have withdrawn from public life. However, King Bel-shaz'-zar, the grandson of Nebuchadnezzar, in the third year of his reign (about 553 B. C.), sent him on a certain mission to Shushan (Susa), which was in the province of Elam. Chap. 8, 1. 2. (Map.) In 538 B. C. he was called in to interpret the handwriting on the wall in Belshazzar's palace. The same night Cy'-rus the Great, the Persian, captured Babylon. "Daniel prospered in the reign of Cyrus." Chap. 6, 28. He was reinstated as prime minister. The first year of Cyrus was 538 B. C. From the prophecy of Jeremiah (Jer. 29, 10) Daniel understood that this year marked the seventieth year of the captivity and the end thereof. Chap. 9, 2. He fasted and prayed and made confession of Israel's sins (chap. 9, 3—27); and it seems the Lord used him to influence Cyrus to issue his decree permitting the Jews to return to their country. The last prophetic utterance of Daniel is dated in the year 534 B. C., the third year of Cyrus. Chap. 10, 1 ff. Accordingly, it seems that his ministry extended over a period of about seventy-two years.

CHARACTER OF DANIEL'S WORK. — Daniel and Ezekiel were contemporaries and lived and wrote in the same country, the kingdom of Babylon. But while Ezekiel labored among his captive countrymen on the banks of the Chebar (Ke'-bar), Daniel preached the name of God in the court of the king who had conquered the Jews. His preaching produced a profound impression. Nebuchadnezzar declared at different times that he was greatly moved by the words of Daniel. Chap. 2, 47; 3, 29; 4, 33 f. King Da-ri'-us spoke in a similar vein. Chap. 6, 26 f. This does not imply, however, that these great kings became true believers of the Gospel; history shows that they did not experience a real change of heart; they continued to worship their heathen idols and died as idolaters. — Due to the peculiar circumstances under which Daniel spoke, his style is also peculiar. He does not use the common prophetic expression, "Thus saith the Lord"; nor does he, as the prophets usually do, address the people of his time. His predictions are highly symbolical. Regarding the final revelation he writes: "And I heard, but I understood not." Chap. 12, 8. 9.

MESSIANIC PROPHECY. — Chap. 2, 44 tells of the kingdom of heaven which God Himself was to establish by the Messiah. See also chap. 7, 13 f. From this passage Christ chose for Himself His favorite self-designation "Son of Man," used by Him 82 times in the gospels. Chap. 9, 24 ff. symbolically specifies the time when "Messiah, the Prince," would come ("seventy weeks," that is, 7 times 70 years). Christ Himself refers to this prophecy Matt. 24, 15. — Chap. 11, 36 ff. is a prophecy regarding the Roman Antichrist. Comp. 2 Thess. 2, 4.

SUMMARY OF CONTENTS. — I. Historical Section. Chaps. 1 to 6: Education and faithfulness of Daniel; he interprets Nebuchadnezzar's forgotten dream of the four monarchies; the three men in the fiery furnace; Nebuchadnezzar's second dream and its fulfilment; Belshazzar's impious feast and his destruction; Daniel in the lions' den. — II. Prophetic Visions of the Coming Monarchies and of the Eternal Kingdom of Christ. Chaps. 7 to 12: The vision of the four beasts and the Ancient of Days; the ram-and-rough-goat vision; vision of the seventy weeks; having humbled himself, Daniel sees the vision of the glory of God; from Da-ri'-us to the Man of Sin; the great tribulation.

CHAPTER 24.

Hosea, Joel, Amos.

HOSEA.

THE PROPHET. — Ho-se´-a, whose name signifies De-liverance, heads the list of twelve minor prophets. The designation "minor" = lesser, smaller, does not refer to quality, but to quantity, or size; the books are shorter than the books of the major prophets. According to the inscription of his book, Hosea prophesied in the reign of Uz-zi´-ah, Jotham, Ahaz, and Hezekiah, kings of Judah, and in the reign of Jer-o-bo´-am II, king of Israel. Reckoning even from the last year of Jeroboam's reign (about 783 B. C.) merely to the first of Hezekiah's (about 727 B. C.), his career must have extended over fifty-five years. He was an early contemporary of Isaiah and Micah. But while these two prophets preached in the Southern Kingdom of Judah and Benjamin, Hosea prophesied in the Northern Kingdom of the ten tribes (Israel). He was the last of the prophets of the Northern Kingdom. This kingdom was completely overthrown by the Assyrians 722 B. C. 2 Kings 17, 6—23.

THE PERIOD. — When Hosea entered on his prophetic career, the Northern Kingdom stood in the zenith of its power and prosperity. Jeroboam had greatly enlarged the borders of the land. 2 Kings 14, 25. 28. The country had become rich. Hos. 12, 8; 2, 8. Israel was a luxuriant vine. Chap. 10, 1 (R. V.). But this material prosperity covered and decorated moral corruption. Hosea paints a frightful picture of the deep moral corruption prevailing in this period when he says: "There is no truth nor mercy nor knowledge of God in the land. There is naught but swearing and breaking of faith, and killing, and stealing, and committing adultery; they break out, and blood toucheth blood." Chap. 4, 1. 2 (*R. V.*). The root of all these evils and their greatest sin was idolatry, shameful idolatry. They forgot and forsook the Lord and followed after false gods. Chap. 1, 2; 2, 5. 13; 3, 1; 4, 17. Of their silver and gold they made themselves molten images of Baal and of calves; these idols they kissed and said to them, "Ye are our gods!" Chap. 8, 4; 10, 1; 13, 2; 14, 3. They sacrificed to these idols and burned incense to their graven images on the tops of the mountains, on the hills, under oaks, poplars, and elms, because the shadow thereof was good. Chap. 4, 13; 2, 13; 11, 2, etc.

THE BOOK. — In the first three chapters, which furnish the key to the whole, Hosea reproves the ten tribes for their idolatry, or spiritual adultery, and calls them to repentance. In the remaining chapters, 4 to 14, he exposes the manifold sins of the priests, people, and princes of Israel, announces to them the wrath and displeasure of God on account of the multitude of their sins, foretells their rejection by God and the Assyrian Captivity, and declares that return to God is the only remedy for existing and impending evils. The purpose of these reproofs and threats is to soften their hearts and to bring them back to God. Therefore his direct threatenings of wrath are mingled with precious promises of mercy.

MESSIANIC PROPHECIES. — Hosea speaks clearly and most comfortingly of the coming Messiah (Christ) and of the condition of His people after His coming.

1. Having declared that He would reject and disown Israel, the Lord immediately proceeds to predict that notwithstanding this rejection He would gather for Himself a numerous people. Chap. 1, 8—11; 2, 23. This true people of God consists not only of such as are Israelites according to the flesh, but also of such as formerly were not

God's people, of Gentiles, or heathen, who are converted to Christ. Rom. 9, 24—26 Paul quotes the Messianic prophecy before us as a passage proving the conversion of the Gentiles in Gospel-days.

2. Hos. 3, 5 God predicts that "in the latter days," *i. e.*, in the days of the Messiah, the true Israel shall return and seek the Lord, their God, and David, their King, *i. e.*, the second David, which is Christ, and shall fear the Lord and His goodness. Chap. 11, 10. 11.

3. St. Matthew (chap. 2, 15) explains Hos. 11, 1 as a reference to Christ's childhood.

4. The words in chap. 13, 14 assured the people of God in the Old Testament that the promised Redeemer would deliver them from the power of death. 1 Cor. 15, 54.

SUMMARY OF CONTENTS. — *I. The Book of Symbols.* Chaps. 1 to 3: The painful and pathetic personal history of the prophet, which he uses to symbolize the people's separation from God and their restoration to the privileges of His worship and favor. — *II. Reproof.* Chaps. 4 to 6: Hosea charges gross iniquity against the people, priests, and princes. — *III. Threats.* Chaps. 7 to 10: He threatens punishment, to culminate in exile. — *IV. Remonstrances.* Chaps. 11 to 13: Hopeful remonstrances and tender expostulation. — *V. Entreaty and Promises.* Chap. 14.

JOEL.

THE PROPHET. — Joel (*Jehovah is God*) prophesied in Judah, probably in Jerusalem. Chap. 1, 14; 2, 1; 3, 5. Concerning the circumstances of his life we know nothing; nor are we certain of the exact period in which he preached; but it is probable that he prophesied about 850 B. C. He is therefore the second prophet in point of time.

THE BOOK. — The Book of Joel opens with a graphic and powerful description of the devastation caused by swarms of locusts and by an extreme drought. The prophet summons his countrymen to fasting and sincere repentance that the divine judgment might be averted. In this great calamity Joel beholds a token and presage of a greater judgment on the Day of the Lord = Judgment Day. Is. 2, 12. This Day of the Lord forms the main thought of his book. He describes it most vividly: The Day of the Lord is great and very terrible; and who can abide it? It is a day of darkness and gloominess, a day of clouds and of thick darkness. The sun and the moon shall be dark and the stars shall withdraw their shining. The Lord will appear in the clouds; but He will not come alone; a great army, i. e., all His holy angels, will accompany Him. A fire devoureth before them, and behind them a flame burneth. The earth shall quake before them; the heavens shall tremble. At their presence the peoples are in anguish, all faces are waxed (grown) pale. Chap. 2, 1—11. The Lord will gather all nations and bring them down into the Valley of Je-hosh'-a-phat, i. e., the Valley of the Judgment of Jehovah. There He will sit to judge all the nations round about. He will say to His heavenly host: "Put ye in the sickle, for the harvest is ripe; come, get you down, for the press is full, the vats overflow, for their wickedness is great." Chap. 3, 13. Great and terrible as is this Day of the Lord, the children of God need not fear it, for "the Lord will be the Hope of [a Refuge unto] His people." Chap. 3, 16.

MESSIANIC PROPHECY. — Chap. 2, 28. 29 Joel speaks of the great blessings of the Messianic age: "And it shall come to pass afterward [in the days of the Messiah] that I will pour out My Spirit upon all flesh," etc. The fulfilment of this great promise began at Jerusalem on the Day of Pentecost. Acts 2, 16 ff.

SUMMARY OF CONTENTS. — I. An Unprecedented Plague of Locusts in Judah. Chap. 1, 1—20. — II. The Day of the Lord. Chaps. 2, 1—3, 8. — III. Retrospect: The Day of the Lord. Full blessings. Chap. 3, 9—21.

AMOS.

THE PROPHET. — Amos (the name means *Burden*) was
a native of Te-ko´-a, a small fortified town of Judea, lying
on the borders of the Wilderness of Judea, about nine miles
south of Jerusalem. In the beginning, Amos was no
prophet, neither was he a prophet's son (scholar); but he
was a herdsman and a dresser of fig-trees. Chap. 1, 1; 7, 14
(*R. V.*). Though a native of the Southern Kingdom, he
was sent by God to preach in the Northern Kingdom.
From chap. 1, 1 we learn that he prophesied about 787 B. C.
He went to Bethel in Ephraim, about ten miles north of
Jerusalem. Bethel was the chief center of the idolatrous
calf-worship. His holy boldness in reproving the manifold
transgressions and the mighty sins of Israel, as well as his
prediction that the kingdom would be destroyed, brought
down upon him the wrath of the chief priest of Bethel, who
labored to have Amos driven out of the land of Israel for
alleged treason. Chap. 7, 10—17.

THE BOOK. — The key-word of Amos's message is
"punishment." About the only word of Gospel import is
found at the end (chap. 9, 11. 12), which the New Testament explains as referring to the days of the *Messiah,* who
was to restore the spiritual kingdom of Israel and receive
into it former Gentiles. Acts. 15, 16. 17. The prophecy of
Amos has been compared to a thunderstorm rolling over
the surrounding heathen kingdoms, touching Judah and
Jerusalem in its progress, pouring the fulness of its power
on Israel, and passing away with a bright rainbow on its
cloud. Chap. 9, 11—15.

SUMMARY OF CONTENTS.—*I. Judgments on Heathen Nations
Bordering on Israel and also on Judah and Israel.* Chaps. 1 and 2.
II. Three Discourses against Israel, each beginning with the call,
"Hear this word!" Chaps. 3 to 6. — *III. Visions* descriptive of
Israel's punishment. Chap. 7, 1—9, 10. — *IV. Calling of the
Gentiles.* Chap. 9, 11—15.

CHAPTER 25.

Obadiah, Jonah, Micah.

OBADIAH.

The Book of O-ba-di´-ah is the shortest book in the Old Testament, consisting of only 1 chapter of 21 verses. Of its author, the prophet Obadiah (*Servant of Jehovah*), we know nothing. It cannot be decided with certainty just when he lived and labored. Some give the year 587 B. C. as the date of his book. According to this supposition Obadiah lived later than Jeremiah. But this is improbable, for Jeremiah evidently quoted from Obadiah. (Comp. Jer. 49, 7—16 with Obad. 1—9.) Again, there is an evident coincidence of thought and expression between Obadiah and Joel. (Comp. Joel 2, 32 and Obad. 17; Joel 3, 2. 3 and Obad. 11; Joel 3, 4. 7 and Obad. 15; Joel 3, 14 and Obad. 15; Joel 3, 17 and Obad. 17 [margin]; Joel 3, 19 and Obad. 10.) That Joel quoted from Obadiah is considered proved by Joel 2, 32. If Joel quoted from Obadiah, then Obadiah must have written his book before Joel penned his prophecy. Joel, we have learned, probably prophesied 850 B. C. Accordingly, Obadiah wrote his book prior to 850, probably about 880 B. C. Obadiah is the most ancient writing-prophet of the Old Testament. He is the first to use the formula "the Day of the Lord." V. 15. — The prophecy of Obadiah is a denunciation against Edom (Idumea). The Edomites were the descendants of Esau, the brother of Jacob. Edom is therefore called the "brother" of Israel. V. 10. The Edomites and the Israelites were also neighbors. The territory occupied by the former extended from the southern end of the Dead Sea to the Gulf of A´-ka-bah. It is a mountainous country (vv. 3 and 9), 100 miles long and 20 miles wide. Edom, though united to Israel by ties of blood, was a bitter enemy of

Israel. A proof of its hostility is given vv. 10—14. This occurred in the reign of King Joram (889—881 B. C.; see 2 Chron. 21, 16. 17). For this unbrotherly, brutal behavior Edom was to receive its reward; Obadiah foretells its destruction. At the same time he predicts the preservation of the "house of Jacob" (of the descendants of Jacob) and its victories. This prediction is finding its complete fulfilment in the victories of the Church of Christ.

SUMMARY OF CONTENTS. — *I. Certainty of Edom's Complete Destruction. Vv. 1—9. — II. This Punishment is a Consequence of Their Animosity and Active Hostility against God's People. Vv. 10—16. — III. The Certain Deliverance of the True Israel;* the victorious extension of the kingdom of Christ. Vv. 17—21.

JONAH.

THE PROPHET. — Jo´-nah, whose name signifies "Dove," was the son of A-mit´-tai. We have met this prophet before, 2 Kings 14, 25, where we read that he prophesied under King Jer-o-bo´-am II of Israel, who reigned between 824 and 783 B. C. His supposed tomb is shown near Nin´-e-veh. He probably wrote our book about 810 B. C. Jonah was of Gath-hepher, a village of Galilee, about four miles north of Nazareth, and within the confines of the Northern Kingdom. One day our prophet received an extraordinary call from God: the Lord bade him go to Nineveh, that great city, and cry against it, for their wickedness was come up before God. So Jonah was now to be a foreign missionary. Nineveh was in a foreign country, in Assyria, of which it was the capital. It stood on the eastern bank of the river Ti´-gris, opposite the modern Mo´-sul, 500 miles in a direct line northeast of Jerusalem. (Map 1.) Nineveh was a very old and an exceedingly great city, at that time the largest city of the world, its population numbering more than half a million. Our book tells us what happened before and after Jonah preached in this great and wicked city.

HISTORICAL CHARACTER OF THE BOOK. — The Book of Jonah purports to be a narrative of facts; and such it is indeed, all the attacks of its enemies to the contrary notwithstanding. The miraculous element which abounds in this book, particularly the miracle of Jonah and the great fish, has always been a favorite target for the cheap, shopworn arguments and jests of infidels, scoffers, and skeptics. But their attacks cannot shake the faith of those who believe that God is almighty. Moreover, the Son of God, our blessed Lord and Savior, who knows all things and whose mouth speaks the truth, refers to the Book of Jonah as a record of facts and even uses Jonah's experience in the sea-monster as a type and prophecy of His burial and resurrection, saying to the skeptics of His day: "An evil and adulterous generation seeketh after a sign, and there shall no sign be given to it but the sign of the prophet Jonas; for as Jonas was three days and three nights in the whale's belly, so shall the Son of Man be three days and three nights in the heart of the earth." Matt. 12, 39 ff.; 16, 4.

PURPOSE OF THE BOOK. — The chief lesson which the story of Jonah's preaching to the heathen Ninevites was meant to teach the Jews was that God is not the God of the Jews only, but of the Gentiles (heathen) also, that He will have all men, the Gentiles included, to be saved and to come to the knowledge of the truth. Let us remember this God-given lesson and be zealous in mission-work!

SUMMARY OF CONTENTS. — *I. The First Call of Jonah.* His flight and his correction. Chap. 1. — *II. His Prayer in the Sea-monster.* His deliverance. Chap. 2. — *III. The Prophet's Second Commission.* He preaches to the Ninevites, and they repent. God spares the city. Chap. 3. — *IV. Jonah's Consequent Great Displeasure and Bitter Complaint.* The Lord lovingly corrects him. Chap. 4.

MICAH.

THE PROPHET. — Micah ("Who is like Jehovah?") is called the Mo-ras'-thite (chap. 1, 1) because he was a native of Mo'-resh-eth near Gath, a small town of Judah, about twenty miles southwest of Jerusalem. Micah prophesied during the reigns of Jotham, Ahaz, and Hezekiah, kings of Judah (beginning of Jotham's reign, 758 B. C.; end of Hezekiah's reign, 698). He was therefore a younger contemporary of Isaiah and Hosea.

THE BOOK. — It consists of three sections, each of which begins with the call, "Hear!" Chap. 1, 2; 3, 1; 6, 1. Micah addressed his message to Israel (Samaria) and Judah (Jerusalem), mainly to the latter. Chap. 1, 1. 5. He denounces the prevailing sins — idolatry (chap. 1, 5. 7), covetousness and oppression (chap. 2, 1—5. 8. 9), cruelty on the part of the leading people (chap. 3, 1—4. 9. 10), giving heed to false prophets (chap. 2, 6. 7. 11; 3, 5—7. 11), violence practised by the rich (chap. 6, 12), bribery in court (chap. 7, 3); he foretells the destruction of both capitals (Samaria and Jerusalem; chap. 1, 6; 3, 12; 6, 13—16) and the exile of the people (chap. 1, 16; 4, 10), but also the deliverance of the "remnant" (chap. 2, 12. 13; 4, 6. 7; 5, 3. 7. 8; 7, 10 ff.).

MESSIANIC PROPHECIES. — Micah is replete with promises respecting the Messiah, or the Christ.

1. He predicts and specifies the *place* where Christ should be born, saying: "But thou, Bethlehem Ephratah, though thou be little among the thousands of Judah, yet out of thee shall He come forth unto Me that is to be Ruler in Israel, whose goings forth have been from of old, from everlasting." Chap. 5, 2. Accordingly, when King Herod, seven centuries later, on the occasion of the visit of the Wise Men from the East, asked the scribes to tell him where Christ should be born, they answered, "In Bethlehem of Judea," and then proceeded to prove this from the Mes-

sianic prophecy before us. Matt. 2, 1—6; see also John 7, 42.

2. The great Messianic prophecy in chap. 4 is, in part, an exact quotation from Is. 2, 2 ff.

3. The repeated prediction of the return of the remnant from Babylon (chap. 2, 12. 13; 4, 6. 7. 10; 5, 3. 7. 8; 7, 11—13) was not exhausted in the physical, or outward, return of the relatively few Jews from the Babylonian Captivity; it was rather a type and pledge of the full and final redemption for which Israel was looking, the redemption through the promised Messiah, the King of Israel. Luke 2, 38; John 1, 49.

SUMMARY OF CONTENTS. — I. The Case of the Lord against Israel and Judah. The promise to the remnant. Chap. 1. 2. — II. A Rebuke of the Cruel Heads and Princes of the People and of the False Prophets, together with promises of the Messiah and of the spiritual glory of His Church. Chaps. 3 to 5. — III. The Lord's Controversy with His People; injustice is rebuked; the nation's moral corruption is described; its punishment; the voice of the remnant. Chaps. 6. 7.

CHAPTER 26.

Nahum, Habakkuk, Zephaniah.

NAHUM.

THE PROPHET. — Nahum is called the El'-ko-shite because he was a native of Elkosh, which probably was a village in Galilee. Chap. 1, 1. It is supposed that he prophesied between 710 and 700 B. C., during the reign of Hez-e-ki'-ah; for he refers to the miraculous defeat of the Assyrian army before Jerusalem (which occurred in 710) as a thing that was past.

THE BOOK. — Nahum's prophecy bears the title "The Burden of Nineveh." Chap. 1, 1. This name probably points to the threatening character of his message. The prophet vividly predicts the destruction of Nineveh, the capital of the great Assyrian Empire, which at that time was still in the very height of its power, holding sway over a large part of Western Asia. (Map 1.) His *purpose* is to comfort Judah (Nahum signifies "Comforter"). The people of Judah stood in need of comfort. The Assyrians were a powerful, warlike, and cruel nation. They had but recently (in 722 B. C.) "turned away the excellency of Jacob" (of Israel), emptying the Northern Kingdom of its inhabitants and destroying their land. Chap. 2, 2; 2 Kings 17, 6. They had invaded Judah, captured its fortified cities, and compelled the little kingdom to pay a large tribute. 2 Kings 18, 13 ff. Although at a second invasion, a year or two later, God had driven the Assyrian King Sen-nach'-e-rib back to his country, — the angel of the Lord destroyed 185,000 Assyrians during the night, — Assur was still an object of dread. Hence Nahum comforts the people of Judah and Jerusalem, assuring them that the Lord, who is great in power (chap. 1, 2—6), had determined to make an utter end of the great Assyrian world-power, to make its grave, and Judah should rejoice at the joyful news of its ruin. Chap. 1, 14. 15; 3, 19. This prediction came true about a hundred years later. So completely did the army of the Medes and Babylonians destroy Nineveh in 606 B. C. that for centuries its site had been well-nigh lost.

SUMMARY OF CONTENTS.—*I. God Makes Known His Decree Regarding the Utter Destruction of Nineveh.* Chap. 1. — *II. The Execution of the Divine Decree.* Chap. 2. — *III. The Utter Ruin of Nineveh Portrayed in a Song of Lament.* Chap. 3.

HABAKKUK.

THE PROPHET. — Ha-bak'-kuk ("Embrace") probably prophesied in the days of the good King Josiah of Judah, who reigned from 641 to 610 B. C. When he delivered his prophetic message, the predicted invasion of Judah by the Chal-de´-ans (Babylonians), which began in 606 B. C., had not yet come to pass, but was close at hand, so close that the people of Habakkuk's time should live to see it. Chap. 1, 5 ff. He was a contemporary of Zeph-a-ni´-ah and Jeremiah.

THE BOOK. — Habakkuk complains to God that his continued outcry against the wickedness of the land of Judah is unheeded. Chap. 1, 2—4. God answers that He will soon raise up the Chaldeans, that bitter and hasty nation, terrible and dreadful, to punish Judah for its sinfulness, and that this punishment will be fearful. Chap. 1, 5—10. Habakkuk is greatly perplexed over the fact that God has ordained the Chaldeans for judgment and chosen them for correction, because these instruments of punishment were far worse than Judah. Chap. 1, 12—17. Then the Lord shows the prophet in a vision that the proud Chaldeans, too, would certainly — and soon — be overthrown for their many sins, particularly for their insatiable lust of bloody conquest, and that their dead idols would not be able to save them. Chap. 2. The book closes with a psalm, which is called "A Prayer of Habakkuk, the Prophet." Chap. 3. In this psalm the prophet describes the sentiments which God's words regarding the punishment of His people at the hands of the terrible and dreadful Chaldeans had created in his heart: he was afraid. Chap. 3, 2. 16. He begs God, "In wrath remember mercy!" Then he recalls to memory many instances from the history of Israel which show how God in His glorious might had helped His people against their heathen enemies, and thereby strengthens his hope that He would do the same again. Chap. 3, 3—15. Though he foresees the coming of the invading Chaldeans and the destruction of the land of Judah, he confidently exclaims: "Yet I will rejoice in the Lord;

I will joy in the God of my salvation," etc. Chap. 3, 16—19. "The prayer with which this book closes touches the summit of the sublime." The book contains several fine familiar sayings (see chap. 2, 2. 14. 20), the most famous being the one in chap. 2, 4: "The just shall live by his faith." St. Paul repeatedly quotes this statement to prove that we become just in God's sight and obtain life and salvation, not by our own works, but solely by faith. Rom. 1, 17; Gal. 3, 11; see Heb. 10, 38. "It was this word of God which Luther pondered during his famous journey to Rome, which also served to open his eyes to the worthlessness of his attempts at self-justification, even while he made the rounds of the sanctuaries at Rome."

SUMMARY OF CONTENTS. — I. *Judgment upon Judah and the Chaldeans.* Chaps. 1 and 2. — II. *A Psalm of Praise to the Justice of God.* Chap. 3.

ZEPHANIAH.

THE PROPHET. — Zeph-a-ni´-ah ("Jehovah hides") was "the son of Cushi, the son of Gedaliah, the son of Amariah, the son of Hizkiah" = Hezekiah, king of Judah. Chap. 1, 1. Accordingly, our prophet seems to have been of royal blood. He was a contemporary of Ha-bak´-kuk, for he prophesied "in the days of Josiah, the son of Amon, king of Judah." Chap. 1, 1. But in what part of that good king's reign did Zephaniah exercise his prophetic office? Evidently in the earlier part, when the reform of Josiah had begun, but before it was completed, between 630 and 624 B. C. Chap. 1, 4. 5; comp. 2 Chron. 34, 3. 8. By his preaching Zeph-a-ni´-ah supported the king in his work of purging Judah and Jerusalem from idolatry.

THE BOOK. — It contains prophecies which Zephaniah uttered at various times and then gathered into a volume in condensed form. "He writes in a fluent and vivid style." The Day of the Lord, *i. e.,* Judgment Day, occupies a prominent place, being spoken of no less than a dozen times. Chap. 1, 7—10. 14—16. 18; 2, 2. 3; 3, 8. The great hymn on Judgment Day, *Dies irae, dies illa* ("That day of wrath, that dreadful day"), which was written in the 13th century, is based on these passages. But while painting the terrible Day of the Lord, Zephaniah does not fail to send forth, for the comfort of the faithful, most cheering promises of salvation through the *Messiah*. Chap. 3, 9—20.

SUMMARY OF CONTENTS. — *I. Announcement of the Coming of "the Day of the Lord" on Judah and Jerusalem.* Chap. 1. — *II. An Exhortation to Repentance; the impending fall of surrounding and of distant nations hostile to Judah.* Chap. 2. — *III. Woe Denounced on Sinful Jerusalem.* Promise that a remnant (those who seek the Lord) shall be preserved in the midst of the catastrophe. Chap. 3.

CHAPTER 27.

Haggai, Zechariah, Malachi.

HAGGAI.

THE PROPHET. — Hag'-ga-i ("Festive") heads the list of the three postexilic prophets (the three prophets who preached after the Babylonian Exile of the Jews). He delivered his four messages to the returned Jews in the second year of the Persian King Darius, 520 B. C. Chap. 1, 1. He was a contemporary of Zech-a-ri'-ah. Of his own history nothing positive is known.

OCCASION OF HAGGAI'S PROPHECY. — In 536 B. C. King Cy'-rus of Persia gave the Jews permission to return to Palestine. Only about 42,000 at once availed themselves of this opportunity to return to the land of their fathers. Ze-rub'-ba-bel, a direct descendant of King David, and Joshua, the high priest, were their leaders. In the second year after their return they began to rebuild the ruined Temple. Their neighbors to the north, the mixed race of Samaritans, wanted to take part in this work, but the Jews refused to permit it, for such cooperation would have meant sinful union in matters of religion with such as had another religion. This refusal angered the Samaritans, and they succeeded in putting a stop to building operations for about fourteen years. Ezra 4. (See p. 64.) But in 520 King Da-ri´-us of Persia issued a new decree for rebuilding the Temple. Ezra 6. Meanwhile, however, the Jews had grown faint-hearted and indifferent with regard to the erection of the house of God; but at the same time they eagerly built comfortable houses for themselves. Chap. 1, 2. 4. 9. That was the situation which moved God to send Haggai to them.

THE BOOK. — The Book of Hag´-ga-i consists of four messages. All four messages refer to the rebuilding of the Temple. They contain both reproof and encouragement. The prophet reproves the people for being indifferent with regard to rebuilding the house of God and for selfishly erecting ceiled houses for themselves. He points out to them that this has displeased the Lord and provoked Him to punish them with drought and famine. Chap. 1, 5. 6. 9—11; 2, 16. 17. But Haggai's messages mainly speak of comfort and hope and give encouragement. He tells the people and their leaders to be strong and work, for God has promised to be with them and to let His Spirit remain among them. Their work of building the Temple will please the Lord, and He will bless them for it in field and orchard. Chap. 2, 19. The fact that this second Temple will not have as great outward glory as the former Temple had should not dishearten them, for if God wanted to give it such outward glory, He could easily do so, as all the silver and gold in the world belongs to Him. Although externally inferior, this new Temple shall have a greater glory than the first Temple had, for the *Messiah,* the Desire of all nations, will come to it and glorify it with His presence. Chap. 2, 4—9. These words accomplished their purpose. Within twenty-four days of Haggai's first message the people went to work on the Temple again, and within four years it was finished. Chap. 1, 14. 15; Ezra 5, 1. 2; 6, 14.

SUMMARY OF CONTENTS. — *I. Haggai Reproves the People* for neglecting the building of the Temple, shows that the prevailing drought and famine have been sent in punishment, and urges them to go to work on the Temple; the good effect of his preaching. Chap. 1. — *II. The Greater Glory of the Second Temple,* especially because of Christ's coming to it; God's promise to Zerub'-ba-bel. Chap. 2.

ZECHARIAH.

THE PROPHET. — Zech-a-ri'-ah ("Jehovah remembers") began to prophesy only two months after Haggai, at Jerusalem, in 520 B. C. The purpose of his preaching, too, was to encourage the leaders and the people to build the Temple. Chap. 4, 6—9. He belonged to the tribe of Levi and was a priest. Babylon was the place of his birth, and he accompanied the first band of exiles on their return to Palestine in 536 B. C. Neh. 12, 1. 4. 12. 16. When Zech-a-ri'-ah began to prophesy, he was still young. Chap. 2, 4.

CHARACTER OF HIS PROPHECY. — The Book of Zechariah shows a variety of style: visions and symbols, simple prose, and sublime poetical figures. It also abounds in Messianic prophecies. The latter part of the book contains symbolic utterances most difficult to understand. Chaps. 9—14.

MESSIANIC PROPHECIES. — The Book of Zechariah is rich in its predictions of the Messianic King and His kingdom, *i. e.,* His holy Christian Church.

1. Chap. 3, 8; 6, 12, Christ, the Branch (Shoot), is promised.

2. Chap. 9, 9. 10 foretells the coming of Christ, the King, to the Daughter of Zion, *i. e.*, the holy Christian Church, and the wide extension of His peaceable rule. See Matt. 21, 5. The growth of the Church of Christ is predicted also chap. 2, 11; 8, 22. 23. This prediction served to strengthen the small number of exiles who had returned to the Holy Land.

3. Chap. 11, 12. 13 foretells that Christ would be sold for 30 pieces of silver, and that this money would be used to purchase a potter's field. See the fulfilment Matt. 26, 15; 27, 9. 10.

4. Chap. 12, 10 predicts that the inhabitants of Jerusalem would pierce Christ and that many would repent of this great sin. See John 19, 34. 37.

5. Chap. 13, 7 the death of Christ is foretold. The fulfilment of this prophecy is recorded Matt. 26, 31.

6. Chap. 13, 1 promises that in the days of the Messiah a fountain should be opened for sin and for uncleanness.

7. Chap. 14 speaks of the happy state of the Church of Christ after the Day of Judgment.

SUMMARY OF CONTENTS. — *I. Ten Symbolic Visions.* A warning from the past and a call to repent and return to God; a series of eight symbolic visions descriptive of the struggle and the victory of God's kingdom; a symbolical act — the crowning of the high priest Joshua, which shows that the Branch (Christ) shall be both Priest and King. Chaps. 1 to 6. — *II. The Mission from Babylon.* In answer to a question asked by the people about fasting, the prophet tells them in God's name that right living is better than sacrifice and assures them that the time is coming when their fasts shall be to them joy and gladness and cheerful feasts. Chaps. 7 and 8. — *III. The Messiah in Rejection and Afterwards in Power.* Two prophetic sermons on the future destiny of God's people both here and hereafter. Chaps. 9 to 14.

MALACHI.

THE PROPHET. — Mal'-a-chi ("My [God's] messenger") is the last of the twelve minor prophets and of all the Old Testament prophets. He appeared about a hundred years later than Haggai and Zechariah. It is generally supposed that he was a contemporary of Nehemiah and that he prophesied at Jerusalem about 430 B. C. This belief is based on the obvious fact that the evils spoken of in Malachi are the same which Nehemiah denounced. (Comp. Mal. 2, 11—16; 3, 7—12 with Neh. 13, 10—14. 23—30.) The *purpose* of his preaching was to strengthen the hands of Nehemiah in reforming these abuses.

THE OCCASION OF MALACHI'S PROPHECY. — Great disorder prevailed among the priests and people of Judah in Palestine. 1. The priests did not honor and fear the Lord, the great King, but despised His name and profaned it, in that they offered blemished victims for sacrifice on His altar, the blind, the lame, and the sick. They had also become mercenary and would do nothing in the Temple unless they were paid for it. Thus they forfeited the respect of the people. Chap. 1, 6—2, 9. 2. The whole nation had robbed God, had robbed Him in tithes and offerings. Chap. 3, 8—10. 3. Many Jews, even priests, had divorced their lawful wives and married heathen women, who worshiped other gods. Chap. 2, 10—16. 4. The people had wearied the Lord with their words and had spoken stout words against Him, saying that it does not pay to serve Him and to keep His commandments and that He delights in evil-doers, blessing and helping them. Chap. 2, 17; 3, 13—15. These sins were the occasion which called forth Malachi's prophecy.

MESSIANIC PROPHECIES. — While unsparing in his denunciation of the prevailing sins of the people, Malachi cheers the God-fearing Jews with promises of the Messiah.

More than 35 centuries had passed since God had given the
first promise of the Redeemer in Paradise; and He was
now speaking through the last of His holy prophets. During the following 400 years the voice of prophecy is to be
hushed. So God repeats once more the oft-repeated promise
of the coming of the Christ, whom the Old Testament believers sought and desired. He calls the Messiah "the
Messenger of the Covenant" (namely, of the new covenant
of grace), who would soon come to His Temple, His holy
Christian Church. He also foretells the coming of Christ's
herald, or forerunner, John the Baptist, whom He designates as the second Elijah. Chap. 3, 1 ff.; 4, 5 f.

SUMMARY OF CONTENTS. — I. *The Love of God for the Children of Israel.* Mal'-a-chi reproves the sins of the priests and
of the people. Chaps. 1 and 2. — II. *The Day of the Lord.*
Malachi comforts the God-fearing Jews with promises of the
twofold coming of Christ. Chaps. 3 and 4.

B. C.   JEWISH HISTORY AFTER THE EXILE.

444 Nehemiah Governor of Jerusalem. The prophet Mal'-a-chi.

409 Manasseh, the priest, builds a rival temple on Mount Ger'-
i-zim.

350 Many Jews removed to Babylon and elsewhere by Ochus,
king of Persia, for taking part in a revolt.

334 Alexander the Great begins the conquest of the Persians.

332 Alexander the Great subjugates Palestine; he plants Jews
in Alexandria, Egypt.

320 Palestine subject to Egypt till 203.

285 The Greek translation of the Old Testament (Septuagint)
begun.

203 Judea subject to Syria till 140.

200 The sect of the Sad'-du-cees founded.

167 Wars of liberation under the leadership of the Mac'-ca-bees
till 140.

165 Judas Maccabeus restores, purifies, and rededicates the
Temple.

140 The Maccabees govern Judea till 63.

136 John Hyr-ca'-nus succeeds Simon Maccabeus. Hyrcanus
destroys the rival temple on Mount Ger'-i-zim in 130.

135 The sect of the Phar'-i-sees founded.
107 Accession of Ar-is-to-bu'-lus, eldest son of Hyrcanus, under
the title of "king."
63 Pompey, the Roman general, takes Jerusalem. The Roman
rule begins.
54 Crassus, the Roman consul, plunders the Temple.
37 Herod "the Great," a descendant of Esau, became King of
Judea by Rome's aid and reigned thirty-four years.
34 Hil'-lel and Sham'-ma-i, teachers in Jerusalem.
17 Herod begins to restore, enlarge, and beautify the Temple,
which was now about four hundred years old.
11 The outer Temple finished.
4 Birth of Jesus Christ.

CHAPTER 28.

The Apocrypha.

MEANING OF THE NAME. — The term A-poc'-ry-pha is
a Greek word, meaning *hidden* (writings). The Jews applied this term to non-canonical writings, that is, to writings having some pretension to the character of sacred
Scripture, but excluded from the Old Testament canon.
The Greek word *canon* denotes a rule, or standard. In this
connection it signifies a standard of faith and rule of life.
All the books from Moses to Malachi, which had been
given by inspiration of God, constituted the Old Testament
canon and were called canonical books. The religious books
written after the days of Malachi were considered apocryphal and were excluded from the canon because they were
not God-inspired and sacred, but of human origin, the
product of man's wisdom.

CATALOG OF THE APOCRYPHA. — Following is the list
and sequence of the apocryphal books circulated by the
Septuagint (the Greek translation of the Hebrew Old
Testament begun about 285 B. C.): 1. Ezra (Esdras; the
third Book of Ezra). 2. Tobit (Tobias). 3. Judith.

4. Additions to the Book of Esther. 5. The Wisdom of Solomon. 6. The Wisdom of Jesus, the Son of Sirach, or Ecclesiasticus. 7. Baruch (Ba′-ruch). 8. The Epistle of Jeremiah (it forms the sixth chapter of Baruch). 9. The Song of the Three Holy Children. 10. The History of Susanna. 11. The Destruction of Bel and the Dragon. 12 to 14. The three Books of the Maccabees. 15. The Prayer of Manasses.

How the Apocrypha were First Circulated. — In 332 B. C. the Jews passed from Persian to Greek rule, when Alexander the Great conquered Asia. The Greek language now became the universal language. Circumstances called for the translation of the Hebrew Old Testament into the new world language. This task was undertaken by learned Jews of Alexandria in Egypt. It was begun about 285 B. C. This Greek version is known as the Septuagint = "Seventy." The translators, however, did not only render the canonical books of the Old Testament into Greek, but also added, in Greek, the apocryphal writings given in the foregoing paragraph. The Septuagint became the "Bible" of Greek-speaking Christians. And so it came to pass in the days after the death of the holy apostles that many Greek-speaking Christians regarded all the books in the Septuagint, the Apocrypha included, as holy books.

Their Reception by the Church. — The Jews of Palestine carefully guarded the Biblical books collected in the Old Testament canon and never permitted the Apocrypha to be added to this collection of sacred, God-inspired writings. The Greek Church, at the Council of La-od-i-ce′-a (A. D. 360), under the leadership of the great Ath-a-na′-si-us, excluded the Apocrypha from the Old Testament. The Roman Church, however, formally decreed and declared at the Council of Trent (in 1545) that the books in the list of Apocrypha given above (excepting

Nos. 1 and 15) are a part of the Old Testament, and to this very day it anathematizes every one who refuses to receive these apocryphal writings as the true Word of God. Thus the Apocrypha are included in the Roman Catholic Bible. From these human writings they prove some of their human, man-made teachings. The Reformed Churches have gone to the other extreme by rejecting the Apocrypha altogether. At the time of the Reformation in the sixteenth century, and even later, they printed these books at the end of the Old Testament, but later eliminated them entirely. The English and American Bible societies are forbidden by their own laws to print them in connection with the canonical books. "As a consequence, this curious, interesting, and instructive part of Jewish literature is now known only to scholars." Luther took a sensible middle course. Selecting the best of the apocryphal writings, he translated them and incorporated them into his celebrated version, placing them at the end of the Old Testament and under this heading: "Apocrypha: These are the books which are not to be placed on a level with the Holy Scriptures, the reading of which, however, is nevertheless profitable and good."

THEIR DOUBTFUL CHARACTER. — There are many good reasons why the Apocrypha must not be placed on a level with the inspired writings of the Old Testament, and must not be used to establish and confirm articles of faith, or religious teachings. 1. The Apocrypha were issued after the times of the inspired prophets, in a period when inspired prophecy had ceased. Malachi was the last of the prophets of the Old Testament. Until the time of John the Baptist no other prophet appeared. During the intervening 400 years God moved no one to write books that were to go into the Bible. Therefore the Apocrypha, which appeared during this prophetless period, are not holy, God-inspired books, but merely human works. 2. None of these books were admitted into the canon of the Old Testament by the Jews, to whom the oracles of God were committed. Rom. 3, 2. 3. Some of the apocryphal writings are anonymous, while others are pseudonymous, that means to say, some appeared without the name of the respective author and are of unknown authorship, while others were issued under false names. By this pious fraud the real author sought to gain a hearing for his work, fearing that otherwise it would be without authority. 4. These books are never quoted by Christ or the apostles in the New Testament. 5. They contain much that is legendary, false, or even contradictory to Biblical teachings. For example, the Book of Tobit gives instructions for using witchcraft; young Tobit is told to use the liver of a certain fish as a talisman against the attack of evil spirits. Again, prayer for the dead is spoken of with approval: "And making a gathering, he [Judas Maccabeus] sent twelve thousand drachms of silver to Jerusalem for sacrifice to be offered for the sins of the dead, thinking well and religiously concerning the resurrection of the dead. . . . It is therefore a holy and wholesome thought to pray for the dead, that they may be loosed from sins." 2 Macc. 12, 43. 46. The Roman Church uses this passage to prove that its doctrine of the mass and its practise of praying for the souls in purgatory is right and good. Again, suicide, self-murder, is defended and glorified in these words: "Now, as the multitude sought to rush into his [Razia's] house, and to break open the door and to set fire to it, when he was ready to be taken, he struck himself with his sword, choosing to die nobly rather than to fall into the hands of the wicked and to suffer abuses unbecoming his noble birth." 2 Macc. 14, 41. 42. — For these and other reasons the Apocrypha must not be placed on an equality with the Holy Scriptures and must not be used for the establishment of doctrine.

THE NEW TESTAMENT
of Our Lord and Savior Jesus Christ.

CHAPTER 29.

The New Testament.

ITS NAME. — We have now come to the second of the two great divisions of the Bible, the New Testament. This is the name of all those Biblical books which were written after the birth of Christ. The name is derived from 2 Cor. 3, 14. There the apostle calls the God-inspired books written before Christ's coming into the flesh "the Old Testament" (Covenant). Accordingly, the divinely inspired books written *after* the birth of Christ are correctly called "the *New* Testament." The word "testament" is derived from the Latin *testamentum,* which was early adopted as an equivalent for the Greek word meaning "covenant." The Old Covenant, the covenant which God had made with His people at Sinai, was a covenant of works; the New Covenant, which He made when He sent His Son into the world, is a covenant of grace. Jer. 31, 31—34; Heb. 8, 6—13. The full name of this second part of the Bible is: "The New Testament of Our Lord and Savior Jesus Christ."

ITS LANGUAGE. — The Old Testament was written in Hebrew, the ancient language of the Hebrews, or Jews. During and after the Babylonian Captivity (606 to 536 B. C.) the Jews adopted the Ar-a-ma´-ic language, which was a dialect similar to Hebrew. But about 333 B. C. the Greek king Alexander the Great conquered Asia. Now Greek became the language best known throughout the civilized world and was generally used in commerce. It penetrated also into the interior of Palestine, where it was spoken alongside of Aramaic; in some Palestinian cities

Testamentum is equivalent to covenant.

Greek even predominated. It was this universal language in which the New Testament was originally written. This rendered its writings immediately available for practically all the civilized world.

ITS WRITERS. — The New Testament was written by the following eight holy men: Matthew, Mark, Luke, John, Paul, James, Peter, Jude. With the exception of Paul, and probably Luke, these writers were not educated men, but came from the common people. Acts 4, 13 Peter and John are called "unlearned and ignorant men." These terms do not imply that they were rude, uncouth, barbarous. "Unlearned" means that they had no knowledge of Jewish culture beyond the Scriptures. "Ignorant men" was a technical term for those who had not studied in rabbinical schools. They were devoid of special learning, plain persons. Luke had received the education and training of a medical doctor; he was a physician. Col. 4, 14. And Paul had sat at the feet of the great Jewish teacher Ga-ma´-li-el in Jerusalem. He seems to have possessed all the learning which was then current among the Jews and was also familiar with Greek literature and philosophy.

HARMONY OF ITS PARTS. — The different writers of the New Testament differed as to education, training, character, and so forth; still there is perfect agreement among them as to doctrine, or teaching. "Every careful student of the New Testament will admit that certain statements there made, especially in the gospels, are difficult to harmonize; but we feel sure that we fail to see the agreement only because we do not quite understand the statements themselves or because we are not sufficiently informed concerning all the circumstances involved. In fact, all new information brought to light by historical research in late years has tended to corroborate the accounts given in the New Testament in the most remarkable manner." The perfect agreement among the writers of the New Testament as to doctrinal contents plainly points to the divine origin of their writings. They all wrote as they were moved by the Holy Ghost and wrote only those things and those words which the Holy Ghost taught them. 1 Cor. 2, 13.

Its Date. — The books of the New Testament were written at various times, but all in the latter half of the first century after the birth of Christ. There is ample historical evidence to prove that all the books of the New Testament were in existence before the year 100. This evidence would fill a whole book. The following may be adduced: The writings of the Apostolic Fathers, who had been pupils of the apostles, appeared between the years 107 and 175 of the Christian Era. These early writings of the pupils of the apostles contain many unmistakable references to, and actual quotations from, almost all books of the New Testament. But how could the Apostolic Fathers have referred to, and quoted from, these books if these books had not been in existence in their day? They do not speak of these apostolic books as things which had only recently made their appearance, but as well known and long established.

APPROXIMATE DATE OF THE DIFFERENT BOOKS.

1 and 2 Thessalonians...	53	Hebrews	66
Galatians	57	1 and 2 Peter	66
1 and 2 Corinthians	58	James	66
Romans	58	Mark	67
Ephesians	62	Luke	67
Colossians	62	Acts	68
Philemon	62	Jude	68
Matthew	62	Revelation	90
Philippians	63	John	92
1 and 2 Timothy, Titus..	65	Three Epistles of John	95

Classification of Apostolic Writings. — The New Testament is composed of 27 different books. They may be divided into three great sections: historical books (5), doctrinal books (21), and prophetic book (1).

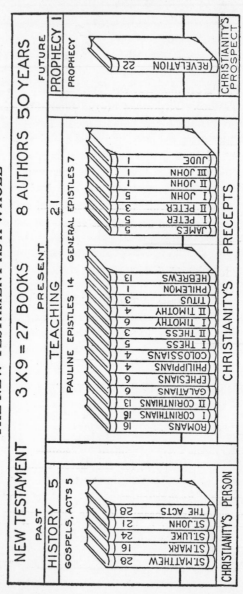

THE NEW TESTAMENT AS A WHOLE

NEW TESTAMENT   3 X 9 = 27 BOOKS   8 AUTHORS   50 YEARS

PAST	PRESENT	FUTURE
HISTORY 5	TEACHING 21	PROPHECY 1
GOSPELS, ACTS 5	PAULINE EPISTLES 14 GENERAL EPISTLES 7	PROPHECY

GOSPELS, ACTS 5

ST. MATTHEW	28
ST. MARK	16
ST. LUKE	24
ST. JOHN	21
THE ACTS	28

PAULINE EPISTLES 14

ROMANS	16
I CORINTHIANS	16
II CORINTHIANS	13
GALATIANS	6
EPHESIANS	6
PHILIPPIANS	4
COLOSSIANS	4
I THESS	5
II THESS	3
I TIMOTHY	6
II TIMOTHY	4
TITUS	3
PHILEMON	1
HEBREWS	13

GENERAL EPISTLES 7

JAMES	5
I PETER	5
II PETER	3
I JOHN	5
II JOHN	1
III JOHN	1
JUDE	1

PROPHECY

| REVELATION | 22 |

CHRISTIANITY'S PERSON   CHRISTIANITY'S TEACHING   CHRISTIANITY'S PRECEPTS   CHRISTIANITY'S PROSPECT

I. The Historical Books: The Gospel according to St. Matthew, the Gospel according to St. Mark, the Gospel according to St. Luke, and the Gospel according to St. John; the Acts of the Apostles.

II. The Doctrinal Books: The Epistles of St. Paul to the Romans, Corinthians (2), Galatians, Ephesians, Philippians, Colossians, Thessalonians (2), Timothy (2), Titus, Philemon, and Hebrews; the Epistle of James; of Peter (2); of John (3); of Jude.

III. The Prophetical Book: The Revelation of St. John.

The historical books tell the story of the life and work of our Lord and Savior Jesus Christ from His birth to His ascension and then describe the founding and extension of the Christian Church up to about A. D. 63. The doctrinal books were written as the needs of the young churches or of individual Christians seemed to demand that the apostles should set forth the Christian doctrine, or teaching, in epistolary form. The Revelation of St. John, the only prophetical book, shows, in symbols and visions, the future of the Church to the end of time.

CHAPTER 30.

The Four Gospels.

THEIR NAME. — The original title of each of these first four books in the New Testament was simply *Gospel.* This is the English equivalent for the Greek name *E-van-gel'-i-on,* from which evangel, evangelical, and evangelist have been derived. *Evangelion* means good news, glad tidings, which is exactly the meaning of the word Gospel. (The word *Gospel* was originally god [good] spell. The "d" and the final "l" were then dropped, and the result was our Gospel. *Spell* is an old word for story, tale.) This name of Gospel was fittingly applied to each of these four books because they tell the good story of our Lord and Savior Jesus Christ, who came into the world to save us poor sinners.

The holy men of God who wrote the four gospels by inspiration of the Holy Ghost are called *evangelists*. Their names are Matthew, Mark, Luke, and John. Matthew and John were apostles, while Mark and Luke were the companions of apostles. When the name of the evangelist was added to his particular book, this was done by placing the phrase "according to" between the word Gospel and his name (the Gospel *according to* St. Matthew, *according to* St. Mark, etc.). This phrase denotes authorship.

THEIR ORIGIN — During the first twenty-five or thirty years after Christ's ascension the Gospel of His life and teaching was proclaimed exclusively by word of mouth. This oral testimony of the apostles and other eye-witnesses of the Savior's ministry was then sufficient. But when false teachers arose, who preached another gospel, and when irresponsible men wrote apocryphal accounts of Christ's life and teaching, then the Holy Spirit moved the holy evangelists to record their testimony of Christ in writing. This written testimony we have in our four gospels.

THE SYNOPTIC GOSPELS. — The first three gospels (Matthew, Mark, and Luke) are called *synoptic* (seeing together) because they give in one common view the same general outline of the ministry of Christ. A striking *similarity* between these three gospels will be observed by the alert reader. Points of similarity: —

I. All three evangelists follow the same general outline. 1. They first give an account of the work of John the Baptist, of Christ's baptism and temptation (in Matthew and Luke this introduction is preceded by incidents from the birth, infancy, and boyhood of Jesus). 2. Then all three relate the story of the Lord's work in Galilee and surrounding countries. 3. In the next section they tell of Christ's journey from Galilee to Jerusalem to the Passover, at which He was crucified. 4. In the following chapters they give an account of incidents on this journey, of Christ's public entry in Jerusalem, and of events in the capital. 5. Next they tell the story of our Savior's sufferings, death, and resurrection. To this most important part of the Gospel-story they devote relatively the most space.

II. In this common outline the three synoptists furnish practically the same subject-matter, the same discourses and utterances of Christ, and the same incidents, and this in about the same sequence, or order.

III. The similarity frequently extends to identity of language; they relate the Gospel-story very often in the same words and expressions. This similarity, however, does not imply that one writer depended on the other. That they worked quite independently appears from the *peculiar features* of each Gospel. Let us briefly note some of these peculiarities.

1. Special features of *Matthew:* He alone has the appearance of the angel to Joseph, the visit of the Wise Men, the flight into Egypt, large portions of the Sermon on the Mount (chaps. 5 to 7), the parables of the tares and of the drag-net (13, 24—30. 47—52), of the unmerciful servant (18, 21—35), of the laborers in the vineyard (20, 1—16), of the wedding-feast and the wedding-robe (22, 1—14), of the ten virgins and of the talents (25, 1—30), of the end of Judas (27, 3—10), of the guards at the tomb (27, 66; 28, 4); no account of Christ's ascension.

2. Peculiarities of *Mark:* He has very few (4) parables; the only parable peculiar to him is that of the seed (4,

Mark in writing to the Romans wants to show Action + doesn't waste words.

26—29); the alarm of Jesus' relatives (3, 21); Christ heals one that was deaf and dumb (7, 32—37) and a blind man at Beth-sa´-i-da (8, 22—26); the flight of the young man (14, 51. 52).

3. Peculiar features of *Luke:* The annunciation of the birth of John the Baptist to Zacharias and of the birth of Christ to the Virgin Mary, together with the Magnificat and the Benedictus; particulars of the birth of Christ at Bethlehem; the circumcision of Jesus and His presentation in the Temple; the journey of the twelve-year-old Jesus to the Passover in Jerusalem; Jesus' first rejection at Nazareth; Peter's draught of fishes (5, 1—11); the raising of the widow's son of Nain; the woman that was a sinner (7, 36—50); the sending out of 70 disciples (10, 1 ff); the parables of the two debtors (7, 41—43), the Good Samaritan (10, 25—37), the rich fool (12, 16—21), the great supper (14, 15—24), the lost piece of silver, the lost sheep, and the lost (prodigal) son (chap. 15), the unjust steward and Dives and Lazarus (chap. 16), the unjust judge and the Pharisee and the publican (18, 1—14); Jesus in the home of Martha and Mary (10, 38—42); healing of ten lepers (17, 12—19), Zac-chae´-us (19, 1—10); Jesus before Herod (23, 6—12); His appearance to the two disciples going to Emmaus (24, 13—35). Luke mentions more miracles (21) than any other gospel.

THE FOURTH GOSPEL. — The Gospel according to St. John is an *autoptic* testimony, that is to say, John declares that he was an eye-witness of that which he writes. The dissimilarity between John's gospel and the three synoptic gospels is even more marked than the difference between the latter. Points of difference: —

1. The synoptists are mostly concerned with Christ's ministry in Galilee, while John deals almost exclusively with the Jerusalem ministry.

2. The synoptists do not positively make mention of more than one Passover during the Lord's public ministry, while John mentions three Passovers.

3. In John the parabolic method of instruction is almost entirely dropped.

4. John omits such extraordinary events as these: the temptation, the Sermon on the Mount, the death of John the Baptist, the transfiguration, Jesus' blessing of little children, the institution of the Lord's Supper, the agony in the Garden, the ascension. On the other hand, he mentions a number of events concerning which the synoptists are silent: the two miracles at Cana (2, 1—11; 4, 46—54), the miracle performed on the impotent man at Be-thes'-da (5, 1—9), Jesus' discourse with the woman of Samaria (4, 1—30), the restoring of eyesight to the man who was born blind (9, 1—7), the raising of Lazarus, Christ's discourses in the Temple, His priceless valedictory discourse (14 to 16), His high-priestly prayer (17).

DIVERSITY EXPLAINED. — Each evangelist had in mind a definite audience and shaped his story accordingly. Matthew wrote primarily for the Jews, Mark for the Romans, Luke for the Greeks, and John for all Christians. Again, each had a particular aim: Matthew's chief aim was to set forth Christ as the King Messiah, the Founder of the kingdom of heaven, who fulfilled all the Old Testament prophecies respecting the Messiah. Mark's particular purpose was to present Christ as the mighty Worker, the Powerful One, who is able to save (miracles). Luke intended to make prominent the fact that Jesus is the Friend of Sinners, the compassionate Savior of the whole human race. John makes known his chief aim in these words (20, 31): "These [few of the many miracles of Jesus] are written that ye might believe that Jesus is the Christ [the Messiah], the Son of God, and that, believing, ye might

KEY TO THE FOURFOLD GOSPEL.

Gospel of	Written to	To Prove	Records Especially	Main Thought	Prominent Word
MATTHEW (Lion — Courage) Angel	Jews	Jesus the Messiah and King	Discourses	Kingship	Fulfilled
MARK (Man — Intellect)	Romans	Jesus the Strong Savior	Miracles	Help	Straightway
LUKE (Ox — Strength)	Greeks	Jesus the Savior of All	Parables	Jesus Friend of Sinners	Compassion
JOHN (Eagle — Swiftness)	Christians	Jesus the Divine Son of God	Discourses	Christ's Deity	Believe

have life through His name." "The understanding of these peculiarities has always been so definite that from the very earliest days pious men declared that the fourfold Gospel was a realization of the wonderful vision recorded by Ezekiel. Chap. 1, 3—21. To Matthew they assigned the figure of a man or angel [sometimes the figure of a lion]; to Mark, that of a lion [sometimes that of a man]; to Luke, that of an ox; to John, that of an eagle."

CHAPTER 31.

The Gospel According to St. Matthew.

ITS AUTHOR. — St. Matthew, who wrote this first gospel by the inspiration of the Holy Ghost, was one of the twelve apostles. He was also called Levi. Mark 2, 14. Matthew means Theodore, the gift of God. He had been a publican, or tax-collector, in Galilee. But Christ graciously converted him and made him one of His twelve apostles. Chap. 9, 9; Luke 5, 27. Matthew had evidently grown rich in the business of collecting custom revenues for the government; for before leaving all to follow Jesus, he made Him and His disciples a great feast in his own house, to which he invited a great company of publicans. Mark 2, 15; Luke 5, 29. During the three years in which he followed the Lord, he heard His gracious words and saw His wonderful works. The things which he heard and saw he recorded in his gospel.

ITS DATE. — When did Matthew write his gospel? Evidently not during the first few years after Christ's ascension. He uses the expression "unto this day" and "until this day." Chaps. 27, 8; 28, 15. This expression implies that a considerable interval of time had passed between the events recorded and the time of writing.

Again, he evidently wrote before the Jewish war and the destruction of Jerusalem, that is, before the years 66 to 70 after the birth of Christ. These were events of immense importance, and Christ had predicted them; Matthew would very probably have recorded the fulfilment of prediction if he had written after these events.

Its Purpose. — Matthew obviously wrote his gospel primarily for Jewish readers, to show them that Jesus is the promised Messiah, who was to save His people from their sins. To this end he quotes so many (about 35) passages from the Old Testament referring to the Messiah and points out their fulfilment in Jesus. In this respect his gospel is fitly placed immediately after the Old Testament.

Its Character. — Our gospel is primarily designed for Jewish readers. This may be inferred from the following facts: 1. Matthew traces the genealogy of Christ back to David and Abraham, one of whom was the great king and the other the great father of the Jews. Chap. 1, 1. 2. He reports many discourses of Christ in which He rebukes the Pharisees, the leading Jewish sect. 3. He mentions Jewish customs, laws, and localities without explaining them. — It is characteristic of our gospel that particular prominence is given to the kingdom of heaven. The expression "kingdom of heaven" occurs 32 times, the expression "kingdom of God" 5 times. Matthew makes us see that the Messianic kingdom has begun. Dan. 2, 44; 7, 13. 14. — Another distinguishing feature of this gospel is the large place assigned in it to the *words* of Jesus, arranged in a *systematic* form, not broken up into fragments, as they are in the other synoptic gospels. Luke, for example, is like "a botanist, who prefers to contemplate a flower in the very place of its birth and in the midst of its natural surroundings, while Matthew is like a gardener, who for some special object puts together large and magnificent bouquets." He also groups many of Christ's miracles (chaps. 8 and 9) and many of His parables the same way. (Chap. 13.) Accordingly, Matthew's arrangement of his material is not chronological.

SUMMARY OF CONTENTS.—I. *Historical Introduction.* Chaps. 1 and 2.—II. *The Messianic Ministry of Jesus in Galilee.* Chaps. 3 to 18.—III. *Continuation of Jesus' Messianic Work in Judea and Jerusalem.* Chaps. 19 to 25.—IV. *Our Savior's Suffering, Death, and Resurrection.* Chap. 26, 1—28, 8.—V. *The Risen Lord Ministering to His Own.* Chap. 28, 9—20.

CHAPTER 32.

The Gospel According to St. Mark.

ITS AUTHOR. — St. Mark, who wrote our second gospel, was not an apostle, but the companion of apostles, of Peter and Paul. From Col. 4, 10. 11 we learn that he was a Jew by birth. His Jewish name was John, his Roman name was Mark. Acts 12, 12. 25; 13, 5. 13; 15, 37. His mother, Mary, was a distinguished member of the church at Jerusalem; at her house the disciples were wont to come together. Here many were gathered together praying for Peter in prison, and thither he betook himself when he was delivered out of prison. Mark was a cousin of Barnabas. Col. 4, 10. He was probably converted by Peter, as may be inferred from the fact that Peter calls him "my son." 1 Pet. 5, 13. He accompanied Paul and Barnabas on their first missionary journey as their "minister" = attendant, assistant. But for some reason he left them at Perga, in Pam-phyl'-i-a, and returned to Jerusalem, much to the dissatisfaction of Paul. Acts 13, 5. 13. Several years later, when Barnabas determined to take Mark with himself and Paul on their second missionary journey, Paul objected, pointing to the fact that Mark had left them the first time. The result was that Paul and Barnabas parted company, Barnabas taking Mark with him to Cyprus, and Paul choosing Silas. Acts 15, 36—40. At a later period, however, we find Mark again associated with Paul, both during his first and his second imprisonment in Rome. In his first imprisonment the apostle refers to him as one of his "fellow-workers unto the kingdom of God," who had been a "comfort" to him: Col. 4, 10. 11;   Philemon 24. Still later, in his second imprisonment, we find Paul request- ing Timothy to bring Mark with him, because "he is useful to me for ministering.", 2 Tim. 4, 11 (R. V.). Mark also accompanied St. Peter, as we learn from 1 Pet. 5, 13. From this apostle he evidently received the particular information which his gospel alone gives us regarding him (Peter. — Chap. 1, 36;   8, 33;   11, 21;   16, 7, etc.). According to tradition Mark was the founder of the church at Alexan- dria, in Egypt.

FOR WHOM IT WAS PRIMARILY WRITTEN. — It is evident that Matthew primarily wrote for Jews; it is equally plain that Mark primarily wrote for non-Jews, for Romans. Proof: 1. Mark does not give the genealogy of Jesus; for that, being Jewish, would not have appealed to a Roman.

2. He explains Jewish words, for example Bo´-a-ner´-ges (3, 17), Talitha, cumi (5, 41), Corban (7, 11), Ephphatha (7, 34), Abba (14, 36).

3. He explains Jewish customs, for example, the cer- emonial washing of hands (7, 2—3), and Passover obser- vances (14, 12;   15, 6. 42).

4. He describes the doctrine of the Sadducees, a Jewish sect (12, 18).

5. He frequently uses Latin words and idioms in his Greek narrative, for example, "legion," "centurion" (in

the history of the crucifixion), "quadrans" (farthing), which was a Roman coin (12, 42).

ITS PURPOSE; DISTINCTIVE FEATURES. — Pursuant to the superscription (chap. 1, 1) Mark purposes to set forth the beginning of the Gospel of Jesus Christ, the Son of God; he purposes, as it were, to prove historically how the Gospel which has gone out into the world has its origin in the person of Jesus Christ and how Jesus Christ by His words has declared Himself, and particularly by His works has shown Himself, to be the Son of God. Accordingly, Mark chiefly presents Him as the mighty Worker and relates His mighty miracles. "This is the Gospel of the works of Christ." It contains only 4 parables, while it records 18 miracles. This feature of presenting Christ as the mighty Worker appealed particularly to the Roman, the man of action, whose watchword was "power." Quickness of action is a prominent mark of this gospel. The word variously translated "straightway," "immediately," etc., occurs in it no less than 42 times. "Mark omits the larger addresses and sermons of Jesus and thus produces a narrative which is remarkable for its quickness of action." — He narrates events in the present tense as if they were just taking place (151 times). — He imparts freshness and light to the whole story by frequently adding certain details of person, number, place, and time that are not to be found in the other, much longer gospels. (Comp. 2, 1—3 with Matt. 9, 1. 2; Mark 3, 5; 5, 2—5. 13; 6, 35—44; 12, 41; 13, 3; 16, 7, etc., with the parallel passages in the other gospels.) All these and many other circumstances give to Mark's gospel a character of its own.

PLACE AND DATE OF WRITING. — An ancient tradition has it that Mark wrote his Gospel at *Rome* for the Christians there. This tradition is probably true. As to the date of this gospel, we may conclude that it was written before

the destruction of Jerusalem, A.D. 70; the probable date
is about A.D. 67.

SUMMARY OF CONTENTS. — *I. Historial Introduction.* Chap.
1, 1—8. — *II. The Messianic Work of Jesus in Galilee.* Chaps.
1, 9—9, 50. — *III. The Messianic Work of Jesus in Judea and
Jerusalem;* it is consummated by His sufferings, death, resurrection, and ascension. Chaps. 10 to 16.

CHAPTER 33.

The Gospel According to St. Luke.

ITS AUTHOR. — Our third gospel, as well as the Book
of Acts, was written by Luke. Chap. 1, 1—4 seems to imply
that Luke did not know Jesus personally. His name occurs
only three times in the New Testament. Philemon 24
Paul calls him one of his fellow-laborers. Col. 4, 14 he
calls him "Luke, the beloved physician." And 2 Tim.
4, 11 Paul writes: "Only Luke is with me" (in my second
imprisonment at Rome). He was associated with the great
apostle at an early date; for he speaks of the occurrences
of Paul's second missionary tour (A.D. 52) as an eye-
witness, using the personal pronouns "we" and "us." Acts
16, 10. After that he seems to have been a constant companion of Paul. He was with the apostle both in his first
and in his second imprisonment at Rome. Acts 27 and 28;
Philemon 24; 2 Tim. 4, 11. That Paul held him in love
and esteem appears from the fact that he calls him "the
beloved physician." Being a physician, Luke was a man
of education and culture.

ITS PURPOSE. — The preface to Luke's gospel (chap.
1, 1—4) shows the primary purpose of the writer. In this
preface he dedicates his book to the "most excellent The-
oph'-i-lus." Who this Theophilus was we do not know.
He evidently was a man in high station. This appears

from the title "most excellent," which Luke always applies to men of high official rank. Acts 23, 26; 24, 3; 26, 25. Again, Theophilus does not seem to have been a former Jew, but a Gentile who lived in Italy. This may be inferred from the following fact: When Luke speaks of Palestine, the land of the Jews, he adds geographical explanations. He tells how far the Mount of Olives and Em-ma´-us were from Jerusalem, that Nazareth and Ca-per´-na-um were cities of Galilee. Luke 1, 26; 4, 31; 24, 13; Acts 1, 12. He even gives information about certain places lying more westward of Palestine. Acts 16, 2; 27, 8. 12. But when he comes to Italy, he refers to some very insignificant villages merely by name, without adding a word of explanation. Acts 28, 12. 13. 15. This makes it quite probable that Theophilus lived in Italy. He had become a convert to Christianity, and Luke wrote his gospel for him that he might know the absolute certainty of those things wherein he had been instructed, or taught, by word of mouth.

That Luke wrote for converts from heathenism (Theophilus and others like him) appears from the absence of the aim to set forth Jesus as the Messiah expected by the Jews. Instead thereof we find numerous references to the fact that Jesus is the Savior of *all mankind* and that the Gospel is intended for all people. Examples showing that Luke aims to set forth Jesus as the Savior of all: —

1. He does not, like Matthew, trace the genealogy of Jesus back only to Abraham, the head of the Jewish race, but back to Adam, the head of the whole human race. Chap. 3, 38. Luther says: "Luke goes back farther and purposes, as it were, to make Christ the common property of all nations. For that reason he carries His genealogy back to Adam. In this way he wishes to show that this Christ is not only for the Jews, but also for Adam and his posterity, that is, for all people in all the world."

2. Luke records the song of Simeon in which this saint says to the Lord: "Mine eyes have seen Thy *salvation,* which Thou hast prepared before the face of all people; a Light to lighten the Gentiles and the Glory of Thy people Israel." Chap. 2, 30—32.

3. Luke lays particular stress on those sermons and parables of Christ in which the universality of salvation is most clearly expressed. Select some of these sermons and parables.

ITS DISTINGUISHING FEATURES. — In the preceding paragraph, as also in chapter 30, several peculiar features of Luke's gospel have been pointed out. In addition, briefly note the following features: its accuracy in medical description, its preservation of inspired hymns (the songs of the angels, Elisabeth, Mary, Zacharias), and the prominence given to women.

WHEN AND WHERE IT WAS WRITTEN. — Luke wrote his gospel before A. D. 70 (the year in which Jerusalem and the Temple were destroyed by the Romans); for neither in his gospel nor in his Book of Acts is there any reference whatever that the Holy City had been destroyed, although Christ's prediction concerning the fall of Jerusalem and of the Temple is fully recorded. Luke 21. From chap. 1, 1—3 we infer that he wrote after Matthew and Mark, that is, about A. D. 67 or 68, after the death of Paul in Rome. As to the place of writing, it is generally believed that it was Rome.

SUMMARY OF CONTENTS. — *I. Historical Introduction.* Chap. 1 to 3: Birth of John the Baptist foretold. The annunciation of the angel to Mary. Mary visits Elisabeth. The Magnificat, or hymn of praise sung by Zach-a-ri´-as. Birth of John the Baptist. The birth of Jesus. His childhood. The ministry of John the Baptist. The gen-e-al´-o-gy of Jesus on His mother's side. — *II. The Prophetic Ministry of Christ in Galilee.* Chaps. 4, 1—9, 50: The temptation of Christ. He returns to Galilee. Jesus in the synagog at Nazareth. He goes to Ca-per´-na-um and

casts out demons. He heals Peter's wife's mother and many
others. The miraculous draught of fishes. Jesus heals a leper
and a paralytic. The call of Matthew. Jesus answers the scribes
and Pharisees. Jesus and the Sabbath. The withered hand
healed. The Twelve chosen. The Sermon on the Mount. The
centurion's servant healed. The widow's son is raised. John the
Baptist sends disciples to question Jesus. Jesus' testimony to
John the Baptist. Jesus explains the unreason of unbelief. Jesus
in the Pharisee's house. Parables of the creditor and two debtors.
The Lord preaches and heals in Galilee. The parable of the
sower. Jesus stills the storm. He casts out demons at Gad'-a-ra.
A woman healed. Jairus's daughter raised. The Twelve are
sent forth to preach. They return. Five thousand people are fed.
Peter's confession of Christ. Jesus foretells His sufferings and
death. The test of discipleship. The transfiguration of Christ.
The powerless disciples. Jesus casts out a demon. He again
foretells His death. The sermon on humility. Final departure
from Galilee. Another test of discipleship. — *III. Discourses and
Parables of Christ,* especially such as illustrate His love of sinners: the Lost Sheep, the Lost Coin, the Lost (Prodigal) Son.
The increasing hatred of the Pharisees. Chap. 10, 1—18, 30. —
IV. Christ's Last Journey to Jerusalem. His suffering, death,
resurrection, and ascension. Chap. 18, 31—24, 53.

CHAPTER 34.

The Gospel According to St. John.

Its Author. — The fourth and last gospel was written
by John the Apostle. He was the son of Zeb'-e-dee, a well-
to-do fisherman of Beth-sa'-i-da, situated on the Sea of
Galilee, and Sa-lo'-me, who was probably a sister of the
Virgin Mary, which would make him a cousin of Jesus.
Salome was one of the most devoted followers of Christ;
she did not forsake Him even when He was hanging on the
cross. Matt. 27, 56; Mark 15, 40. With his elder brother
James, who also became an apostle, John was in the fishing
business at Capernaum, on the northern end of the Sea

of Galilee. Matt. 4, 21; Mark 1, 19. He seems to have owned a home in Jerusalem also. John 19, 27. From chap. 18, 15 it appears that he was acquainted with the foremost man of the Jewish nation, the high priest. He owned boats and had hired servants, which would indicate that he was a man of some means. In all probability he had been a follower of John the Baptist, who later directed him to Jesus. Chap. 1, 35—40. He returned with Christ to Galilee (chap. 2, 2. 12); and when Jesus soon thereafter publicly

Bethsaida, the Birthplace of John.

entered on His Messianic ministry in Galilee, He called John and James to follow Him; both forsook their daily vocation to enter His personal service. Matt. 4, 21. 22. He, his brother James, and Peter became the three intimate disciples of Christ. They alone were privileged to be present at the raising of Jairus's daughter, the transfiguration, and the agony in the Garden. Jesus surnamed James and John Bo-a-ner´-ges (Sons of Thunder) in allusion to the latent fervor and vehemence of their nature. Mark 3, 17. This part of their nature came out when they asked the Lord for permission to "bid fire to come down from heaven and consume" the people of a certain village in Samaria who would not entertain Him. Luke 9, 51—55. At the last Passover, John had the place of honor, reclining next to Christ. Chap. 13, 25; 21, 20. He constantly refers to himself as "the disciple whom Jesus loved." Chap. 13, 23; 19, 26; 20, 2; 21, 7. 20. In his modesty he also simply refers to himself as "the other disciple." When Jesus had been taken in the Garden, John followed Him; he followed Him to Calvary. There the dying Savior gave His mother into his charge, and John took her to his own home. Chap. 19, 27. After Christ's ascension he is repeatedly mentioned among the number of the apostles, particularly in connection with Peter. Acts 3, 1 ff.; 4, 13 ff.; 8, 14. His brother James was killed by Herod A. D. 44, but he escaped. Acts 12, 2. Paul calls him one of the "pillars" of the Church. Gal. 2, 9. After the death of Peter and Paul (A. D. 68) and before the destruction of Jerusalem (A. D. 70) he removed to the city of Eph'-e-sus, in Asia Minor, where, according to ancient tradition, he supervised the churches which had been established by Paul. Under the Roman Emperor Do-mi'-tian, about 90 A. D., he was temporarily banished to the barren little island of Patmos in the Ae-ge'-an Sea, where he wrote the Book of Revelation. Rev. 1, 9. He returned to Ephesus, and I-re-nae'-us, a Church Father, expressly states that John lived till the time of the Roman Emperor Tra'-jan, who reigned from 98 to 117 after Christ. All the ancients relate that he lived to a very great age and that he was the only one of the twelve apostles that died a natural death, the others having died the death of a martyr.

ITS DATE. — John's gospel was probably written a good while after the synoptic gospels, perhaps somewhere about the year 92 after Christ.

ITS PLACE. — It is not positively known where John wrote his gospel, but according to uniform tradition he wrote it at Ephesus, after his return from Patmos.

ITS PURPOSE. — The author himself expressly states his purpose in the words: "And many other signs, truly, did Jesus in the presence of His disciples, which are not written in this book; but these are written that ye might believe that Jesus is the Christ [the Messiah], the Son of God, and that, believing, ye might have life through His name." Chap. 20, 30. 31. One should bear this purpose in mind while reading John's gospel.

"On the other hand, however, the fourth gospel is so unlike the other gospels and so unique in its character that the attentive reader will involuntarily seek for some special reason why this book should have been written. We find it in the fact that in the latter years of John's life the Church began to be threatened by a dangerous heresy, which made it necessary to describe the life of Christ precisely under the point of view which John chose. Under the eyes of the aged apostle a certain Jewish agitator by the name of *Ce-rin'-thus* is said to have denied the essential and true divinity of Jesus Christ, rejecting the statement that the Son of God suffered death for us. That must have been the beginning of the heresy which later became known as *Gnosticism*, the adherents of which essayed to amalgamate the Word of God with heathen philosophy and necessarily fell into blasphemous error. It is well within the limits of possibility that John, recognizing the danger in its beginnings, wrote his gospel against the errors of Cerinthus, since he actually makes it his point to demonstrate the divinity of Christ."

DISTINGUISHING FEATURES. — Chapter 30 pointed out a number of peculiarities of the Gospel according to St. John. The following may here be added: 1. The book is remarkable for its vivid dialog form. See chaps. 1, 3, 4, 5, 6, 7—10, 11, 12, 13, 14, 21. In chaps. 15 and 17 we have monolog. 2. This gospel gives the fullest treatment of the person and work of the Holy Spirit. Chaps. 14—16. 3. Only eight of the thirty-five miracles of Christ are recorded in this gospel, but several of them are treated at some length and become the occasion of extended address to the people. See chaps. 5, 6, 9, 21. Luther says: "Since John records very few of the works of Christ, but very many of His discourses," while the other three evangelists, on the other hand, record many of His works, but few of His words, therefore the Gospel according to St. John is much to be preferred to the other three and to be extolled more highly."

SUMMARY OF CONTENTS. — *I. Historical Introduction.* Chaps. 1 to 4. Chap. 1, 1—18 is commonly called the prolog = the preface, or introduction. It is a brief summary of the whole book and serves as a general introduction. The message of John the Baptist. The marriage at Cana. Jesus and Nic-o-de´-mus. The beginning of Christ's public ministry. — *II. The Beginning of the Conflict between Jesus and the Jews.* Chaps. 5 to 12. — *III. Christ in the Circle of His Disciples.* Chaps. 13 to 17. — *IV. Christ's Sufferings, Death, and Resurrection.* Chaps. 18 to 20. — *V. Addition,* which records how Jesus appeared again to His disciples at the Sea of Galilee, supplied them miraculously with a great draught of fishes, gave a charge to Peter, and foretold Peter's death. Chap. 21.

CHAPTER 35.

The Acts of the Apostles.

THE AUTHOR. — St. Luke, who penned the third gospel, also wrote the Acts of the Apostles and dedicated this book to the same person — to The-oph´-i-lus. (Comp. Acts 1, 1 with Luke 1, 1—3.) The Book of Acts is clearly the continuation of the Gospel according to St. Luke.

Indeed, the same event, Christ's ascension, closes the latter book and opens the former. Moreover, in dedicating the Book of Acts to Theophilus, Luke refers to his former work. Luke himself witnessed, to a great extent, the events he narrates. (See the sections in which he uses the pronoun "we": chap. 16, 10—17; 20, 5—15; 21, 1—18; 27, 1—28, 16.) For further particulars regarding St. Luke go back to chapter 33.

DATE AND PLACE OF WRITING. — From chap. 1, 1 we learn that the Book of Acts was written after the Gospel according to St. Luke; but how long after, is not known. As Luke mentions neither the fall of Jerusalem (A. D. 70) nor the death of St. Paul (in the year 67 or early in 68), it may be set down as fairly certain that he wrote this book before these events. The book closes with the second year of Paul's imprisonment in Rome (A. D. 63). Luke was with Paul during his second imprisonment in Rome. The Book of Acts was probably written A. D. 68 in Rome. That agrees with what Jerome says on this point.

THE PURPOSE. — The Book of Acts is a historical book; it contains history, divinely inspired history. Its title would lead us to believe that it gives the record of the acts, or doings, of all the apostles. The title, however, which is not from the pen of Luke, but was added by a later hand, is not an exact description of the book. True, we find a list of the apostles in chap. 1, 13, and chap. 2, 14 Peter and the Eleven are mentioned; but after chap. 2 most of the twelve apostles are not referred to, and the bulk of the book records the work of others than the Twelve, as Stephen and Philip (chaps. 6—8), Barnabas (chap. 11), and Paul (chap. 9 and 13—28). We have drawn attention to the fact that our book is a continuation of the Gospel according to St. Luke. In that Gospel St. Luke tells us what Jesus did until the time of His ascension, and in the

Acts he goes on to tell us what Jesus did after His ascension. "The former treatise have I made, O Theophilus, of all that Jesus began both to do and teach, until the day in which He was taken up." Acts 1, 1. 2. "The position of the word 'began' is very emphatic in the original, as if to imply that the Acts of the Apostles formed *a continuation of Christ's work*. The writer conceives of Him as still carrying on His work in virtue of His resurrection and ascension; and in the introduction to the book he refers to these events as well as to the prediction of His second advent. Chap. 1, 1—11. So this history is His story, the story of the risen Christ, who sits at the right hand of God the Father Almighty as the Head of His Church and through His Holy Spirit governs and extends it."

The program of Christ and of the book is found chap. 1, 8: "Ye shall receive power after that the Holy Ghost *The* is come upon you; and ye shall be witnesses to Me both in← *Heading* Jerusalem and in all Judea and Samaria and to the uttermost part of the earth." The Book of Acts records the fulfilment of this prophecy. It vividly tells how Jesus' disciples were all filled with the Holy Ghost and then preached the Gospel of Christ first in Jerusalem, next in all Judea and Samaria, and then in the uttermost parts of the then known world. It covers a period of about 30 years (A. D 33 to 63) and graphically points out the gradual growth and development of the early Church. This expansion was accomplished by means of the Gospel, the glad tidings of the grace of God in Christ Jesus. The word *grace* is a favorite word with St. Luke. Luther says in his introduction to the Book of Acts: "This book should be read and regarded not merely as St. Luke's record of the personal acts or history of the apostles, but this is the point one should rather note, *viz.*, that with this book St. Luke teaches all Christendom to the end of the world the really chief article of Christian doctrine, which tells us that we must all be justified alone by faith in Jesus Christ, without the Law or our own works."

THE HOLY SPIRIT IN ACTS. — Some one has called this book "The Acts of the Holy Spirit." His agency and ministry are specially prominent, being expressly referred to about 70 times. Let the student in his reading of this book make a note of all those passages containing such references. The book opens with a reference to the promise of the Father that He would send the Holy Ghost on the disciples. The second chapter records how a beginning of the fulfilment of this promise was made on the Day of Pentecost. The rest of the book is a description of the disciples at work under the influence of the Spirit of Christ. Note particularly how each of the three sections telling of the beginning of the work in Jerusalem, in all Judea and Samaria, and among the Gentiles is marked by a notable outpouring of the Holy Spirit. Chap. 2, 1—4; 8, 17; 10, 44—48.

ACTS A BOOK OF MISSIONS. — "The dominant note of the book is the missionary cause." The book is replete with missionary thoughts. Let the student read it with pencil in hand and note on paper some of the passages which point out: 1. Missionary motives (why we should engage in mission-work). 2. Missionary means (the Gospel is the only means, and an effectual means). 3. Missions and prayer. 4. Proof that Home Missions come first, then Foreign Missions. 5. How did God show that He wants black people brought to the knowledge of Christ? 6. Who were prejudiced against Foreign Missions, and how was their prejudice overcome? 7. Where do we find an example of a church hearing a report on Foreign Mission work? Etc.

SUMMARY OF CONTENTS. — *I. Historical Introduction.* Last instructions of the risen Lord during the forty days between His resurrection and ascension; ten days of prayer; Matthias is chosen in place of Judas. Chap. 1. — *II. Establishing the Church in Palestine.* 1. In Jerusalem. The Day of Pentecost; the first sermon and the first baptism (about 3,000 souls). The brotherhood of the first believers. Peter and John heal a lame beggar at the door Beautiful; Peter preaches to the multitude which gathered; Peter and John are imprisoned; Peter's bold address before the Council; he and John are let go, and the disciples unite in praise and prayer. Voluntary community of goods. The sin of Ananias and Sapphira. Believers are multiplied in Jerusalem. The apostles, again imprisoned, are divinely delivered and preach. The appointment of the first deacons. The ministry and martyrdom of Stephen. Chaps. 2 to 7. 2. Establishing the Church in Judea and Samaria: First great persecution under Saul and consequent extended preaching of the Word in wider circles. The Samaritans receive the Gospel at the hands of Philip, the deacon; the Ethiopian eunuch is converted and baptized by Philip. The conversion of Saul of Tarsus. Further miracles by Peter. He is shown by means of a vision what should be his attitude toward the Gentiles; he obeys the vision and preaches in the house of the former Gentile Cornelius; the hearers receive the Holy Spirit and are baptized. Accused for going to the Gentiles, Peter justifies his conduct before the church at Jerusalem. The Gospel is brought to Antioch, which becomes the starting-point of foreign missions. King Herod kills James the Elder and imprisons Peter; Peter is liberated by an angel. Chaps. 8 to 12. — *III. Establishing the Church in Heathen Countries under the Ministry of Paul.* 1. First missionary journey of Paul with Barnabas. The Apostolic Council at Jerusalem concerning the reception of Gentiles. The second missionary journey of Paul. His third missionary journey. (Map 3.) 2. Paul goes to Jerusalem, where he is arrested and is in great danger; he makes his defense before the Sanhedrin (Jewish Council), before Felix, Festus, and Herod Agrippa at Caesarea; he appeals to Caesar and is sent to Rome to be tried; his voyage to Rome. As prisoner Paul preaches the Gospel in Rome two years. Chap. 13 to 28.

CHAPTER 36.

The Life of St. Paul.

DOCTRINAL BOOKS OF THE NEW TESTAMENT. — The four gospels and the Acts of the Apostles are the 5 historical books of the New Testament. The 21 books which follow are doctrinal; they chiefly contain doctrine, or teaching. They set forth the significance of the gospel facts. Fourteen of these 21 books were written by St. Paul. This circumstance alone calls for a special lesson on the life of this great apostle of Christ.

PAUL'S EARLY LIFE AND EDUCATION. — Paul was born at Tar´-sus, a city in the Province of Ci-li´-ci-a, Asia Minor. His parents were Jews of the tribe of Benjamin. Phil. 3, 5; 2 Cor. 11, 22. His father had acquired the Roman citizenship; so the son, too, was a Roman in law. Acts 16, 37; 22, 25—28. He was circumcised the eighth day and received the name Saul = Asked for. After Acts 13, 7 he is commonly called Paul = Little. It seems he was small of stature. Tarsus was "no mean city." Acts 21, 39. It was a famous seat of Greek learning. The opportunities for mental improvement it afforded were, no doubt, diligently improved by Paul. That he obtained a good knowledge of Greek and Greek literature appears from his epistles. At a suitable age his parents sent him to Jerusalem to study Jewish theology in the school of the great Ga-ma´-li-el, the most distinguished Rabbi of that age. Acts 22, 3. At his feet he became thoroughly versed in rabbinical literature. Following the example of his father and of his teacher, he became a Pharisee, a member of "the straitest sect" of the Jewish religion. Acts 26, 5. Looking back to the days in which he had been a young, ardent Pharisee, he later wrote to the Galatians: "I advanced in the Jews' religion beyond many of mine own age among my countrymen,

St. Paul.

being more exceedingly zealous for the traditions of my fathers." Gal. 1, 14. According to the pharisaic standard he led a blameless life and stood high in the confidence of the leading men of the Jewish nation. Phil. 3, 6; Acts 7, 58. In accordance with the rule observed among the Jews that every person should learn some trade, he became a tent-maker; in later years he was thus in a position to support himself without depending on the gifts of the churches. Acts 18, 3; 20, 34; 2 Thess. 3, 8.

PAUL THE PERSECUTOR. — In the Bible we first find him at Jerusalem, a young man apparently thirty years of age, taking part in the persecution of the Christians at Jerusalem. Acts 7, 58. Filled with burning zeal for the Jewish religion, he took a prominent part in the persecution of the primitive Christians. He "laid waste the Church, entering into every house, and haling [dragging] men and women, committed them to prison." Acts 8, 3. His mad fanaticism made him go even to other cities to persecute the Church of Christ. Acts 26, 11. He did it ignorantly, in unbelief. 1 Tim. 1, 13. He thought he was doing God service.

PAUL IS CONVERTED. — In the midst of his mad career he was "apprehended of Christ Jesus." He was on the way to Damascus, a very old city in Syria, about 150 miles northeast of Jerusalem, to bring Christians bound to Jerusalem to punish them, when Jesus appeared to him, converting his heart and calling him to be His apostle to the Gentiles. Acts 9, 3—19; 22, 6—16; 26, 11—18. This was the most important event in the history of the New Testament Church.

PAUL THE PERSECUTED. — Before entering on his apostolic career, he remained certain days with the Christians at Damascus and then went to Arabia, where he lived in solitary retirement for a short period. Gal. 1, 17.

Damascus. (See Map 1.)

Returning to Damascus, he preached Christ with great power. The unbelieving Jews resolved to kill him. But with the assistance of the believers he quickly and quietly escaped and fled to Jerusalem. 2 Cor. 11, 32. 33; Acts 9, 23—28. This was three years after his conversion. Gal. 1, 18. The Christians at Jerusalem were at first all afraid of him, but Bar'-na-bas told them of his conversion and preaching. Paul stayed in Jerusalem only fifteen days. The hostile Jews were seeking to kill him. But the Christians sent him forth to Tarsus, his home city. Acts 9, 29. 30; 22, 17—21. When Barnabas had found an abundance of work in An'-ti-och of Syria, he departed to Tarsus to seek Paul; and when he had found him, he brought him to Antioch. Here both taught much people a whole year. Acts 11, 25. 26. (Map 1.)

PAUL'S FIRST MISSIONARY JOURNEY. — When Paul and Barnabas had returned from Jerusalem, whither they had taken a collection of the Antioch church for the suffering Christians at Jerusalem, the church at Antioch solemnly set him and Barnabas apart for the work of preaching the Gospel in more distant countries. This was the beginning of his great missionary activity as the Apostle of the Gentiles. He and Barnabas set sail for the island of Cy'-prus, the latter's home. (Map 1.) Crossing over to Per'-ga, in the Province of Pam-phyl'-i-a, they proceeded to Antioch in Pi-sid'-i-a, where Paul preached in the synagog. But the hostile Jews stirred up a persecution against Paul and Barnabas and expelled them out of their borders. They came to I-co'-ni-um, where they were again persecuted. They fled to Lys'-tra and Der'-be in Ly-ca-o'-ni-a. The miracle performed on a lame man led the heathen people to worship them; but the apostles protested. Soon, however, the unbelieving Jews who followed them from Antioch and Iconium persuaded the people to persecute Paul and Barnabas. They stoned Paul and dragged him out of the city, supposing that he was dead. But he recovered, and the next day he left with Barnabas for Derbe, where they preached and made many disciples. Then they returned to Lystra and to Iconium and to Antioch, confirming the souls of their converts and exhorting them to continue in the faith. Passing through Pi-sid'-i-a, Pam-phyl'-i-a, and

At-ta´-li-a, they returned to their home base in Antioch of Syria and reported to the church there on their first missionary work among the Gentiles. They had been absent about two years (from 45 to 47). The full story of their tour is recorded Acts 13 and 14, and their itinerary is marked on the map. (Map 3.)

THE COUNCIL AT JERUSALEM. — After the return from their first missionary expedition, Paul and Barnabas remained at Antioch "no little time," about a year or so. Former Pharisees who had joined the church at Jerusalem came from that city to Antioch and caused a great disturbance by telling the Christians who had been Gentiles, "Except ye be circumcised after the manner of Moses, ye cannot be saved." The church now sent Paul and Barnabas and others to Jerusalem to discuss this question. The conference held there showed that Paul and the other apostles perfectly agreed in saying that it is not necessary to salvation to be circumcised or to keep any ceremonial commandments given to the people of God in the Old Testament. This conference was held fourteen years after Paul's conversion, about A. D. 51. Read Acts 15, 1—35; Gal. 2, 1—10.

SECOND MISSIONARY JOURNEY. — Soon after Paul's return from Jerusalem, he set out on his second missionary journey. First he and Si´-las visited the churches which he had established to see how they fared. This done, he intended to penetrate into new portions of Asia. But the Lord commanded him to go over into Europe to preach the Gospel there. In Europe he planted the first church at Phi-lip´-pi; next he established churches at Thes-sa-lo-ni´-ca and Be-re´-a. After preaching in Ath´-ens, he proceeded to Cor´-inth, where he remained eighteen months. During his stay at Corinth he wrote the two epistles to the Thessalonians. From Corinth he started on his fourth visit to

Jerusalem. Having saluted the church at Jerusalem, he returned to Antioch, where he spent some time. This second missionary tour had lasted about two years, from 52 to 54. It is recorded Acts 15, 36—18, 22. (Map 3.)

THIRD MISSIONARY JOURNEY. — Leaving Antioch, Paul first visited churches which he had established and then came to Eph´-e-sus, where he made his headquarters for about three years. During his stay at Ephesus he wrote the Epistle to the Galatians and the First Epistle to the Corinthians. Passing through Troas and Mac-e-do´-ni-a, he dispatched the Second Epistle to the Corinthians from Phi-lip´-pi and then proceeded to Corinth himself, where he remained three months. At Corinth he wrote the Epistle to the Romans. His intention was to see Rome. Acts 19, 21; Rom. 15, 24—28. But before visiting Rome, he wished to go to Jerusalem at Pentecost. The third missionary journey was made about 55 to 58. Read Acts 18, 23—20, 3. (Map 3.)

PAUL'S FIFTH AND LAST VISIT AT JERUSALEM. — Leaving Corinth, Paul traveled by way of Philippi, Troas, Mi-le´-tus, Tyre, Ptol-e-ma´-is, and Caes-a-re´-a. Acts 20, 3—21, 15. In Jerusalem he was mobbed by the infuriated Jews. The Roman captain saved him from being torn to pieces and sent him to Felix, the governor, at Caesarea.

PAUL'S IMPRISONMENT. — Paul was now a Roman prisoner for nearly five years. Felix unjustly left him in bonds for two years at Caesarea. Under the next governor, Festus, Paul was finally constrained to appeal to Caesar. Accordingly, Festus sent him to Rome, where he arrived in the spring of 61. Here he was a prisoner for two years. He wrote the epistles to the Ephesians and Colossians, to Philemon, and to the Philippians. Read Acts 21, 17—28, 31.

PAUL IS RELEASED. — The account in the Acts ends with Paul's imprisonment at Rome. But there is an early and general tradition to the effect that he obtained his liberty again for a time, just as he had confidently expected. Philemon 22; Phil. 1, 25. 26; 2, 24. After his release he visited Crete (Titus 1, 5), Miletus, Troas, Macedonia, and Corinth (1 Tim. 1, 3; 2 Tim. 4, 13. 20). While in Macedonia, he wrote the First Epistle to Timothy and the Epistle to Titus. After his liberation he also carried out his long-cherished wish to preach the Gospel in Spain. Rom. 15, 24. 28.

His Second Roman Imprisonment and Death. — In the fall of 66 he was again a prisoner at Rome. This time he expected his imprisonment to end with his death. 2 Tim. 2, 9; 4, 6—18. He is said to have died a martyr's death under bloody Nero, in 67.

CHAPTER 37.

The Epistle of Paul to the Romans.

Order of Paul's Epistles. — The epistles of Paul do not follow in chronological order in the Bible. Not the sequence of time in which they were written, but their length, importance, etc., determined their arrangement. The Epistle to the Romans comes first. It is the most important of all the epistles of Paul. *Luther* pronounces it "the chief book of the New Testament and the purest Gospel. It would be quite proper for a Christian not only to know it by heart word for word, but also daily to use it as daily bread of the soul; for you can never read and study it too much and too well. The more one uses it, the more precious it becomes, and the better it tastes."

To Whom It was Written. — "To all that are in Rome, beloved of God, called to be saints." Chap. 1, 7.

Origin of the Church at Rome. — From chaps. 1, 8

and 16, 19 it appears that the church at Rome had existed for some time when Paul wrote this epistle. How had it been founded? Evidently not through the services of St. Paul himself. When he wrote his letter (in 58), he had never been in Rome. Chap. 1, 10. 13; 15, 23. The Roman Catholic Church of to-day claims that St. Peter was the founder of the church in Rome and that he guided its destinies for twenty-five years as its first bishop. This claim has no foundation in the Bible. Indeed, it is contrary to all the evidence of the New Testament. Here is some of the evidence: —

1. Up to the time of the Apostolic Council in 51 St. Peter was still at Jerusalem. Acts 12, 4; 15, 7; Gal. 2, 1 ff. Trustworthy tradition has it that he died in 67. From 51 to 67, however, is not twenty-five years.

2. St. Paul wrote his Epistle to the Romans early in 58. But in this epistle he makes no mention whatever of St. Peter, as he surely would have done if so prominent an apostle had planted the Roman church.

3. In his epistle (chap. 16, 3—16) St. Paul sends special greetings to a large number of Christians in Rome. But St. Peter's name is not mentioned in the long list of those whom he greets. What does that mean? It can only mean that St. Peter was not in Rome at the time. It is clear, then, that neither St. Peter nor St. Paul founded the church at Rome.

Nor have we any evidence to the effect that any other apostle was the founder. The origin of this church must probably be accounted for in the following manner: Rome, the mistress and metropolis of the world, had a large number of Jewish inhabitants in those days. Some of these were present in Jerusalem on the great Day of Pentecost when the Holy Ghost was poured out on the disciples. Acts 2, 10. In all probability some of these "sojourners

The Forum, or Market-Place, in Rome.

from Rome" were among the three thousand who were converted and baptized. When they returned to Rome, these
converts carried the Gospel of Christ with them. That
was the beginning of the church at Rome. About twenty-
five years had now passed since that Pentecost. In the
mean time Christians from other places had moved to the

metropolis and had helped to increase the growth of the church. When Paul wrote his epistle, it seems to have been a large church. At any rate, it had attracted wide attention. St. Paul says: "Your faith is spoken of throughout the whole [Christian] world." Chap. 1, 8; 16, 19.

PURPOSE OF THE EPISTLE. — Paul had long intended to visit the church in Rome, but had so far been prevented from carrying out his purpose. His plan now was to take a collection of the churches in Greece for the poor Christians in Jerusalem to the latter place and then pass through Rome on a mission-journey to Spain. Chap. 15, 25—28; Acts 19, 21. But before going to Rome, he desired to get in touch with the church there by means of a personal letter. The conditions for sending such a letter were favorable, inasmuch as Phoebe, a deaconess of Cen-chre´-a, a port of Corinth, was just on the point of going to Rome. Chap. 16, 1. 2. Although the church at Rome was far and favorably known for its faith, it had not enjoyed the benefit of thorough apostolic instruction. Such instruction St. Paul sends in his full and exhaustive doctrinal treatise. Again, the church was composed of both former Jews and former Gentiles. Chap. 1, 13; 2, 17—24, etc. The Gentile Christians seem to have constituted the main body. But the two classes had not yet formed one harmonious whole. The members who had come from the Jewish Church clung to the idea that the Jews as such should enjoy special privileges in the kingdom of God, while the Gentile Christians were inclined to despise the Jews, who had so often rejected the Word and grace of God that God had finally rejected them. Chap. 11, 14. 15. Paul's wish is to unify these two elements. Finally, the church at Rome evidently stood in need of admonition regarding particular duties, for example, regarding the duty of not offending such as are weak in knowledge and faith, regarding the duty of obeying even a wicked government, etc. Chaps. 13 to 15.

Where and When Written. — Paul wrote this epistle from Corinth, in the early spring of 58, just before leaving for Jerusalem. It was dictated by him to Tertius in the house of Ga´-ius at Corinth. Rom. 16, 22. 23, comp. with 1 Cor. 1, 14; Rom. 15, 25—28, comp. with Acts 19, 21.

Summary of Contents. — I. *Salutation and Introduction.* Chap. 1, 1—17. At the end of the introduction (vv. 16. 17) the apostle states the great theme of the epistle: Justification by faith. — II. *Doctrinal Part of the Letter.* Chap. 1, 18—11, 36. 1. Paul proves to both Jews and Gentiles that they are all under sin, that all the world is guilty before God and subject to His wrath. Chap. 1, 18—3, 20. 2. The divine method of rescue. God has set forth Christ to be a propitiation through faith in His blood. In Christ Jesus there is redemption and righteousness for all. This righteousness is obtained by faith alone. Chap. 3, 21—31. That a man is justified by faith without the deeds of the Law is exemplified in Abraham. Chap. 4. 3. The advantages of justification by faith: We have peace with God, a joyful hope of eternal life and glory, and present joy even in tribulation. A parallel between Adam and Christ: Adam brought sin and death into the world; Christ brought righteousness and life. Chap. 5. 4. The objection made to the doctrine of free justifying grace is that it tends to encourage sin. Paul's answer to this objection: Free grace does not multiply sin; on the contrary, it emancipates from the dominion, or ruling power, of sin and is the only way to true holiness and final glory. Chap. 6 to 8. 5. In the following three chapters (9—11) Paul takes up the problem of the unbelief of the Jews. He expresses his deep sorrow for the Jews, his kinsmen according to the flesh, because of their exclusion from salvation in Christ, but at the same time points out that they are not all Israel which are of Israel, but that only those are in truth Israelites and children of God who believe. (Chap. 9, 1—13; 3, 28. 29.) He points to the sovereignty of God according to which He converts some and hardens others; at the same time he shows from history how God endured with much long-suffering the vessels of wrath fitted to destruction, and how He made known the riches of His glory on the vessels of mercy. (Chap. 9, 14—29.) The apostle deplores the fact that, while the Gentiles, who followed not after righteousness, have attained to righteousness, even the righteousness which is of faith,

— the last few chapters deal with the table of duties,
the last chapter deals with the salutations.

Israel, which followed after the Law of righteousness, has not attained to the Law of righteousness, because they sought it not by faith, but, as it were, by the works of the Law, and in unbelief rejected God's righteousness and salvation which is so near to all and open to all. Their unbelief was foretold in the writings of the prophets. (Chap. 9, 30—10, 21.) Through Israel's fall salvation has come to the Gentiles. The Gentile Christians, however, must not boast against Israel because of their preference to them, but should beware of unbelief, lest they, too, be rejected. The rejection of Israel is partial ("in part"), not total; God has reserved a remnant according to the election of grace, although the mass of the Jews are hardened; this remnant of Israel will be converted and saved. Paul admires and adores the wisdom of God. (Chap. 11.) — *III. Practical Part of the Letter,* containing divers exhortations to holiness of life. (Chap. 12, 1—15, 13.) — *IV. Conclusion:* Personal news, numerous greetings to individual Christians at Rome, warning against false teachers, doxology. (Chap. 15, 14—16, 27.)

CHAPTER 38.

The Epistles of Paul to the Corinthians.

FIRST EPISTLE.

THE CITY OF CORINTH. — Corinth was the capital of A-cha´-ia (Greece), situated on the isthmus, or neck of land, which connects the upper and lower parts of Greece. It lay at the northern foot of a great rock rising about 2,000 feet above the sea. Lying in the direct route between Ephesus and Rome, Corinth became the chief commercial emporium of Europe; over half of the traffic of the East and West poured through its gates. It contained nearly half a million inhabitants, drawn from many lands — Greeks, Jews, Italians, and a mixed multitude. Its flourishing commerce brought wealth, and wealth brought luxury and licentiousness. A "Corinthian life" was a synonym for luxury and licentiousness. Immorality was not only

Licence to do any thing you please, 6 commandment etc.

openly tolerated, it was consecrated here by the worship of
Aph-ro-di´-te (Venus), the Greek goddess of love, who had
a great temple here in which a thousand women were kept.
At the same time the inhabitants made such pretensions
to philosophy and literature that "Corinthian words" was
a phrase meaning polished and cultivated speech.   To this
city Paul came on his second missionary journey in
A. D. 52 and founded a church.

THE CHURCH AT CORINTH. — In Corinth, Paul found
a certain Jew named Aq´-ui-la, born in Pon´-tus, lately
come from Italy, with his wife Pris-cil´-la, because the
Emperor Clau´-di-us had commanded all the Jews to depart
from Rome; and he came to them; and because he was of
the same trade, he abode with them, and they wrought;
for by their trade they were tent-makers. Acts 18, 1—3.
Every Sabbath, Paul went to the Jewish synagog and sought
to persuade Jews and Greeks.   The Jews, however, showed
such determined opposition that he left them to their fate
and turned to the Gentiles.   Next to the synagog stood
a house belonging to a Gentile converted to Judaism whose
name was Justus; this house now served as meeting-place.
Many of the Corinthians who heard Paul preach believed
and were baptized, and thus a large and flourishing congregation was gathered.   And he dwelt there a year and
six months, teaching the Word of God among them. Acts
18, 4—18.   His converts were chiefly Gentiles and seem to
have been drawn, in the main, from the lower classes.
1 Cor. 1, 26—29; 12, 2.   They were not free from the
prevailing tendency to intellectual pride (chap. 1, 17; 2,
1 f.; 8, 1), accompanied with a proneness to sensual sin,
equally characteristic of their city (chap. 5, 1—11; 6,
15—18; 11, 21).   At the end of eighteen months Paul
resumed his missionary travels.   He was succeeded at

Corinth, for a time, by a certain Jew named A-pol'-los, born at <u>Alexandria</u> in Egypt, an eloquent man and mighty in the Scriptures, who had become a Christian. Acts 18, 24—19, 1. Ere long, however, other teachers appeared and began to make trouble.

OCCASION OF THE FIRST EPISTLE. — Paul had now labored nearly three years at Ephesus, when disquieting reports reached him from Corinth. He<u> heard that the Corinthian church had been split into factions.</u> One Corinthian said, <u>"I am of Paul,"</u> another, <u>"I am of Apol-los,"</u> another, "I<u> am of Ce'-phas,"</u> another, "<u>I am of Christ.</u>" Chap. 1, 11. 12; 3, 4; 11, 18. The quarrel among these parties brought other evils in its train. <u>Church dis-cipline was neglected;</u> the congregation said nothing to a certain young member who had committed the scandalous sin of incest. Chap. 4, 19—5, 1. O<u>ne member went to law against another, and that before the unrighteous, or un-believers, in the civil courts of the heathen.</u> Chap. 6, 1—7. Various forms of licentiousness were practised. Chap. 6, 13. <u>Common decorum came to be disregarded in the church-meetings.</u> Chap. 11, 1—15; 14, 34. <u>Even the observance of the Lord's Supper was made the occasion for offensive behavior.</u> Chap. 11, 20 ff. The <u>gifts of the Holy Spirit</u> which had been bestowed on the Corinthian church were often misused. Chaps. 12 to 14. And, finally, dangerous errors regarding the <u>resurrection of the dead had crept in and were tolera</u>ted. Chap. 15, 12 ff. Moreover, the con-gregation had sent a delegation to Paul in Ephesus to sub-mit to him a series of questions on which information and advice was desired. Chap. 16, 17; 7, 1. <u>Such were the circumstances which called forth the first letter to the Corinthians.</u> The <u>sentiment in which Paul wrote</u> it he describes thus: "Ou<u>t of much affliction and anguish of heart I wrote unto you with many tears; not that ye should</u>

be made sorry, but that ye might know the love which
I have more abundantly unto you." 2 Cor. 2, 4.

WHEN AND WHERE WRITTEN.—Paul wrote this epistle
at Ephesus (chap. 16, 8. 19 comp. with Acts 18), at the end
of his three years' sojourn at Ephesus (chap. 16, 3 f.),
before Pentecost (chap. 16, 8), probably around Easter
in 58 (chap. 16, 6—8).

SUMMARY OF CONTENTS. — I. Salutation and Thanksgiving.
Chap. 1, 1—9. — II. Paul Exhorts the Corinthians to Unity, reproving their dissensions. The manner of his preaching: He
preached the Gospel of Christ Crucified not with enticing words
of man's wisdom, but in demonstration of the Spirit and of
power; his preaching excelled the wisdom of this world and
human sense. Chaps. 1, 17—2, 16. The jealousy and strife and
factions among the Corinthians were due to the fact that they
gloried in men, each party priding itself on the supposed superiority of the teacher whom it had chosen and making invidious
comparisons. Paul points out that every minister has his gifts
from God and that it is God who gives success to his labors.
Ministers are stewards; the Lord is their sole Judge. Warning.
Chap. 3. — III. Concerning Church-discipline. Chap. 5: The
apostle sharply condemns the flagrant case of fornication which
had occurred in the Corinthian congregation, and the indifference
with which the members treated the scandal, and urges the exclusion of the incestuous young man. — IV. Litigation among
Church-members. A Christian should not go to law with his
Christian brother in heathen courts. Chap. 6, 1—8. He should
avoid all sin and shame and flee fornication. Chap. 6, 9—20. —
V. Instruction Regarding Marriage, etc. Paul next answers the
questions which the congregation had submitted to him concerning marriage and celibacy (chap. 7) and concerning the law-
fulness of eating meats that had been used in making sacrifices to
heathen idols. In this connection he cites his own example of
self-denial even in things lawful. The duty of supporting the
ministry. Chaps. 8 and 9. From the history of Israel under Moses,
Paul adduces examples to enforce his warning against carnal
security. Chap. 10. He points out the decorum to be observed
by both men and women in church-meetings, and rebukes the

disorders at the Lord's Table in Corinth. Chap. 11. — *VI. Spiritual Gifts.* What estimate is to be placed on spiritual gifts; the incomparable excellence of Christian love; the use and abuse of the gifts of the Spirit. Chaps. 12 to 14. — *VII. Conclusion.* The resurrection. Chap. 15. Directions for the collection to be taken for the poor Christians in Jerusalem; Paul's traveling plans; recommendations; greetings. Chap. 16.

Second Epistle.

Having dispatched his first epistle, Paul sent Timothy to Corinth. 1 Cor. 4, 17; 16, 10. Next he sent Titus. 2 Cor. 7, 13 f.; 8, 6. 16; 12, 18. (See chapter 45.) Then he departed from Ephesus to go to Macedonia. Acts 20, 1. On the way there he stopped at Troas, where he anxiously expected the arrival of Titus, who was to bring word regarding the effect of his epistle. But when he did not find Titus at Troas, he proceeded to Macedonia. Chap. 2, 12. 13. There Titus came to him. Chap. 7, 5. 6. Titus brought both good and bad news from Corinth. He reported that as a result of hearing Paul's epistle, they had excluded the incestuous young man (chap. 2, 6 f.) and taken steps to gather the collection for the poor saints at Jerusalem. Chap. 8, 1 f.; 9, 1 f. On the other hand, Titus reported several unfavorable conditions: some of the members still were prejudiced against Paul (chap. 3, 1 f.); others had been made sorry with the letter (chap. 2, 2; 7, 8); and the Judaizing party was more bitter against him than ever before (chaps. 10 to 12). All this moved him to write his second epistle before going to Corinth in person. He wrote it in Macedonia, probably from Philippi, in the summer of 58. Chap. 8, 1; 9, 4.

Summary of Contents. — *I. Salutation and Introductory Remarks.* Chap. 1: Reasons why Paul had not come to Corinth as yet. — *II. The Glory of the Gospel Ministry.* Chap. 2, 1—7, 1. Paul advises the Corinthians to forgive the young person excommunicated for incest, who had now repented (chap. 2, 5—11), and then shows over against his opponents the glory of the Gospel-ministry and his own apostolic methods, earnestly exhorting the readers to receive and live the Gospel which he preached and to separate themselves from the world. — *III. The Need of Liberality toward the Needy.* After briefly explaining the aim of his foregoing letter and expressing his pleasure at the good results it had brought about, he exhorts them to a prompt and liberal fulfilment of their promise to contribute for the relief of the needy brethren at Jerusalem. Chaps. 7, 2—9, 15. — *IV. Paul Defends His Apostolic Office.* At the beginning of chap. 9 there is a sudden change in the apostle's tone and speech. He still addresses his remarks to all, but chiefly has in view his detractors, defends himself against their charges, sets forth the gifts he received from God and his apostolic labors, and threatens severe measures against obstinate offenders. Chap. 10, 1—13, 10. — *V. Conclusion.* Chap. 13, 11—14.

CHAPTER 39.

Main Point: Not by the works or deeds of the Law

St. Paul's Epistle to the Galatians. *Know the surrounding Seas.*

THE GALATIANS. — Ga-la´-ti-a was a fertile and beautiful country in the heart of Asia Minor. Its name was derived from the Galati = Celts, or Gauls. The Galati had originally come from Gaul, the France of to-day. About 280 B. C. great hordes of these wild people had migrated eastward; some attempted to swarm into Greece and finally found a home in the heart of Asia Minor. They were conquered by the Romans 189 B. C., yet remained self-governed, but tributary, till 26 B. C., when Caesar Augustus converted Galatia into a Roman province under a governor. The language of the Galati was partly Gallic (Celtic), partly Greek. The commercial advantages which the country afforded attracted many Jews. (Map 1.)

THE CHURCHES OF GALATIA. — Paul came to Galatia in the course of his second missionary journey, probably in 51 or 52. Acts 15, 40; 16, 6. His first visit seems to have been brief. He had an attack of his painful and humiliating bodily malady, "an infirmity of the flesh." But they responded to his faithful preaching of Christ Crucified with great enthusiasm and zealous attachment. Chap. 3, 1; 4, 13—15. He was able to plant a number of churches. These churches were mainly composed of converts from heathenism. Chap. 4, 8; 5, 2; 6, 12. Paul gives them the testimony, "Ye did run well." Chap. 5, 7. During his second missionary tour, about the year 54, the apostle visited them again, "strengthening all the disciples." Acts 18, 23. Shortly after that, however, Judaizing teachers arose in these churches of Galatia and troubled (disquieted) them. Chap. 1, 7. They were former Jews, who now professed Christianity. But they insisted that faith in Christ was not enough to obtain righteousness before God, life, and salvation. They told the Galatians that it was necessary to salvation to keep the Ceremonial Law of the Jews, submit to circumcision, observe the Jewish feasts, etc. Paul had taught the Galatians that in order to become righteous in God's sight and obtain life and salvation, nothing more was needed than faith in Christ. To destroy this doctrine, these Judaizing teachers hinted that Paul was no true apostle of Christ, that he had never seen the Lord, and that he owed his knowledge of the Gospel to the apostles who had their headquarters at Jerusalem. They were prompted by unworthy motives. Chap. 4, 17; 6, 13. They soon succeeded in winning over the greater part of the churches. What made their success easy was the fact that some members hoped to escape persecution if they would enter into outward fellowship with the Jews. Chap. 6, 12. Many were ready to receive circumcision, etc. Chap. 3, 1; 4, 9 ff.; 6, 13. These were the circumstances which called forth Paul's Epistle to the Galatians.

THE EPISTLE. — Paul wrote this letter about the year 56

or 57 from Ephesus. The subscription added later to this letter, "Unto the Galatians written from Rome," is erroneous. (Gal. 2, 11 f., compared with Acts 15; Gal. 4, 13, comp. with Acts 16, 6; 18, 23; 19, 1 ff.) Paul seems to have written this letter with his "own hand," not by an amanuensis, as usually. Chap. 6, 11. He wrote it in holy zeal, "in great agitation, but free from passionate anger, speaking to the Galatians as a father to his children." Chap. 1, 8. 9; 5, 12; 4, 19.

This letter is *a doctrinal epistle*. "Together with the Epistle to the Romans, Galatians ranks first in doctrinal importance, because Paul both here and there discusses the fundamental doctrine of the Christian faith," the doctrine of justification by faith. He presents this great doctrine from every side, particularly from the side of Christian liberty. "It has done more than any other book of the New Testament for the emancipation of Christians, not only from the yoke of Judaism, but from every other form of externalism that has ever threatened the freedom and spirituality of the Gospel. It was Luther's favorite epistle, to which he was 'wedded,' as he said; and from it he largely drew his inspiration in his conflict with the Church of Rome." Luther's *Commentary on Galatians* is one of his most valuable books.

SUMMARY OF CONTENTS. — *I. Salutation and Introduction.* Chap. 1, 1—5. — *II. Doctrinal Part of the Letter.* Chap. 1, 6—4, 31: Paul expresses surprise that the Galatians have so soon been estranged from him and his Gospel. He defends his apostleship, which had been challenged, by showing that he received his apostleship and his Gospel not from man, but directly from Christ Himself. Chap. 1, 6—2, 14. He forcibly presents the great doctrine of Christianity — justification by faith — and proves that his doctrinal position is correct. Chap. 2, 15—4, 31. A man is not justified, or regarded as righteous and holy, in consequence of doing the works prescribed by the Law of Moses, but only through faith in Jesus Christ; for by the works of the Law shall no flesh be justified. If righteousness is through the Law, then Christ died in vain and for naught. That we gain righteousness, life, and salvation by believing in Christ and not by the works prescribed in the Law of Moses is proved by the experience of the Galatians themselves as well as by the example of Abraham. The Galatian churches had received the Spirit through the Gospel of Christ and by faith in that Gospel, not by the works of the Law, even as Abraham believed God and this was reckoned to him for righteousness. Those who endeavor to obtain the blessing — life and salvation — by the works of the Law will never gain it; they will rather come under the curse; for it is written: "Cursed is every one that continueth not in *all* things which are written in the book of the Law to do them." Christ has redeemed us from the curse of the Law, being made a curse for us when He died on the accursed tree. Through Christ the blessing of Abraham comes on all that believe. The promise of blessing was given over 400 years before the Law was published on Sinai. The giving of the Law was not meant to set aside the Gospel-promise of blessing in Christ, nor was the Law intended to serve as a means whereby life and salvation might be given. "If there had been a law given which could have given life, verily, righteousness should have been by the Law." But the Scripture proves that none keep the Law perfectly, that all are, therefore, sinners and under the curse of the Law. There is, then, but one way left open for obtaining life: faith in God's promise. But if the purpose of the Law was not to give life, what, then, was its purpose? It was to serve as a tutor for the people of God in the Old Testament, during the time prior to Christ's coming into the world. They were treated as minors and had no freedom, but were bound by the Law. The Law was to them a yoke of bondage. This condition was to obtain only for a time. When the fulness of time was come, God sent forth His Son, made of a woman, made under the Law, to redeem them that were under the Law, that we might receive the adoption of sons. Those who believe in God's Son are no more servants, but God's free children. This is illustrated by the story of Hagar and Ishmael, on the one hand, and Rebekah and Isaac, on the other. — III. *Practical Application of This Teaching*. Chap. 5, 1—6, 10: Stand fast, therefore, in the liberty wherewith Christ hath made us free and be not entangled again with the yoke of bondage. If you submit to circumcision with the intention of becoming righteous thereby, Christ will profit you nothing. They are severed from Christ who would be justified by the Law; they are fallen away from grace. You have been called to liberty; only use not your liberty for an occasion to the flesh, but by love serve one another. For all the Law is fulfilled in one word, even in this, "Thou shalt love thy neighbor as thyself." The works of the flesh and the fruits of the Spirit. Deal mildly with a brother who has slipped. Be liberal in your support of the man who teaches you the Word of God. — *IV. Conclusion.* Chap. 6, 11—18.

CHAPTER 40.

St. Paul's Epistle to the Ephesians.

THE CITY OF EPH'-E-SUS. — Ephesus was the capital of the large and important province of proconsular Asia, the western part of Asia Minor. It was a great and busy center of commerce. The historian Strabo calls it the greatest place of trade of all the places of Asia west of the Taurus. Ephesus was celebrated not only for its commerce, but also for the great and magnificent temple erected to the heathen goddess Di-an'-a (Ar'-te-mis), which was renowned as one of the seven wonders of the ancient world. Acts 19, 23 ff. The site of the once great and opulent city is now occupied by some wretched villages.

PAUL'S VISITS TO EPHESUS. — Paul paid his first visit to Ephesus on his journey from Corinth to Jerusalem at the close of his second missionary tour in the year 54. He remained but three months. During this brief stay he entered the Jewish synagog and reasoned with the Jews. And when they asked him to tarry a longer time, he consented not, but, taking his leave of them and saying, "I must by all means keep this feast that cometh in Jerusalem; but I will return again to you, if God will," he sailed from Ephesus. Acts 18, 18—21. Priscilla and Aq'-ui-la, whom he left there, and Apollos, who came soon after, did preparatory work. Paul returned during his third missionary journey and remained for nearly three years (54—57). The Lord abundantly blessed his ceaseless labors, and a large and flourishing church was gathered from among the Jews and especially from among the Gentiles. Acts 19, 10. 20; Eph. 2, 11; 3, 1. Here the student should read without fail St. Luke's account of Paul's

Ruins of Ancient City of Ephesus.

activity in Ephesus in Acts 19, 1—20, 1, also Paul's charge to the elders, or pastors, of Ephesus at Mi-le'-tus before his last visit to Jerusalem. Acts 20, 16—38. After Paul's death, in 67, St. John is said to have made Ephesus his home. One of the messages which Christ gave to John on Patmos for the seven churches in Asia Minor was for the Church at Ephesus. (See Rev. 2, 1—7.)

WHEN AND WHERE EPHESIANS WAS WRITTEN. — It is plain that Paul wrote this epistle while he was a prisoner. Chap. 3, 1; 4, 1; 6, 20. The subscription correctly states that it was "written from Rome unto the Ephesians by Tych´-i-cus." Paul's first Roman imprisonment, during which it was written, began in 61 and ended in 63. The date of this letter is probably A. D. 62.

To Whom Written. — "To the saints which are at Ephesus and to the faithful in Christ Jesus." Chap. 1, 1.

Character of the Epistle. — While the Epistle to the Galatians was obviously written in great agitation, that to the Ephesians has the atmosphere of quiet meditation. The diction and style assume an exaltation such as is hardly found in any other of Paul's letters. "It is one of the richest and most valuable of the epistles, having a singular fulness of matter, depth of doctrine, solemnity of style, and warmth of emotion, which render it precious to the Christian of every land." "It embraces every doctrine of Christianity," but the doctrine of the holy Christian Church, the communion of saints, plainly stands in the foreground. Other doctrines are interwoven into the presentation of this prominent doctrine.

Summary of Contents. — I. Salutation. Chap. 1, 1. 2. — II. Doctrinal Part of the Letter. Chap. 1, 3—4, 16: Paul breaks out into a glorious hymn of praise on behalf of the Ephesians for all the spiritual blessings bestowed on them by God in Christ, the Redeemer, tracing these blessings to their ultimate source, the elective grace of God. Chap. 1, 3—14. Then he thanks God for the faith and love of the Ephesian Christians and earnestly prays that they may learn to realize more and more (1) the glory of their heavenly inheritance, (2) the exceeding greatness of God's power to which they owe their faith, and (3) the great honor and dignity of the Church — it has for its Head the exalted Christ. Chap. 1, 15—23. He reminds his readers of the great love, grace, and kindness of God which they experienced: When they were dead in trespasses and sins and the children of wrath, God quickened them (made them alive), converted them, and saved them. No atom of this was due to themselves; it was all of grace. Chap. 2, 1—10. Next the apostle reminds those of his readers who once were Gentiles, and at that time aliens and

afar off, that they have now, through Christ, been brought nigh
to God's people and made members of the body of Christ. Chap.
2, 11—22. He praises the particular grace of God which was
given him that he should preach among the Gentiles the Gospel
of Christ and thereby help to carry out the eternal purpose of
God to save the Gentiles as well as His chosen people Israel.
Chap. 3, 1—13. Repeated prayer that Christians may be able
more and more to comprehend the ecumenical character and great
dimensions of the Christian Church. Chap. 3, 14—21. —
III. *Practical Part of the Letter.* Chap. 4, 1—6: The apostle exhorts the Church and each individual member to walk worthily of
the calling whereby they were called, endeavoring to keep the
unity of the Spirit in the bond of peace, to serve one another
with the special gift of grace given to each one of them, and thus
to promote the increase of the whole body of Christ, of the whole
Church. He dwells particularly on the chief gifts of the ascended
Lord, that is to say, on the holy ministry, and on its purpose.
Chap. 4, 1—16. He further exhorts his Christian readers to lead
a life different from that which the Gentiles lead, to put away
"the old man" and to put on "the new man," to walk as children
of light, and to subject themselves one to another in the fear of
Christ. Chap. 4, 17—5, 21. He next inculcates domestic duties
on Christian wives, children, and servants, on the one hand, and
on Christian men, fathers, and masters, on the other. Chap.
5, 22—6, 9. Finally he exhorts his Christian readers to put on the
whole armor of God for the Christian warfare against the devil
and his wicked host. Chap. 6, 10—20. — *IV. Conclusion.* Chap.
6, 21—24: The mission of Tychicus. Closing benediction.

CHAPTER 41.

St. Paul's Epistle to the Philippians.

THE CITY OF PHILIPPI. — Phi-lip'-pi was the chief city
of Eastern Macedonia. It was situated near the border of
Thrace, to which it originally belonged, in a very fertile
plain between two mountain ranges. While it belonged to
Thrace, its name was Crenides, or "Fountains," from its
copious springs. On account of the gold-mines in the sur-

rounding district, Philip, king of Macedonia and father of
Alexander the Great, took it from the Thracians in
358 B. C., renaming it Philippi in his honor and strongly
fortifying and garrisoning it.   About 300 years later, in
42 B. C., a famous battle was fought on the plain of
Philippi, in which Octavius (who later became Caesar
Augustus) and Mark Antony gained a decisive victory over
Brutus and Cassius, the murderers of Julius Caesar.
Later, when Octavius had become the Emperor Augustus,
he gave Philippi the rank of a Roman colony and trans-

Ruins at Philippi.

ported Roman citizens to it; the people were governed by
their own magistrates and possessed the rights of Roman
citizens.   As the city offered no attractions as a place of
commerce, only few Jews were to be found here.   They
had no synagog, but worshiped on the bank of the river.
Acts 16, 13.   At present only ruins mark the site of ancient
Philippi.

THE CHURCH OF PHILIPPI. — In the year 52 St. Paul,
accompanied by Silas, Timothy, and Luke, set his foot for
the first time on European soil.   This was in response to
the cry which he had heard in a vision, "Come over into

Macedonia and help us!" The first place at which he preached in Europe was Philippi, on a Sabbath-day, without the gate by a riverside, where the Jews met for prayer; and his first audience consisted of women. The first convert was Lydia, a seller of purple goods. She constrained Paul and his companions to lodge at her house. After many days Paul wrought a miracle of healing on a slave girl who had a spirit of divination and brought her master much gain by soothsaying. This excited the opposition of the master and other mercenary men, who dragged Paul and Silas into the market-place before the rulers and had the magistrates order that both be beaten and thrown into prison. In the night the jailer was converted and baptized and then secured the discharge of the apostles with honor the next morning. (See Acts 16, 9—40.) About six years later (in 58) Paul was able to revisit Philippi. The account of this visit is very brief. Acts 20, 3—6.

The first European church which St. Paul had founded during his first visit was very near and dear to him. In our letter he calls the members "my brethren dearly beloved and longed for, my joy and crown." Chap. 4, 1. They, in turn, showed their warm attachment to him by sending him financial aid in need on several occasions; and theirs was the only church from which he accepted such aid. Chap. 4, 15. 16; 2 Cor. 11, 8. 9. When they heard that Paul was in prison at Rome and unable to earn a living by tent-making, they sent E-paph-ro-di'-tus all the way from Philippi to Rome, a distance of 700 miles, to bring some money which they had collected for him. Chap. 2, 25; 4, 18. This Epaphroditus, who was probably one of the "bishops" (overseers, pastors) of the Philippian church, became the bearer of the epistle on his return.

THE EPISTLE. — This epistle was written by Paul at a time when he was a prisoner, but had hopes of being released ere long. Chap. 1, 7. 13. 16. 25; 2, 23. 24. This fits his first Roman imprisonment, which lasted from A. D. 61 to 63. That he was in Rome at the time of writing appears from the fact that he mentions members of Caesar's household. Chap. 4, 22. Again, the letter must have been written toward the *end* of his two-year imprisonment, in 63, for he speaks as one who expects to be released before long. Epaphroditus, who had been taken sick, was at length able to return to Philippi. Paul takes this opportunity to write this letter to his beloved Philippians. The whole tone of the letter is one of cordial intimacy and devoted attachment. "Joy" is its key-note; the words "joy" and "rejoice" occur no less than 16 times. (See, for example, chap. 3, 1; 4, 4.)

SUMMARY OF CONTENTS. — *I. Salutation and Information Concerning Paul.* St. Paul tells the Philippians that he thanks God for their fellowship in the Gospel, that he cherishes a confident persuasion that God will keep them in the true faith until the end, and that he prays God to increase their love. Chap. 1, 3—11. He then adverts to his own circumstances and informs his readers that his imprisonment has now fallen out rather to the progress of the Gospel and declares his readiness to glorify Christ by life or by death, although he has a strong impression that he will be delivered and be permitted to visit the Philippians once more. Chap. 1, 12—26. — *II. He exhorts them* to steadfastness in their sufferings for Christ's sake, to unity, humility, and unselfishness, according to the example of Christ, to an upright and blameless life. Chap. 1, 27—2, 18. Chap. 2, 5—11 we have the great doctrinal passage of the epistle in which Christ's states of humiliation and exaltation are fully set forth. Paul hopes soon to send to the Philippians his and their trusty friend Timothy with news of his prospects, and in return he hopes to hear of their state before he visits them in person. Meanwhile he is sending to them Epaphroditus, the messenger of their bounty, who has been of invaluable service to him since his arrival, but whose recent illness and anxiety on their account render it expedient that he should return to Philippi. Chap. 2, 19—30. — *III. He Warns the Christians at Philippi against Judaizing*

Teachers, who speak much of circumcision and other works of the Ceremonial Law as the source of their righteousness, and shows by means of his own example that the only true gain is to know Christ as one's Savior and Lord and in Him to reach righteousness and the resurrection from the dead. Chap. 3, 1—11. He admonishes his readers to follow his example in pressing on toward the goal of perfection and the heavenly prize and cautions them against the example of many nominal Christians, who refuse to take up their cross and follow Christ; for they mind earthly things which please the body. But their end is perdition. Chap. 3, 12—21. — *IV. Final Exhortations.* The holy apostle exhorts his readers once more to rejoice in the Lord, to take everything to the Lord in prayer, and to follow all good things. The precept in chap. 4, 8 is one of the most beautiful in the New Testament. He thanks the Philippians warmly for their gifts of love, which he welcomes not so much on his own account as for the evidence it affords of their devotion to the Gospel. For their kindness to him God will yet reward them with the higher treasures that are hid in Christ Jesus. Doxology. Parting salutations. Benediction. Chap. 4, 9—23.

CHAPTER 42.

St. Paul's Epistle to the Co-los´-sians.

THE CITY OF CO-LOS´-SAE. — Colossae was a city in the province of Phryg´-i-a, in the interior of Asia Minor. It lay on the river Lycus, a tributary of the famous Mae-an´-der, about a hundred miles east of Ephesus and about ten miles east of La-od-i-ce´-a and Hi-er-ap´-o-lis on the Roman road from Ephesus to the Euphrates. The inhabitants of Phrygia were of a mixed character — Phrygians, Greeks, and Jews. About 200 years before Christ Antiochus the Great transported 2,000 Jewish families from Mesopotamia to Lydia and Phrygia. The Colossians were noted for their skill in dyeing wool. Philemon, to whom St. Paul wrote an epistle, and his runaway slave O-nes´-i-mus were natives of Colossae. Ancient writers describe Colossae as "a populous city, prosperous and great"; but in later times it was eclipsed by Laodicea and Hierapolis and finally disappeared from history. Recent excavations near the present town of Chonas have uncovered certain ruins which have practically been identified as those of ancient Colossae. The region is "somber and melancholy," covered with the traces of volcanic action.

THE CHURCH AT COLOSSAE. — Chap. 2, 1 St. Paul says to the Christians at Colossae: "For I would that ye knew what great conflict [concern, anxiety] I have for you and for them at Laodicea, and for as many as have not seen my face in the flesh." From this the conclusion is drawn that the Colossians were among those who had not seen his face. If they had not seen his face, then he had never been in their city; and if he had not been in their city, then he had not directly introduced the Gospel among them and founded their church. We have no account of St. Paul's visiting Colossae or doing any work in it. It is true, he twice traversed Phryg'-i-a, in which Colossae lay. He went through this province during his second missionary journey and again in his third. Acts 16, 6; 18, 23. But if he took the direct route, he did not pass through Colossae; for the direct route lay through the northeastern section of the country, toward the boundary of Galatia.

But if the Colossian church was not planted by St. Paul, how, then, did it come into existence? We have learned that the apostle lived and labored at Ephesus nearly three years. From Ephesus his influence spread far and wide, "almost throughout all [the province of] Asia." St. Luke records "that all they which dwelt in Asia heard the Word of the Lord Jesus, both Jews and Greeks." Acts 19, 10. 26. The word of the truth of the Gospel also came to the Colossians. Col. 1, 6. 23. They learned it from Ep'-a-phras. Chap. 1, 7. This Epaphras was a Colossian. Chap. 4, 12.

He was one of Paul's disciples and assistants and became
the minister of the Colossian church. Chap. 1, 7. He
probably gathered this and the neighboring churches at
Laodicea and Hierapolis. Chap. 4, 13.

OCCASION OF THE EPISTLE. — What prompted St. Paul
to write his letter to the Colossian Christians? Epaphras
had made a journey to Rome during the apostle's first imprisonment there and had reported to him on the internal
state and condition of the Colossian church. The report
was favorable and gave St. Paul joy. Epaphras was able
to tell of their love in the Spirit, of their order, and of
the steadfastness of their faith in Christ. Chap. 1, 8; 2, 5.
But at the same time he had to acquaint Paul with certain
dangers that were threatening the young church. These
dangers arose from certain errorists, or false teachers, who
professed to be Christians, but clung to, and endeavored
to spread, Jewish ideas. Regarding these ideas, we may
gather the following from our epistle: —

The errorists told the Colossians that the Christianity
which they had received was still incomplete and insufficient,
that it had not brought them to a state of perfection and
would not bring them to heaven. They would have to have
a higher wisdom and knowledge than this simple Christianity and would have to adopt stricter rules of life than
those furnished by the preaching of the apostles. They —
the false teachers — could give them this higher wisdom
and knowledge and teach them such rules. They said:
"Be circumcised and observe the rest of the rules of the
Ceremonial Law which God gave through Moses. Abstain
from such meat and drink as was forbidden by Moses;
touch not; taste not; handle not. Keep the holy-day, the
day of the new moon, and the Sabbath-days." Chap. 2,
11. 16. 21. They called their teaching "philosophy," and it
had indeed a show of wisdom. Chap. 2, 8. 23. They used

enticing words, plausible discourse. Chap. 2, 4. They pretended to be humble. Chap. 2, 18. 23. They practised strict self-denial and subjected their body to hard treatment. Chap. 2, 23. They worshiped angels, intruding into the things which they had not seen. Chap. 2, 18. So the Colossian heresy was serious and perilous. The Colossians were in danger of being beguiled of their reward, robbed of their prize. To meet and overmaster this heresy, St. Paul wrote his Epistle to the Colossians. In this epistle the doctrine of the dignity and divinity of Christ and of the sufficiency of His work is most prominent.

WHERE AND WHEN WRITTEN. — The Epistle to the Colossians was written at the same place and time as the Epistle to the Ephesians, that is to say, toward the end of Paul's first imprisonment in Rome, probably toward the end of the year 62. (Chap. 4, 3. 10. 18.) Both epistles are closely related in thought and language, which indicates that Paul composed both under similar conditions and in a similar frame of mind. Again, Paul sent both letters by the hand of one and the same bearer, Tych´-i-cus, "that beloved brother and faithful minister and fellow-servant in the Lord." Col. 4, 7. 8; Eph. 6, 21. 22.

SUMMARY OF CONTENTS. — I. Address and Opening Salutation. Chap. 1, 1. 2. — II. Doctrinal and Polemical Part of the Letter. Chap. 1, 3—2, 23: Paul thanks God for the faith, love, and hope of the Colossians, of which he heard through Epaphras (chap. 1, 3—8), and prays for their progress in a fuller knowledge of God and His will and in gratitude for their deliverance from the power of the devil and for their redemption from sins. Chap. 1, 9—14. Then follows the fundamental doctrinal statement of the epistle concerning the person and office of Christ, the Redeemer; it sets forth who He is and what place He fills in the universe and in the Church. Chap. 1, 15—20. Next Paul reminds his readers of what Christ did for them when they were Gentiles (chap. 1, 21—23), and then tells them of his apostolic work among the Gentiles. Chap. 1, 24—29. — III. Warning *against False Philosophy.* Chap. 2. In chap. 2 begins the polemic part, in which Paul opposes the Colossian teachers of error and attacks their heresy. In this he is prompted by his intense interest in, and deep concern for, the Colossian and neighboring churches; it is his desire to preserve them from being beguiled, or deluded, with enticing words (with persuasiveness of speech, R. V., chap. 2, 1—7). He cautions them to beware lest any man will make them his spoil through his "philosophy," which is nothing but vain deceit = empty deception. He calls the specific teachings of the deceivers "the tradition of men" (they are no part of God's Word), and their teachings regarding circumcision, distinction of meat and drink, holidays, etc., he calls "the rudiments of the world" = elementary teachings, which have reference only to things of this world and are far from being "philosophy." The Christians have no need of observing the old Jewish Ceremonial Law, for they are complete in Christ and in Him have all that is required for their present and final salvation. The insistence of these errorists on the observance of the Ceremonial Law is obsolete, out of date; for the Ceremonial Law is a thing of the past, Christ having abolished it. The commandments and doctrines which they teach are the commandments and doctrines of *men,* not of God, and their worshiping of angels and neglecting of the body is merely "will-worship," the invention of their own mind and will. Chap. 2, 8—23. — *IV. Practical Parts of the Letter.* Chap. 3, 1—4, 6: In opposition to the false worship of those false teachers, St. Paul now points out what are truly good works in God's sight. He urges his readers to seek supremely those things which are in heaven (chap. 3, 1—4), to put off their old vices, impurity, malice, falsehood, etc., and to put on the new Christian virtues, especially gentleness, forgiveness, love, and to this end to let the Word of Christ dwell in them richly in all wisdom. Chap. 3, 5—17. He enforces particularly domestic duties, telling Christian wives and husbands, children and parents, servants and masters, how to conduct themselves. Chap. 3, 18—4, 1. He exhorts his Christian readers to continue steadfast in prayer and intercession (chap. 4, 2—4), to walk in wisdom toward them that are without the Church, and to seize every opportunity to win them for Christ. Chap. 4, 5. 6. — *V. Conclusion.* Chap. 4, 7—18: The mission of Tych'-i-cus. Divers salutations. Autograph salutation and benediction.

CHAPTER 43.

The Epistles of Paul to the Thessalonians.

FIRST EPISTLE.

THE CITY OF THESSALONICA. — Thes-sa-lo-ni′-ca is a city and seaport of Macedonia at the northeast end of the Thermaic Gulf, now called the Gulf of Sa-lo-ni′-ki. It is one of the oldest cities of Europe and has a fine harbor. Its ancient name was Therma = Hot Springs, there being hot springs in the neighborhood. About 315 B. C. Cassander, brother-in-law of Alexander the Great, named it Thessalonica in honor of his wife; this name has become Saloniki. When Macedonia became a Roman province in 148 B. C., Thessalonica was made its capital. In the time of St. Paul it was a populous and flourishing town. It was inhabited chiefly by Greeks, with a mixture of Romans. The Jews also were attracted to it in great numbers on account of its commerce, and they had a synagog here. Acts 17, 1. The Turks captured Thessalonica A. D. 1430. Its present population is about 90,000. "It rises from the shore along the face of a hill. The city is enclosed by white walls, partly ancient and partly medieval, about five miles in circuit, and is surrounded by cypresses and other evergreens. As seen from the sea, it presents a bright and beautiful appearance; but its internal aspect is miserable in the extreme. The principal buildings are mosques, most of which were previously Christian churches." *Mosmedan church.*

THE CHURCH. — In Acts 17, 1—10 we have an account of the origin of the church at Thessalonica. The student should read this account. In the course of his second great missionary journey (A. D. 52) Paul, together with Silas and Timothy, came from Philippi to Thessalonica. 1 Thess. 2, 2. He preached in the synagog of the Jews for three successive Sabbath-days with considerable success. Some of the Jews were converted to Christ; but especially did a great number of such Greeks as had adopted the Jewish religion accept the Gospel, and of the chief women not a few. And thus the church of the Thessalonians was formed.

This church was very dear to Paul. Chap. 2, 8. But before long the Jews who believed not persecuted him and his companions. Being driven from Thessalonica, he went to Be-re´-a, which was about one hundred miles south, and preached there until the Jews of Thessalonica came down and stirred up the people against him. Some of the Berean believers brought him to Athens, where he waited for Silas and Timothy to join him. Acts 17, 10—15. He greatly longed to see the Thessalonians and twice planned to visit them in their persecution and affliction; but Satan hindered him each time. Chap. 2, 17. 18. So he sent Timothy to strengthen them and to comfort them concerning their faith. Chap. 3, 1—5.

OCCASION OF THE FIRST EPISTLE. — When Timothy returned to Paul, who had meanwhile gone to Corinth, he brought him a favorable report. The members of the young Thessalonian church had remained steadfast in the faith in the midst of persecution and had become shining examples of faith and love. These glad tidings led Paul to write the First Epistle. This was about the close of the year 52 or early in 53. As far as we know, this is the first letter of St. Paul and the earliest of the books of the New Testament. In some editions of the Bible there is a note at the end of the epistle which states that it was written from Athens. This note is erroneous. The epistle was written at Corinth. (See Acts 18, 1. 5.)

SUMMARY OF CONTENTS. — I. Personal Address and Salutation. Chap. 1, 1. 2. — II. Historical Part of the Letter. Chap. 1, 3—3, 13: Paul assures the Thessalonians that he is constantly mindful of them in thanksgiving and prayer and tells them how well he is persuaded of the truth and sincerity of their faith and conversion to God. Chap. 1. He reminds them in what manner he brought and preached the Gospel to them and how they accepted it; he had sought neither their money nor praise from them. He explains why he has been absent from them for a short season and why he is so greatly desirous to see them. Chap. 2. He testifies his great love to them partly by sending Timothy to them to strengthen and to comfort them, partly by rejoicing in their well-doing and partly by praying God to grant him soon a safe journey to them. Chap. 3. — III. *The Model Walk, the Believer's Hope, and the Day of the Lord.* Chaps. 4 and 5: He exhorts the Thessalonians to make progress continually in all manner of godliness, to abstain from the conventional sins and vices of the heathen (personal impurity and fraud), to increase more and more in brotherly love, to be diligent in the performance of their earthly duties, and to earn their own living. He further exhorts them to sorrow moderately for their Christian dead. To this exhortation he adds a brief description of the resurrection and of the second coming of Christ. Then follows a series of detached exhortations and precepts to cultivate various Christian virtues. — IV. *Salutation and Benediction.* Chap. 5, 26—28.

SECOND EPISTLE.

In his First Epistle (chap. 4, 15 ff.) St. Paul had already taken cognizance of the question agitating the mind of the Thessalonians concerning the second advent of Christ. Many misapprehended his meaning, however. In the midst of the increasing persecutions to which they were exposed their hope of the advent which was to deliver them from every evil grew into the mistaken idea that the Day of the Lord (Judgment Day) was just at hand, that Christ's coming would take place immediately. Chap. 2, 1. 2. "Mistaken and enthusiastic men had also nourished this deception by appealing to visions and to the traditionary sayings of the apostle; and it would even appear that an epistle had been forged in the name of the apostle. The church was thrown into a state of wild excitement; an impatient and fanatical longing for the instant when Christ would come seized upon one portion. . . . The consequence was that many of the Thessalonians were neglecting their secular business and living idle and useless lives, conceiving that there was no use of working in a world which was so soon to be destroyed." Chap. 2, 2. 3; 3, 11. 12. Hearing of this state of affairs in the Thessalonian church, the apostle dispatched his Second Epistle. He wrote it from Corinth (not "from Athens"), a few months after the First Epistle, probably early in A. D. 53. His main object was to correct the erroneous notions concerning the imminent advent of Christ.

SUMMARY OF CONTENTS. — *I. Salutation.* Chap. 1, 1. 2. — *II. Doctrinal Part of the Letter.* Chap. 1, 3—2, 12: St. Paul renders thanks to God for the Thessalonians' growth in faith and for their steadfastness amid all the persecutions and tribulations which they endured. He comforts and encourages them under their sufferings by assuring them that Christ will infallibly return with the angels of His power to punish their persecutors and to give rest to those who are troubled. He prays God to keep them in the true faith to the glory of our Lord Jesus Christ. Chap. 1. Touching the second coming of Christ, he beseeches them not to suffer themselves to be led astray as if the Day of the Lord would *immediately appear;* he reminds them of his former instruction in this matter, *viz.,* that this Day will not come except the great apostasy come first and the man of sin be revealed, the son of perdition. He describes this man of sin as the great Antichrist. The apostle then thanks God because He has chosen the Thessalonians to salvation; he exhorts them to stand fast in the doctrine which he has taught them and prays for their consolation. Chap. 2. — *III. Practical Part of the Letter.* Paul craves their prayers that he may preach the Gospel unhindered; he expresses his confidence in the Lord that they will follow his teaching and prays that the Lord direct their hearts into the love of God and into the patient waiting for Christ. He then proceeds to admonish them on account of the disorderly conduct which many of them exhibited in that they desisted from their secular work and ate other men's bread. Chap. 3, 1—15. — *IV. Conclusion.* Chap. 3, 16—18: Autographic attestation and apostolic benediction.

CHAPTER 44.

The Two Epistles of Paul to Timothy.

THE PASTORAL EPISTLES. — First and Second Timothy and Titus are called the Pastoral Epistles. Timothy and Titus, to whom they were addressed, were pastors, and the contents of all three letters relate chiefly to the pastoral care of churches. They were written subsequently to Paul's release from his first Roman imprisonment (A. D. 63; see chap. 36). His main purpose in writing these letters was to give Timothy and Titus directions regarding their conduct in their pastoral office.

THE FIRST EPISTLE OF PAUL TO TIMOTHY.

TIMOTHY. — Timothy's father was a Greek and a Gentile, but his mother Eu´-nice and his grandmother Lo´-is were devout Christian converts from Judaism, who instructed him in the Scriptures of the Old Testament from his earliest childhood. Acts 16, 1—3; 2 Tim. 1, 5; 3, 15. He lived at Lystra, in Lyc-a-o´-ni-a, Asia Minor, and seems to have been converted to Christ during Paul's first visit to Lystra and Der´-be, about the year 48. On the apostle's second visit to that quarter, about three years afterward, Timothy was a disciple so highly spoken of by the brethren at Lystra and I-co´-ni-um as to be deemed worthy of being associated with Paul as a laborer in the Gospel. Acts 14, 9—21; 16, 1—3. Having been converted by Paul, he is called by him "my own son in the faith" and "my dearly beloved son." 1 Tim. 1, 2. 18; 2 Tim. 1, 2. Before taking Timothy with him on his missionary tour, however, Paul first circumcised him to disarm the prejudice of the Jews. Acts 16, 3. Thereafter we find him constantly associated with the apostle as his companion or as his delegate to churches at a distance. He was his attendant during his first imprisonment at Rome. Phil. 1, 1; 2, 19—23; Col.

1, 1; Philemon 1. After his release from this imprisonment, Paul took him with him on another missionary tour,
but left him for a time in charge of the church at Ephesus.
1 Tim. 1, 3; 3, 14. It was while in this trying and respon-
sible position that Timothy received the two letters called
by his name. He was a much younger man than Paul.
1 Tim. 4, 12; 1 Cor. 16, 10. 11; Phil. 2, 22. But his work
was so excellent that Paul finds reason for the highest
praise. 1 Cor. 16, 10.

PURPOSE OF THE FIRST EPISTLE.—Having left Timothy
in temporary charge of the Ephesian church, Paul desired
to give him directions for teaching the Christians in
Ephesus and warning them against errors. Chap. 1, 3; etc.

WHEN WRITTEN. — Paul wrote First Timothy between
the year 64 (the year after his release from the first imprisonment at Rome) and 67, shortly before his death,
probably in 65.

SUMMARY OF CONTENTS. — I. *Apostolic Address and Greeting.* Chap. 1, 1. 2. — II. *Timothy's Care for the Church as a
Whole.* Chap. 1, 3—4: Timothy is put in mind of the former
charge given him by Paul at his going to Mac-e-do'-ni-a to com-
mand certain men not to preach Judaic fancies. Chap. 1, 3—7.
The right use and end of the Law. Chap. 1, 8—11. Paul's
thanksgiving for the grace of God given to him. Chap. 1, 12—17.
Timothy is charged to war a good warfare and to beware of
apostasy. Chap. 1, 18—20. Paul exhorts to pray for all men and
for those in authority on the ground of Christ's mediatorial death.
How Christian women should be attired; they are not permitted
to preach or to usurp authority over the men; their calling.
Chap. 2. The ideal bishop, or pastor; the ideal deacon. Paul
intends to visit Timothy. Purpose of this epistle. An ascription
of praise. Chap. 3. Paul mentions certain errors of doctrine which
shall arise in the latter times and shows how to combat them.
To the end that Timothy might not fail in doing his duty as
pastor, Paul furnishes him with divers pastoral directions. Chap. 4.
— III. *The Work of a "Good Minister of Jesus Christ."* Chaps.
5 and 6: Rules to be observed in reproving old and young in

the Church. How pastor and people are to treat widows. Support of the ministry. Discipline of offenders. The minister must be impartial. A precept for Timothy's health, etc. Chap. 5. Relation of masters and servants. Paul characterizes Judaic teachers. Godliness is great gain, and love of money is the root of all evil. What Timothy is to flee and what to follow. Whereof to admonish the rich. Final admonitions. Apostolic benediction. Chap. 6.

THE SECOND EPISTLE TO TIMOTHY.

WHEN WRITTEN. — From chap. 1, 8. 16. 17 and 2, 9 it is evident that this epistle was written by Paul while he was a prisoner at Rome. Some suppose this to have been his first Roman imprisonment, the imprisonment recorded by St. Luke Acts 28, 16—31. However, there are a number of circumstances which make this supposition appear improbable. 1. During his first Roman imprisonment Paul enjoyed comparative freedom, being suffered to dwell by himself with a soldier who kept him, to receive visitors in his lodging, his own hired house, and to preach without let or hindrance. During the imprisonment in which he wrote Second Timothy, his condition was entirely different: he suffered trouble as an evil-doer, even unto bonds. Chap. 2, 9. 2. The apostle confidently expected that he would be released from his first imprisonment. Phil. 2, 24; Philemon 22. He has no such expectation, however, with regard to the imprisonment at Rome in which he wrote this epistle to Timothy; he anticipates a fatal ending: "I am now ready to be offered, and the time of my departure is at hand. I have fought a good fight; I have finished my course; I have kept the faith." Chap. 4, 6. 7. 3. Timothy, Demas, and Mark were with Paul during his first imprisonment at Rome (Phil. 1, 1; Col. 1, 1; Philemon 1; Col. 4, 10. 14) ; but they were not with him during the imprisonment in which he wrote Second Timothy. Chap. 1, 2; 4, 10. 11. These and other circumstances are strong

evidence against the belief that this epistle was written by
Paul during his first imprisonment at Rome. — Many editions of the Bible append the note: "The Second Epistle
unto Timothy . . . was written from Rome when Paul was
brought before Nero the second time." This agrees with
a tradition current in the early days of the Church. It was
probably written in the year 66 or 67. It is the last message
the great apostle penned, for not long after he suffered
martyrdom.

ITS CHARACTER. — "In this last epistle, Paul, as it
were, takes leave from all his labors on earth, bequeathing
to Timothy, his faithful helper, this testamentary instruction concerning the work of the ministry. This letter is
much more personal in character than the first one; for
this reason Paul here takes less pains than usually to follow a connected line of thought. Nevertheless, the latter
plainly consists of two main sections. In the first, St. Paul
exhorts Timothy to be steadfast in affliction and faithful
in preaching the Gospel; in the second, he foretells coming
departures from the truth and warns against their baneful
influence." "A peculiarity of this as of the other pastoral
epistles is the introduction of short and weighty sayings
with the words, 'Faithful is the saying.' In 2, 11—13 we
have what is probably part of a Christian hymn, expressing
the faith in which the apostle would have Timothy meet
his trials."

SUMMARY OF CONTENTS. — *I. Address and Greeting.* Chap.
1, 1. 2. — *II. Exhortation to Faithfulness and Perseverance.* Chap.
1, 3—2, 14: Paul's love to Timothy and the unfeigned faith which
was in Timothy himself, his mother, and his grandmother. Paul
exhorts him to stir up the gift of God which was in him, to be
steadfast and patient in persecution, and to persist in the form
and truth of that doctrine which he had learned of him. He
deplores the fact that certain men had all left him and highly
commends On-e-siph'-o-rus, who was faithful amid desertions.

Chap. 1. He exhorts Timothy to constancy and perseverance in his pastoral office as well as in his faith and conduct. — *III. The Right Discharge of the Ministerial Office in the Congregation with Respect to Various Circumstances.* Chap. 2, 15—4, 8: Timothy is told to divide the Word of God aright and to shun profane and vain babblings. Of vessels to honor and of vessels to dishonor. Paul teaches him whereof to beware and what to follow after and in what manner the minister of God ought to behave himself. He foretells that in the last days grievous times shall come because of false teachers and false brethren, whom he describes. Then he propounds to him his own example, calls on him to continue in the things which he had learned, and commends the Holy Scriptures. He solemnly charges him to his duty as pastor with all care and diligence and certifies him of the nearness of his death. — *IV. Personal Matters. Greetings. Benediction.* Chap. 4, 9—22.

CHAPTER 45.

Paul's Epistles to Titus and Phi-le´-mon.

THE EPISTLE TO TITUS.

TITUS. — Less is known of Titus than of Timothy. In the Book of Acts his name is never mentioned. Titus was a Greek, *i. e.*, Gentile, by birth. Gal. 2, 3. Paul tells the Galatians that he took Titus with him when he and Barnabas were sent from Antioch to Jerusalem to attend the apostolic convention (A. D. 51). At Jerusalem some false brethren insisted that Titus should be circumcised as commanded in the Law of Moses. In the case of Timothy Paul had ordered his circumcision out of tender regard for weak Jewish Christians. But in this case he refused to yield. Why? "Because of the false brethren unawares brought in privily to spy out our liberty which we have in Christ Jesus, that they might bring us into bondage; to whom we gave place by subjection, no, not for an hour, that the truth of the Gospel might continue with you."

Gal. 2, 1—5. Soon thereafter Paul set out on his second missionary journey, Titus being a "partner and fellow-helper." 2 Cor. 8, 23. Titus served in this capacity during the remaining years of Paul's life. Paul calls him his "own [true] son after the common faith" (Titus 1, 4), not only because he had been converted under his preaching, but also because he resembled the apostle so much in his moral make-up. Paul twice sent him as a confidential messenger to the church at Corinth. He dispatched him to Corinth to see for him what impression his first letter to the Corinthians had made. That was a very delicate mission; for the strife and confusion in the Corinthian church was threatening to destroy the apostle's influence. Titus discharged his duty so successfully that Paul made him the bearer of his Second Epistle to the Corinthians, at the same time instructing him to manage the Corinthian collection for the relief of the poor brethren in Judea. 2 Cor. 8, 6. 16—18. Having been liberated from his first imprisonment at Rome in the year 63, Paul also visited the island of Crete. When he departed, he selected Titus for the important and trying position of continuing and completing the work which he had to leave unfinished. Titus 1, 5. The task was difficult because of the natural character of the people and because of the many teachers of error. Chap. 1, 10—12. Before winter set in, Paul sent one of his other assistants to Crete to relieve Titus and asked Titus to give diligence to come to him to Nicopolis, a city of Epirus, where he had determined to winter. Chap. 3, 12. Nothing more concerning Titus is certainly known. According to ancient tradition he labored for many years in Crete and suffered martyrdom there at the age of 94.

WHERE AND WHEN THE EPISTLE TO TITUS WAS WRITTEN. — There is a striking resemblance between this epistle and the First Epistle to Timothy. This resemblance justifies the conclusion that both were written at about the same time, say about A. D. 65. The place of writing probably was Ephesus or some other place on Paul's way to Ni-cop'-o-lis.

OCCASION OF THE EPISTLE. — Paul had left Titus in Crete as his representative to complete the work of appointing elders, i. e., pastors, in every city. For that difficult work this letter was to give him directions.

MEMORABLE SAYINGS. — "The Epistle contains a number of memorable sayings, including several of the most comprehensive statements of Christian truth to be found in the New Testament. Chap. 2, 11—14; 3, 4—7. In 2, 11—14 we have an excellent illustration of that 'doctrine which is according to godliness,' that sober-minded union of faith and practise, which is the ripest fruit of Christianity and which forms the chief burden of this most salutary letter." Memorize these memorable sayings.

SUMMARY OF CONTENTS. — I. Address and Apostolic Greeting. Chap. 1, 1—4. — II. Picture of a True Pastor. Chap. 1, 5—16. — III. Pastoral Instruction and Advice. Chap. 2, 1—3, 11. IV. Paul Wishes to Meet Titus and Greets Him. Chap. 3, 11—15.

THE EPISTLE TO PHILEMON.

PHILEMON AND ONESIMUS. — Phi-le'-mon was a prominent member of the Christian church at Colossae, in Phrygia, Asia Minor. That Colossae was the residence of Philemon may be inferred from the following facts: 1. Archip'-pus, who was one of the recipients of this epistle (v. 2), is spoken of as a minister in the Colossian congregation. Col. 4, 17. 2. O-nes'-i-mus (Philemon's slave) is expressly called one of the Colossians. Col. 4, 9. — Ap'-phi-a (v. 2) seems to have been the wife of Philemon, and Archippus, the minister, probably was their son. We gather from this letter that Philemon had been converted to Christianity through the instrumentality of Paul (v. 19) and had since then earned a reputation for faith and love (vv. 5 and 7). In his house the Christians at Colossae gathered for divine worship. V. 2. That was the custom in the early days when the Christians had no churches of their own — they met for worship in private homes. Onesimus (the Greek name means Profitable, v. 11) was Philemon's "servant," that is to say, bond-servant, or slave. But he had not lived up to his good name, for he had run away from his master and gone to the great city of Rome (vv. 11. 15. 16), perhaps with the aid of money stolen from his master (v. 18). At Rome he was providentially brought under the influence of Paul and converted by him. V. 10. He was very profitable to the aged apostle, who was still a prisoner, ministering to him in the bonds of the Gospel. Vv. 11. 13. By his grateful and devoted services he greatly endeared himself to Paul. The latter calls him his own heart, a brother beloved, a faithful and beloved brother. Vv. 12. 16; Col. 4, 9. As he was Philemon's lawful slave, Paul could not think of retaining him permanently in his service. He therefore took the opportunity afforded by the mission of Tych'-i-cus to Colossae (Col. 4, 7) to send him back to his master. V. 12. — "Thus the apostle establishes the principle that the Gospel does not invalidate human ordinances that are not in themselves against the Moral Law. On the other hand, he reminds Philemon that he must now recognize his slave Onesimus as a brother in Christ."

WHEN AND WHERE WRITTEN. — Paul was still a prisoner in Rome when writing this letter (v. 1); but his imprisonment was drawing to a close (v. 22). He was set free from this first imprisonment in 63. Accordingly, this epistle was penned by him (v. 19) in 62 or 63.

PURPOSE OF THE EPISTLE. — The Roman law permitted severe and cruel punishment to be inflicted on runaway

slaves, even to the extent of death. Paul pleads with
Philemon to pardon his Christian slave Onesimus and to
treat him as a brother beloved. "The whole tone and
structure of the letter was well fitted to bring out the better
nature of Philemon." The letter "exhibits an exquisite
tenderness and delicacy of feeling, with all that tact and
subtlety of address by which Paul was wont to find his
way into the innermost hearts of men." Luther calls it
"a masterfully beautiful example of Christian love."

SUMMARY OF CONTENTS. — *I. Address and Salutation.*
Vv. 1—3. — *II. Sincere Appreciation of Philemon's Christian
Worth and Work.* Vv. 4—7. — *III. Statement of the Object of
the Letter.* Vv. 8—20. — *IV. Conclusion.* Paul expects a speedy
release from imprisonment and asks that a lodging be prepared
for him at Colossae. Salutation and benediction.

CHAPTER 46.

The Epistle to the Hebrews.

WHO WROTE IT. — Luther, who suggested Apollos as
the likeliest author of this epistle, says: "It is unknown who
wrote it and will probably also remain unknown for
a while." The epistle itself is anonymous; the writer never
mentions his own name. Various authors have been suggested: Luke, Barnabas, Timothy, Paul, and others. In
our English Bible this book immediately follows the epistles
of Paul and bears the title: "The Epistle of Paul the
Apostle to the Hebrews." The following are some of the
arguments advanced in favor of the Pauline authorship:
1. The writer was a prisoner. Chap. 10, 34. 2. He refers
to Timothy as a special friend. Chap. 13, 23. 3. He closes
his letter with salutations and benedictions in the Pauline
style. 4. The contents of the letter are Pauline. Compare
chap. 10, 30 with Rom. 12, 19; chap. 10, 38 with Rom. 1, 17

and Gal. 3, 11; chap. 12, 14 with Rom. 12, 18; chap. 2, 8 with 1 Cor. 15, 27; 2, 10 with Rom. 11, 36; 2, 14 with 2 Tim. 1, 10 and 1 Cor. 15, 26; 5, 12—14 with 1 Cor. 3, 2; 6, 10 with 1 Thess. 1, 3. Speaking of the probable origin of Hebrews, Luther says: "Be that as it may, it is a wonderfully fine epistle, which masterfully and thoroughly speaks from Scripture of the priesthood of Christ and also beautifully and abundantly explains the Old Testament."

To Whom Written. — "To the Hebrews," that is, to Christians of the Jewish race. The whole tenor of the epistle implies that it was written for Jewish Christians. (See also chap. 1, 1: "the fathers" = the ancestors of the Jews; chap. 2, 11: "brethren"; chap. 2, 16: "He took on Him the seed of Abraham.") From chap. 9, 7—15 it may be inferred that the letter was originally intended for Jewish Christians in Palestine, because here the Levitical service in the Temple is spoken of as going on before the eyes of the readers. "Moreover, it was in Palestine that the temptations to relapse into Judaism, against which the writer is so anxious to guard his readers, were most formidable. The sacerdotal splendor of the ancient Sanctuary threw into the shade the simple forms of Christian worship; and the flames of patriotic zeal burned more fiercely in the Holy Land than among the Jews of the Dispersion."

Purpose. — The purpose of the writer of the epistle is apparently to encourage and admonish the Jewish Christians to persevere in the profession of their faith. They were in great danger of falling away from Christianity and relapsing into Judaism. Chap. 6, 4—6. One of the sources of danger has been referred to in the preceding paragraph. Another peril lurked in this, that they were being persecuted by their countrymen and had suffered the spoiling of their goods on account of their belief in Christ. Perhaps some had already gone back to Judaism, while others were ready to return. Chap. 10, 25. To prevent further apostasy, the apostle wrote this letter. "Its one idea is to restrain Hebrew Christians from abandoning their new faith." To accomplish this purpose, the apostle points out that Christianity is in every way superior to Judaism with all its pomp and ceremony. Thirteen times we find the word "better" in this letter: Jesus better than the angels (1, 4); a better hope (7, 19); a better covenant, better promises (7, 22; 8, 6); better sacrifices (9, 23); a better substance (10, 34); a better country (11, 16); better things (11, 40; 12, 24); etc. The idea of the superiority of Christ and Christianity over the religion of the Jews pervades the entire epistle.

WHEN AND WHERE WRITTEN. — It must have been written before the destruction of Jerusalem and the Temple by Titus in the year 70. This is inferred from the absence of any allusion to the overthrow of the Temple. The Sanctuary is spoken of again and again; but there is not a word about its having been destroyed. Had the Temple been overthrown when this epistle was written, the apostle would certainly have alluded to this important event; it would have furnished one of the strongest links in the chain of argument to prove the temporary nature of the Jewish worship. There is here not only an absence of any allusion to the destruction of the Temple, but the writer repeatedly refers to the Temple as being still in existence and the sacrifices as being offered. Chap. 8, 4; 9, 6. 7; 10, 1; etc. While the year 70 is the limit in one direction, the year 61 is the limit in the other; for Paul sends greetings from Italy (chap. 13, 24), but he did not come to Italy before 61 (Acts 28, 13 ff.). The epistle was probably penned in 66. The reference to Italy points to Rome as the place of writing.

CHAPTER ELEVEN. — This is the greatest chapter on faith in the entire Bible. Read it carefully.

SUMMARY OF CONTENTS. — *I. Christ, the Eternal Son of God, Our High Priest.* Chap. 1, 1—4, 13: Christ is superior to the angels, for He is the true and eternal Son of God and sits at the right hand of the Majesty on high, while the angels are but ministering (serving) spirits. Chap. 1. Therefore we ought to give the more earnest heed to His doctrine. Jesus was made a little lower than the angels when He became true man and our brother in order that He might suffer death for every man and thus deliver us from sin, death, and the devil. Chap. 2. Christ has been counted worthy of more glory than Moses, the great leader of the Jews; for Moses was merely a faithful *servant* in God's house, but Christ is the Son of God and thus Master over God's house (the Church); if we, therefore, do not believe in Him to the end, we shall be more worthy of punishment than hard-hearted, backsliding Israel under Moses in the wilderness. Let us labor therefore to enter into that rest, lest any man fall after the same example of unbelief. Chap. 3, 1—4, 13. — *II. The Priestly Office of Christ Greater than That of Aaron.* Chaps. 4, 14—7, 28: We have a great High Priest, who has passed into the temple of heaven, Jesus, the Son of God; let us therefore hold fast our profession. The nature of the priestly office and work in general. Our Savior is a divinely appointed High Priest and possesses all the qualifications of a true high priest. The apostle reproves the Hebrews for their dulness of hearing, which kept them from becoming capable of studying the more advanced truths of the Christian religion. He exhorts them not to fall back from the Christian faith, but to be steadfast, diligent, and patient, to wait upon God, because He is most sure in His promises. Jesus is a High Priest after the order of Mel-chiz'-e-dek and so far more excellent than the priests of Aaron's order. Their priesthood was changeable, His is unchangeable, eternal; they were made priests after the law of a carnal commandment, but He after the power of an endless life; those priests were made without an oath, but He with an oath by Him that said unto Him, "The Lord sware and will not repent: Thou art a Priest forever after the order of Melchizedek." — *III. Christ Far Excels the Jewish Priests also with Regard to His Sacrifice.* Chaps. 8, 1—10, 18: He is the Mediator of a better covenant, or testament, than was the temporal covenant made with the Jews at Mount Sinai; for the new covenant of the Gospel is eternal and has been established on better promises. Description of the Jewish rites and sacrifices. They were far inferior to the dignity and perfection of the blood and sacrifice of Christ. They could not in themselves take away sin and had to be repeated; but He has by His one offering, the offering of Himself, perfected forever them that are sanctified, obtaining eternal redemption by the sacrifice of Himself. — *IV. Having such a High Priest, let us hold fast the profession of our faith without wavering and in good behavior.* Chaps. 10, 19—13, 17: The consequences of apostasy are terrible. Patiently continue to bear your afflictions; the Helper will soon come. To draw back means perdition. Faith defined. A great cloud of witnesses: examples of faith found in the Old Testament setting forth the triumph of faith. Past triumphs should be present incitements. The heavenly Father's chastening is for our profit. Exhortation to godliness and a warning from Esau's case. A striking contrast between the terrors of Sinai and the attractive glories of Mount Zion. Let us obey and serve God, who is a consuming fire. A number of salutary counsels and admonitions as to charity, chastity, contentment, right regard for departed teachers, to beware of divers and strange doctrines (teachings), to bear the reproach of Christ, to praise God, to give alms, to obey pastors. — *V. Conclusion.* Chap. 13, 18—25: The apostle bespeaks their prayer for him and then offers up a beautiful prayer for them. News of Timothy's release. Salutation. Benediction.

CHAPTER 47.

The Epistle of James.

THE CATHOLIC EPISTLES. — The seven epistles which now follow (the Epistle of James, the two epistles of Peter, the three epistles of John, and the Epistle of Jude) are called *catholic* (not Roman Catholic nor Greek Catholic). The word catholic means *general*. Thus we have the title "The General Epistle of James," "The First Epistle General of Peter," etc. They are called catholic, or general,

Only the first Epistle of John is called a General Epistle not the II a III.

in the sense of being circular letters and intended for more than one church, for whole groups of churches.

WHO WROTE THE EPISTLE OF JAMES. — The writer of this letter styles himself "James, a servant of God and of the Lord Jesus Christ." Chap. 1, 1. The term "servant" here is an official designation; it points out that James held the office of an apostle. In the college of the twelve apostles there were two Jameses. 1. James the Elder, the brother of John. He cannot have been the author of this letter, for he suffered martyrdom as early as the year 42 or 44 (Acts 12, 2), while this letter bears marks of having been written at a later date, as will be seen under the heading "When Written." 2. There was another James, James the Less (Greek: the Little = of shorter stature; Mark 15, 40), the son of Al-phae´-us (or Cle´-o-phas, Matt. 10, 3; John 19, 25). He was a "brother" = a relative of Christ; for Alphaeus and Joseph, the foster-father of Jesus, were brothers. James the Less resided at Jerusalem, seems to have been married (1 Cor. 9, 5), and was an acknowledged leader in the mother church at Jerusalem. Acts 12, 17; 21, 18. He seems to have presided over the Apostolic Council held at Jerusalem or at any rate was one of the chief speakers at this important meeting (A. D. 51. — Acts 15, 13—22). Paul calls him, along with Peter and John, a pillar of the Church. Gal. 2, 9. He was surnamed "the Just" even among the Christ-hating Jews because of the religious and righteous life which he led. This fact regarding the integrity of his life throws light on his epistle. He was slain by the Jewish rulers A. D. 69.

TO WHOM WRITTEN. — "To the twelve tribes which are scattered abroad" (Greek: which are in the *Diaspora* = Dispersion, chap. 1, 1). This expression originally denoted all Jews who lived outside the Holy Land among heathen nations. John 7, 35. But here it cannot mean all these

Writing to Christian Jews

that lived
outside of
Palestine

Jews; for James addresses his Jewish readers as "brethren" (chap. 4, 11; 5, 19), "my brethren" (chap. 1, 2; 2, 1; 3, 1. 10; 5, 12), "my beloved brethren" (chap. 1, 16. 19; 2, 5), who hold the faith of our Lord Jesus Christ, the Lord of Glory (chap. 2, 1), bear that worthy name (chap. 2, 7), and wait for the coming of the Lord (chap. 5, 7). This makes it perfectly clear that he is writing to Christian Jews outside Judea and Jerusalem. Of these there were many thousands. Acts 21, 22. The Christian Jews to whom this epistle is addressed were exposed to manifold trials, which called for the exercise of patience. Chap. 1, 2. 4; 5, 7—18. They were also threatened with spiritual dangers, as may be seen from the numerous warnings and admonitions addressed to them.

WHEN WRITTEN. — Some suppose the Epistle of James to be the oldest New Testament writing in existence. But there are several arguments against this supposition and in favor of a late date. 1. When this letter was written, the danger of trusting in a dead orthodoxy had already set in. This points to a later period. Chap. 2, 14—26. 2. James clearly alludes to the Gospel according to St. Matthew in a number of instances. (Compare chap. 1, 22 and Matt. 7, 21; 2, 13 and Matt. 6, 14. 15; 3, 15 and Matt. 7, 16; 4, 10 and Matt. 23, 12; 4, 11 and Matt. 7, 1—5; 4, 12 and Matt. 7, 1; 5, 2 and Matt. 6, 19; 5, 12 and Matt. 5, 34—37, etc.) Now, the Gospel according to St. Matthew was written A. D. 62; therefore James must have written his epistle between the years 62 and 69. As he seems never to have left Jerusalem, he probably wrote it in that city.

CHARACTER OF THE EPISTLE. — This epistle is less doctrinal than any other in the New Testament. "The purpose of the writer is not so much to instruct as to exhort and admonish." "This is the Epistle of Holy Living. Great stress is laid upon works, not apart from faith, but as both the proof and fruit of faith." "The style of the epistle is sententious and forcible, passing swiftly, and sometimes without any apparent logical formation, from one topic to another." Boldly denouncing sin in strong terms and polished, poetical language, St. James reminds us of one of the old Hebrew prophets.

AGREEMENT BETWEEN JAMES AND PAUL. — Chap. 2, 14—26 has led some to believe that James contradicts Paul with regard to the great doctrine of justification by faith. Both make use of the term *to be justified*. The word *justify* here means to declare righteous and free from sins, to absolve one from eternal punishment for the sake of Christ's righteousness, and to adopt one into sonship and heirship of eternal life. Now Paul says: "We conclude that a man is justified by faith, without the deeds of the Law." Rom. 3, 28. But St. James says: "Ye see, then, how that *by works* a man is justified, and not by faith *only*." Chap. 2, 24. Again, Paul writes: "What saith the Scripture? Abraham believed God, and it was counted unto him for righteousness." Rom. 4, 3; Gal. 3, 6. But James says: "Was not Abraham, our father, justified by *works?*" Chap. 2, 21. That this contradiction is not real, but only apparent will be made clear by the following considerations: —

1. Paul is writing against the self-righteous man, who does not want to be justified and saved alone by the grace of God in Christ Jesus, but insists that good works are necessary to salvation. James, however, is writing against the vain, foolish man who trusts for salvation in a mere barren orthodoxy, imagining that a mere intellectual knowledge of religious truths, which is barren of good works, is faith and will save him.

2. Not only St. Paul, but St. James as well, says and believes what Scripture says: "Abraham believed God, and

it was imputed unto him for righteousness." Jas. 2, 23. So both teach that faith, or belief, is the instrument or means whereby Abraham was justified.

3. Both Paul and James teach that true faith is not barren of good works, but fruitful of good works. Paul writes to Titus (chap. 3, 8) : "These things I will that thou affirm constantly, that they which have believed in God might be careful to maintain good works." Again: "Our Savior Jesus Christ gave Himself for us that He might redeem us from all iniquity and purify unto Himself a peculiar people, zealous of good works." Titus 2, 14. Gal. 5, 6 St. Paul defines true faith as "faith which worketh by love." True faith is a working faith. A "faith" which is barren of good works is a mere figment of the mind, which has no reality, no existence. "Faith without works is dead." Jas. 2, 20. 26. Such a dead faith does not profit, cannot save. Jas. 2, 14. When James says "that by works a man is justified, and not by faith only," he evidently means that imaginary faith which is without good works. There is, then, no real contradiction between Paul and James; both agree perfectly. (See Apology of the Augsburg Confession, Art. III, 123—132; Formula of Concord, Thorough Declaration, Art. III, 42—44.)

SUMMARY OF CONTENTS. — *I. Address and Salutation.* Chap. 1, 1. — *II. The Testing of Faith.* Chap. 1: Trials and temptations should be borne with joy; they try our faith and result in patience. The wisdom to use them in the right way is obtained by prayer. Afflictions come alike on rich and poor; but great blessing is the reward of endurance. In our trials and temptations we are not to impute our weakness or sins to God; for temptations to evil do not come from Him, but from our lust; He sends us only good and perfect gifts. His best gift is the Word of Truth, for it regenerates, renews, and saves. Therefore let every man be swift to hear; but not only to hear, but also to do thereafter. Parts of pure religion. — *III. True Faith Is Active in Love.* Chap. 2: It is not agreeable to Christian profession to regard the rich and despise the poor brethren; we should rather be loving and merciful. Do not boast of faith where no deeds are, which is but a dead faith of the head and mouth, the faith of devils, not of Abraham and Rahab. — *IV. A True Faith will Control the Tongue.* Chap. 3: We are not rashly or arrogantly to reprove others, but rather to bridle the tongue, — a little member, but a powerful instrument of much good and great harm. Those who are truly wise are mild and peaceable, without bitter envying and strife. — *V. The Rebuke of Fleshly Lusts.* Chap. 4: Quarrels arise from covetousness and fleshly lusts. To be a lover of the world is to be a spiritual adulterer. The remedy is found in submission to God, resisting the devil, cleansing the heart. The apostle warns against censorious depreciation of others, denounces overweening confidence in our own plans and our ability to carry them out; we should ever be mindful of the uncertainty of this life and commit ourselves and our affairs to God's providence. — *VI. The Rich Warned.* Chap. 5, 1—6: Rebuke of the rich who oppress the poor; dire calamities will surely be visited upon them. — *VII. Exhortations in View of the Coming of the Lord.* Chap. 5, 7—20: We ought to be patient in afflictions, after the example of the prophets and Job; to avoid all needless oaths, to pray in adversity, to sing in prosperity; the sick are to have prayer offered for them by the elders of the church; the erring brother is to be reclaimed.

CHAPTER 48.

The Two Epistles of St. Peter.

Questions will be asked concerning Peter's life.

ST. PETER. — The life and character of the apostle who wrote the two letters which we are about to study is of sufficient importance and interest to call for a special lesson. We shall understand his epistles better if we know his life. St. Peter was the son of a certain Jonas. Matt. 16, 17 Christ calls him Simon Bar-jona = Simon, the son of Jona. John 1, 42. Who this Jonas was is not known. Andrew, one of the twelve apostles, was Peter's brother. Matt. 10, 2. Peter's original name was Simon, which is a contraction of Simeon. Acts 15, 14. This Hebrew name signifies "Hearing." Gen. 29, 33. At his very first meeting with Jesus, the Master conferred on him the new name of Ce'-phas = Stone. John 1, 40—42. The Greek name for Cephas is Petros. The bestowal of this new name was a prophecy and a promise: By the Lord's power and grace Simon was to become a stone, or rock. It is to be observed that after this first interview, Jesus invariably called him Simon, save on the occasion of Peter's great confession: "Thou art the Christ [the Messiah], the Son of the living God." On this occasion the Savior solemnly and with a direct reference to the meaning of the name said to him: "Thou art Peter, and upon this rock will I build My Church." Matt. 16, 16—18. The rock (Greek: *petra*) on which Christ built His Church was not St. Peter (*Petros*), but Christ Himself. "For other foundation can no man lay than that is laid, which is Jesus Christ." 1 Cor. 3, 11.

Simon and his brother Andrew were natives of Beth-sa'-i-da ("Fisherton"), a city in Galilee, on the north-western shore of the Sea of Galilee, a little northeast of Ca-per'-na-um. John 1, 44. Their occupation was that of fishers, and both were devoid of special learning. Acts 4, 13. (See chapter 29.) Peter was evidently married. We read: "When Jesus was come into Peter's house [at Capernaum], He saw *his wife's* mother laid and sick of a fever." Matt. 8, 14. Whether or not he had any children we do not know. The fact that his mother-in-law was still living would lead us to infer that he was not an old man at the time when he became a disciple of Christ. About three years later the Lord said to him, "When thou shalt be old," implying that he was not old at the time. John 21, 18. Twenty-five years later his wife was still living, accompanying him on his mission-journeys. 1 Cor. 9, 5. The Pope of Rome, who claims to be St. Peter's successor as head of the Church, religiously practises celibacy and forbids his priests to marry. If such celibacy were according to the mind of the Master, would He have chosen Peter, who was married, as one of His apostles?

Simon and his brother Andrew, who introduced him to Jesus, were both disciples of John the Baptist before finding the Messiah. After their first meeting with Him, which is described John 1, 35—42, they resumed their work of fishing. One day, while casting a net into the Sea of Galilee, they heard Jesus say to them, "Follow Me [be My disciples], and I will make you fishers of men." And immediately they left their nets and followed Him. Matt. 4, 18—22. With James and John, Simon Peter was one of the three most intimate disciples of our Lord, this trio being privileged to be with Him on special occasions. Matt. 17, 1—8; 26, 37—46; Mark 5, 37 ff.

In the four catalogs of the apostles, Peter is named first. Matt. 10, 2—4; Mark 3, 16—19; Luke 6, 14—16; Acts 1, 13. This points to his being regarded as first among equals. "It is quite unscriptural and smacks of Romanism to call Peter the Prince of the Apostles or the Supreme Shepherd, as some Protestant writers have done. It is true that Peter excelled among his companions by personal gifts and tireless willingness to work, so that they probably conceded to him a certain leadership. But this privilege of Peter, if it existed, was not of divine appointment; on the contrary, Christ forestalled all ambitions of church supremacy by abolishing all differences of rank among His followers, including the apostles." (See Matt. 23, 8, and comp. Luke 22, 24—30.) "As Peter was of an impulsive, decided character, it happened quite without design that he often appeared as spokesman of the disciples when Christ addressed important questions to them all (Matt. 16, 16;

19, 27) ; for this reason also he had to bear the brunt of serious rebukes which were meant for all disciples (Matt. 16, 23; Luke 22, 31) ."

St. Peter is a prominent actor in the story of Christ's sufferings, death, and resurrection. The Lord sent him and John into Jerusalem to prepare the last passover for Him and His disciples. In the evening, after the passover-meal, he at first refused to let the Lord wash his feet. John 13, 6 ff. After the institution of the Lord's Supper, when they went out to the Mount of Olives, he boastfully pledged to adhere to His Master under all circumstances. In the Garden of Gethsemane his impulsiveness prompted him to draw his sword in defense of the Lord and to cut off the servant's ear. John 18, 19. Presuming on his own strength, he followed into the palace of the high priest, where fear for his safety seized him and caused him to deny his Savior thrice in succession. But the mercy of the Lord led him to repentance; he went out and wept bitterly. When the holy women, on Easter morning, reported what they had heard and seen at the sepulcher, Peter was one of the first to arise and run to the sepulcher. Some time during the day the risen Redeemer appeared to him. He was therefore the first of the apostles to behold Jesus after His resurrection. Luke 24, 34; 1 Cor. 15, 5. At His appearance at the Sea of Galilee the Lord solemnly reinstated him in the apostolate, charging him to feed His lambs and His sheep. At the same time He predicted that Peter would die a martyr's death. John 21.

St. Peter is prominent in word and deed through the first 12 chapters of Acts. He suggested the election of an apostle in place of the betrayer. On the Day of Pentecost he preached his first sermon, the very first sermon in the New Testament Church, which resulted in the conversion of about 3,000 souls. Going with John to the Temple at the hour of prayer, he healed the lame beggar at the Gate Beautiful, preached to the people, was imprisoned with John, brought before the Council, boldly confessed Christ, and was released, the Council straitly threatening them that they speak henceforth to no man in Jesus' name. Again, Peter was the spokesman when Ananias and Sapphira were punished for lying to the Holy Ghost. As a result of the miracles wrought by him the people of Jerusalem brought forth the sick into the streets and laid them on beds and couches that at least the shadow of Peter, passing by, might overshadow some of them. Then he and the other apostles were imprisoned; but God sent an angel to deliver them. The next year Peter and John were sent to Samaria to confirm and enlarge the Samaritan Church. On their return they preached the Gospel in many villages of the Samaritans. Passing through all parts, Peter came down also to the saints who dwelt at Lydda, where he healed Ae-ne´-as and at near-by Joppa restored Tab´-i-tha to life. He tarried many days at Joppa with one Simon, a tanner. From Joppa, God sent him up to the City of Caes-a-re´-a to do a new thing, *viz.*, to receive Gentiles into the Christian Church in the person of the Roman centurion Cornelius and his household. About that time King Herod imprisoned Peter in Jerusalem. But when the Christians prayed for him, an angel was sent to deliver him. Six years later, at the Apostolic Council of Jerusalem (A. D. 51), Peter made one of the principal addresses in favor of the emancipation of the Gentile Christians from the bondage of the Jewish Law. On this occasion the missionary outlook was also discussed, James, Peter, and John agreeing with Paul that the latter should go and preach principally to the heathen and they to the Jews. Gal. 2, 9. Not long after this meeting, Peter came to Antioch in Syria, Paul's headquarters. At first he freely mingled with Gentile

Christians; but when certain Jewish Christians came from Jerusalem, he withdrew and separated himself, fearing those Jewish Christians from Jerusalem. For this inconsistent conduct Paul had to take him to task publicly. Gal. 2, 11 ff. Paul mentions him again in the year 57 as being engaged in missionary labors, in company with his wife (1 Cor. 9, 5), perhaps among the dispersed Jews in Asia Minor (1 Pet. 1, 1).

Regarding St. Peter's subsequent life, scarcely any information is furnished by the New Testament. But there is an ancient and quite general tradition that he suffered martyrdom at Rome along with St. Paul during the persecution in the reign of Nero in 67 or 68. He is said to have been crucified. Thus passed away one of the "pillars" of the Church. Gal. 2, 9.

CHAPTER 49.

The Two Epistles General of St. Peter.

FIRST EPISTLE.

To Whom Written. — "To the elect who are sojourners of the Dispersion in Pontus, Galatia, Cap-pa-do'-ci-a, Asia [the Province of Asia], and Bi-thyn'-i-a." Chap. 1, 1 (R. V.). Pon'-tus was a Roman province south of the Black Sea and north of the province of Cap-pa-do'-ci-a. Ga-la'-tia was a province southwest of Pon'-tus. Cappadocia, the largest ancient province in Asia Minor, lay south of Pontus. Bithynia lay across from Constantinople. (See map.) The Christian churches in these four provinces of Asia Minor had been founded by Paul and his associates. Paul was now probably on his last great missionary journey, which took him to Spain; during his absence St. Peter looked after these churches and sent them this letter. He addresses his Christian readers as "sojourners of the Dispersion." They were dispersed here and there among the heathen of those provinces. The designation "sojourners," "sojourners and pilgrims" (chap. 2, 11), is to remind them that earth is not their home, that they are here only for a while, that they are on their way to the heavenly Canaan.

WHEN AND WHERE WRITTEN. — St. Peter wrote this epistle at Babylon. Chap. 5, 13. There is no evidence to prove that he ever was in the city of Babylon on the Eu-phra´-tes; hence the name must probably be taken figuratively. Babylon was the cruel oppressor of God's people in the Old Testament. In the New Testament, Rome became the seat of cruelty and oppression of the people of God. Here the first great bloody persecution of the Christians under Nero had broken out about two years before St. Peter wrote this epistle. Babylon here signifies Rome. St. Peter died a martyr's death at Rome in 67 or early in 68. Hence he probably wrote this letter in 66. He sent it by Sil-va´-nus (Silas), a former companion of Paul. Chap. 5, 12.

THE OCCASION. — The Christians of Asia Minor to whom this letter was addressed were "in heaviness through manifold temptations," or trials. Chap. 1, 6; 4, 12. Again and again the apostle speaks of their sufferings. In fact, there is no other apostolic writing that treats of the sufferings of the Christians so extensively as does this letter. What was the nature of these sufferings? There is nothing in our epistle to indicate that the Christians of Asia Minor were at the time enduring physical or legal persecutions. The persecutions to which they were being subjected were rather social, proceeding from suspicion and ill will on the part of the non-Christian members of the community.

They were reproached for the name of Christ. Chap. 4, 14. They suffered for their religion, as Christians. Chap. 4, 16. The unbelievers spoke evil of them, as of evil-doers. Chap. 2, 12; 3, 16; 4, 4. That was a fiery trial. Chap. 4, 12. In view of these afflictions St. Peter sent them this comforting and encouraging letter.

PURPOSE OF THE LETTER. — St. Peter himself states the object of his letter in these words: "I have written unto you briefly, exhorting and testifying that this is the true grace of God; stand ye fast therein." Chap. 5, 12 (R. V.). The whole letter abounds in exhortation and admonition. Again and again the apostle exhorts and admonishes his Christian readers to lead a godly life and thus to disprove the suspicion and slander that they are evil-doers.

But they were also in great need of comfort and encouragement. This St. Peter freely weaves into his exhortation and admonition. He assures them that their sufferings are for their good and for the glory of God. He tells them that their experience is nothing strange and unusual, but that the same afflictions are accomplished in their brethren that are in the world, and that they should really rejoice, inasmuch as they were partakers of Christ's sufferings. He reminds them that their sufferings shall last but a while and that hereafter in heaven they shall enjoy great and eternal salvation. Thus he illumes their dark night of sufferings with the bright rays of Christian hope. St. Peter has often and truly been called "the Apostle of Hope."

Luther's matchless explanation of the Second Article of the Creed rests on chap. 1, 18. 19: "Ye were not redeemed with corruptible things, as silver and gold, from your vain conversation received by tradition from your fathers, but with the precious blood of Christ."

SUMMARY OF CONTENTS. — I. Address and Salutation. Chap. 1, 1. 2. — II. Christian Suffering and Conduct in the Light of

Full Salvation. Chaps. 1, 3—2, 10: St. Peter thanks God for the living hope of the great salvation in Christ which his readers shall enjoy in heaven after their brief sufferings here below. He exhorts them accordingly to a holy conversation in general, because He that called them is holy and a just Judge and because Christ has redeemed them at such great cost. They should love one another with a pure heart fervently because they are now born anew by the living Word of God. Things conflicting with such love are laid aside, and progress in love is promoted by a diligent use of the Word of God. The Christians are a holy temple, built on Christ, the precious Corner-stone, by the grace of God; "ye are a chosen generation, a royal priesthood, a holy nation, a peculiar people" (a people for God's own possession); therefore you should thank Him with your lips and your lives. — *III. Proper Conduct before Pagans.* Chap. 2, 11—3, 17: The apostle beseeches his readers to abstain from fleshly lusts and to lead a decent life among their evil-speaking heathen neighbors; they should be law-abiding citizens, obedient servants, chaste and respectful wives, sensible husbands. He exhorts all to unity, love, and peace. — *IV. Comfort for Such as Suffer for Well-doing and Exhortation to Cease from Sin.* Chap. 3, 18—4, 19. — *V. Divers Exhortations to the Elders and to the Younger.* Doxology. Greetings. Chap. 5.

SECOND EPISTLE.

St. Peter addressed this epistle to the same readers as the former one. Chap. 3, 1. He wrote it when he knew that the putting off of his tabernacle was coming swiftly. Chap. 1, 14. This would make the year 67 the probable date of writing and Rome the place of writing.

In his First Epistle, St. Peter sought to guard the Christians against dangers from without the Church; in this Second Epistle he guards them against dangers from within the Church, resulting from erroneous beliefs and evil practises. The dangers arose 1) from false teachers, 2) from scoffers, or mockers. Certain false teachers, who are characterized chap. 2, were enticing unsteadfast souls, promising them liberty, while they themselves were slaves of corruption. The scoffers referred to mocked at the belief in the coming of Christ to judge the quick and the dead at the end of the world. These dangers led the apostle to write this letter, in which he intended to put the readers on their guard against those teachers of error and those mockers.

SUMMARY OF CONTENTS. — *I. Address and Salutation.* Chap. 1, 1. 2. — *II. Exhortations to Progress in Christian Life.* Chap. 1: St. Peter urges his readers to give all diligence, in the strength of God's promises and of fellowship with God, to add one Christian grace to another and thus to show that they are not idle and unfruitful as to the knowledge of our Lord Jesus Christ, and also to make their calling and election sure. He is careful to put them in remembrance of these things, knowing that his death is at hand. What he and his fellow-apostles had made known to them concerning Christ is absolutely certain and true; for they had seen Christ's majesty and had heard the voice of God from heaven testifying, "This is My beloved Son"; and the prophets of the Old Testament bore trustworthy witness of Christ. — *III. Warning against False Teachers.* Chap. 2: False teachers shall arise among the Christians, who shall privily and for their own gain bring in destructive heresies, and many shall follow their lascivious doings. These false and ungodly teachers shall certainly be punished. The impurity, presumption, railing, and covetousness of these teachers of error. — *IV. Certainty of Christ's Second Coming.* Chap. 3: St. Peter tells how the scoffers mock at the promise of Christ's coming. Just as certainly as the world was once destroyed by water, it shall be destroyed by fire on the Day of Judgment. The delay of the Lord's judicial advent is only apparent. First, "one day is with the Lord as a thousand years, and a thousand years as one day." Secondly, "the Lord is not slack concerning His promise, as some men count slackness; but is long-suffering to us-ward, not willing that any should perish, but that all should come to repentance." The Day of the Lord will come, and that suddenly, when least expected. The manner how the world shall be destroyed on the Last Day. We should, therefore, lead a holy life. Warning against wresting the epistles of Paul and against being led away with the error of the wicked. Doxology. Chap. 3.

CHAPTER 50.

The Three Epistles of John. — The Epistle of Jude.

FIRST EPISTLE OF JOHN.

Besides his gospel the Apostle John also wrote three epistles. The first of these is a general epistle, while the second and the third are addressed to individuals. From the tone in which John speaks to the readers of the First Epistle it appears that he was well known to them and they to him. It is generally supposed that they were members of Christian churches in Asia Minor. These churches had been founded by Paul or his associates. But after Paul had died a martyr's death at Rome, A. D. 67, and before the destruction of Jerusalem, John left the latter city and went to Eph´-e-sus in Asia Minor. During the remaining thirty-odd years of his life he had the oversight of the churches in Asia Minor. He probably wrote his first epistle from Ephesus about the year 95, he being the only surviving apostle. The tone of the letter (also of the second and third letters) is such as would befit an aged apostle addressing men of a later generation ("my little children," etc.).

The churches to whom the first epistle is addressed were exposed to the seductions of false teachers, whom John calls antichrists = opponents of Christ. Chap. 2, 18—26; 4, 1—6. They denied that Jesus is the Son of God and the Savior of the world and also led the people to think of sin but lightly. This was incipient *Gnosticism*. (Gnosticism = a kind of "philosophy" in the first ages of Christianity. The name is derived from the Greek word *gnosis* = knowledge. The Gnostics pretended to a higher knowledge than that possessed by the ordinary believer in the Bible, but did not trouble themselves much about their conduct. Indeed, there were many things commonly regarded as bad which the true Gnostic would not shun, but seek, as a means of enlarging his experience. Such teaching made righteousness of no account in comparison with knowledge; it also made the work of Christ of no account, for there could be no need of an atonement if there were no real evil in sin.) To warn his readers against those particular teachers and their false teachings, John wrote this epistle, in which he points out that holiness of life, particularly love of the brethren, must necessarily be adjoined to true faith.

Luther says in his preface to this epistle: "Having in his gospel taught faith, St. John now in this epistle opposes such as boasted of faith without works, teaching us in various ways that works do not remain absent where there is faith; but if they do remain absent, faith is not genuine, but a lie and darkness."

SUMMARY OF CONTENTS. — *I. Introduction.* Chap. 1, 1—4. Subject-matter and purpose of the epistle. — *II. God Is Light.* Chap. 1, 5—2, 29: Walking in the light means fellowship with God and with the brethren; consciousness and confession of sin; keeping God's commandments. Walking in the light excludes hatred of the brethren, love of the world, and following false teachers. — *III. God Is Love.* Chap. 3, 1—5, 12: We are called children of God by the singular love of God. The evidence of sonship: righteousness and brotherly love. Warnings not to believe all teachers who boast of the Spirit. Exhortation to believers to love one another and to be like God, who is Love and in His love sent His Son to be our Savior. Faith in Christ is the source of love. The witnesses of our faith. — *IV. Conclusion.* Chap. 5, 13—21.

SECOND EPISTLE OF JOHN.

This letter is addressed "unto the elect lady and her children." Some take these words in a figurative sense as the designation of a church and its members. But since the words taken as they read make excellent sense, the figurative interpretation is forbidden. The word translated "lady" is Kuria, which may have been the name of this Christian matron. St. John congratulates her on the con-

sistent Christian conduct of her children. V. 4. He beseeches her to walk after God's commandments, loving God
and her fellow-Christians, and then warns her against the
insidious and corrupting influence of certain false teachers
who were going about denying the reality of Christ's coming in the flesh, of Christ's humanity. He tells her how to
treat teachers who abide not in the doctrine (teaching) of
Christ: "If there come any unto you and bring not this
doctrine, receive him not into your house, neither bid him
Godspeed; for he that biddeth him Godspeed is partaker of
his evil deeds." Here we are forbidden to aid false
teachers 1) by our hospitality, 2) by wishing them success.
This reminds us of the story of St. John and Ce-rin'-thus,
a false teacher who had come to Ephesus. Finding Cerinthus in a public bath, the apostle immediately left the place,
saying to those about him, "Let us flee home, lest even the
bath fall on us, because Cerinthus, that enemy of the
truth, is within."

THIRD EPISTLE OF JOHN.

Like the two preceding epistles, this also was probably
written about A. D. 95 from Ephesus. The aged apostle
wrote it to "the well-beloved Ga'-ius," who was a sincere
and charitable member of the Church. Vv. 1—6. While
commending Gaius for his piety and his hospitality shown
to strangers who were traveling as Christian missionaries,
John complains of the factious and intolerant conduct of
an arrogant and ambitious ecclesiastic named Di-ot'-re-phes,
who had gone so far as to close his doors on "the brethren"
whom the apostle had sent with a letter to the church, and
excommunicated the members who had taken them in.
The aged apostle writes that he will attend to this case
when he visits the church. De-me'-tri-us, apparently the
bearer of this third epistle, is a trustworthy man. The
apostle hopes soon to visit Gaius, when they will have a talk.

CHAPTER 51.

The General Epistle of Jude.

This last of the epistles as we have them in our New Testament was written by "Jude [Judas], the servant [apostle] of Jesus Christ and brother of James" (the Less, the writer of the epistle that bears his name). It is a "catholic," or general, epistle, written to no individual church or Christian, but in general "to them that are sanctified by [in] God the Father and preserved in [kept for] Jesus Christ, and called." Christians in Palestine are supposed to have been the recipients. The date of writing is somewhat uncertain. However, the letter shows a marked resemblance to 2 Pet. 2, 10 ff., which suggests the idea that it was probably written later than Second Peter (A. D. 66). Again, Jerusalem was destroyed A. D. 70. The fact that St. Jude does not mention this greatest of divine visitations among those found in his letter justifies the inference that it was written prior to that great event, probably in the year 68.

St. Jude exhorts his readers to *contend earnestly for the faith* which was once for all delivered unto the saints, seeing that false teachers had crept in unawares to seduce them. He sharply denounces these teachers and predicts that dreadful judgments will be inflicted on them. He shows how the believers should keep themselves safe and recover others out of the snares of those deceivers. The epistle closes with one of the most beautiful doxologies to be found in the New Testament. Origen, a learned Christian writer, who lived between A. D. 186 and 253, says: "Jude wrote an epistle consisting of few lines, indeed, but filled with the vigorous words of heavenly grace."

"The epistle is remarkable for several allusions to matters of ancient history that are not recorded in the Old Testament. In v. 14 we have a quotation from an a-poc´-

ry-phal book of Enoch (of which several copies of an Ethiopian version were brought from Abyssinia by the traveler Bruce in 1773); and v. 9 seems to have been derived from a book called 'The Assumption of Moses,' only a small part of which has been preserved to us. These allusions are no more at variance with the doctrine of inspiration than the quotations in the Old Testament from the 'Book of Jasher,' etc., Paul's allusions to 'Jannes and Jambres', or his quotations from heathen writers."

CHAPTER 52.

The Revelation of St. John the Divine.

The Angel Reveals to John what is going to happen from the Apostolic Times to the End

THE PROPHETIC BOOK. — Christ conferred upon the Apostolic Church the gift of prophecy. Accordingly, ordinary Christians as well as the apostles predicted future events. Such predictions we found here and there in the doctrinal books of the New Testament, in the epistles. The last book of the New Testament, which forms the subject of our present study, consists almost entirely of prophecy. Chap. 22, 6. 9. 10. It bears the title, "The *Revelation* of St. John the Divine." From the Greek word translated "Revelation" we have the title A-poc'-a-lypse = an unveiling. The veil covering the future is here drawn aside, and "the things which are and the things which shall be hereafter" are shown. Chap. 1, 1. 19; 4, 1; 22, 6. We have here a symbolic history of the fortunes of the Church from the first century to the end of time. In a series of vivid pictures John was shown how the Church would develop, pass through dreadful conflicts with the wicked powers of earth and hell, and ultimately gain the victory.

THE AUTHOR. — The writer repeatedly calls himself *John.* Chap. 1, 1. 4. 9; 21, 2; 22, 8. That he is the *Apostle* John is pointed out by the surname "the Divine." (The

the Epistle was sent to seven churches in Ephesus

Greek word translated Divine is *theo-log'-os* = one who knows God and divine things and discourses about them.)

WHERE JOHN RECEIVED THE REVELATION. — He states: "I, John, was in the isle that is called Pat'-mos." Chap. 1, 9. Patmos is one of the innumerable little islands which lie in the southeastern Ae-ge'-an Sea, off the cost of Asia Minor. It is about twenty-five miles distant from Mi-le'-tus on the mainland, and Eph'-e-sus is about the same distance north of Miletus. The island is quite small, only about twenty-five miles in circumference, mountainous and almost barren. It was used by the Romans as a place of exile for criminals. To this lonely little island John had been banished by the Roman Emperor "for the Word of God and the testimony of Jesus." Chap. 1, 9. In the side of the high hill, near the little town of La Scala, on the eastern side of Patmos, a grotto is pointed out to travelers which tradition assigns as the place where the exiled apostle saw and recorded his prophetic visions.

WHEN DID JOHN RECEIVE THE REVELATION? — He writes: "I was in the spirit on the Lord's Day" = Sunday. Chap. 1, 10. On this particular Lord's Day, John was "in the spirit." He uses the same expression chap. 4, 2; 17, 3; 21, 10. With this expression he wishes to point out that he was in an extraordinary state or condition. Therefore he does not mean the Holy Spirit in this place, for he was in the Holy Spirit, like all other Christians, at all times. The word *spirit* here signifies the *human* spirit, the soul, the mind. On this particular Sunday, John was in his mind *only*, that is to say, his mind, or inner life, was separate from the whole range of sensuous perceptions; he was entirely wrapped up in what occurred in his mind only, and so he could be with his thoughts in another place while his mind and body were on Patmos. Chap. 17, 3; 21, 10.

DATE OF WRITING. — John was directed by the Lord to

commit to writing what he had seen and heard in the spirit. Chap. 1, 1. 19. But it is not clearly stated whether or not he wrote the entire book at once or after he had left the island and returned to Eph'-e-sus. From chap. 1, 11 and 10, 4 it would appear that he wrote it immediately while still an exile in Patmos. When was this? Ancient tradition informs us that John was condemned to Patmos during a persecution under the Roman Emperor Do-mi'-tian, who reigned from A. D. 81 to 96. Accordingly, many surmise that the A-poc'-a-lypse was written about A. D. 90.

To Whom Written. — "To the seven churches which are in Asia." Chap. 1, 4. This Asia was a Roman province in Asia Minor. The seven churches are named chap. 1, 11: Eph'-e-sus, Smyr'-na, Per'-ga-mos, Thy-a-ti'-ra, Sar'-dis, Phi-la-del'-phi-a, and La-od-i-ce'-a. These churches were in the vicinity of the city of Ephesus, where St. John lived and labored till his death. The book was intended to be read to the seven churches. Chap. 1, 3. Like all the books of the New Testament the Book of Revelation met an immediate need on the part of those to whom it was addressed. But it was far more than a pamphlet for the times. The Book of Revelation is intended for *all* times.

Its Purpose. — The A-poc'-a-lypse was designed to be a book of consolation for the children of God in the manifold trials and tribulations which were to come upon the Christian Church till the end of time. And very well does the book meet this purpose of consolation. The prophecy of the ultimate triumph of the kingdom of God over all hostile forces of earth and hell, the promise of the coming of Christ, the pictures of heaven with its glory and its joys, have been a source of cheer and comfort and courage to millions of Christians.

A Book of Unique Character. — God *signified* the revelation by His angel unto His servant John, that is,

He represented it by signs, or symbols. Chap. 1, 1. Accordingly, the book contains a succession of symbols in which the actual meaning is set forth with striking impressiveness. In this regard the prophecy of Revelation closely resembles the prophecies contained in the second part of E-ze′-ki-el's book and in the visions of Daniel. About fifty symbols are interpreted: Chap. 1, 20; 4, 5; 5, 6. 8; 12, 9; 16, 13. 14; 17, 18; 19, 8; 20, 14, etc. Many of the rest of the symbols remain more or less inexplicable. It is not possible to be sure about the meaning of all such images as the seals, the vials, the horses, the scorpions, etc. Only time can make these symbols plain by their fulfilment. In spite of the symbols that are difficult of interpretation, the general scope of the book is intelligible to all readers of average human intelligence.

RULES TO BE REMEMBERED BY THE READER. — The Revelation is a symbolic history of the fortunes of the Christian Church from the first century of the Christian Era to the end of time. This does not mean, however, that the events are recorded in chronological order from chapter to chapter. In the prophecy of this book, as in Old Testament prophecies, we have 1. anticipation, 2. repetition and amplification, 3. recapitulation. STOP

1. *Anticipation.* Christ's coming to Judgment will be the end of time. Yet this end is anticipated at the very opening, chap. 1, 7: "Behold, He cometh with clouds; and every eye shall see Him."

2. *Repetition and amplification.* Prophecies often repeat substantially the same things in successive pictures to show them from a different point of view and to set them forth more clearly and impressively. Take the example of Christ's coming to Judgment and the end of the world, which is the main subject of the book. Having introduced this subject at the outset in chap. 1, 7, John comes back to it

again and again, each time adding something new. Chap.
6, 12—17; 10; 11, 15—19; 20, 11—15.

3. *Recapitulation.*   After unfolding the events, the
writer, before closing, often pauses to give a summary of
what has been revealed.   Such a recapitulation is found
chap. 20.

THE "MILLENNIUM." — In the first seven verses of
chap. 20 the expression "a thousand years" is found six
times.   From this expression has been formed the Latin
word *mil-len'-ni-um* = a thousand years' time.   The Greek
word for a thousand is *chil'-i-oi,* from which we have Chil'-
i-ast and Chil'-i-asm.   Chiliast is the term applied to those
who take these thousand years in a literal sense as meaning
years of 365 days each.   They believe that a thousand
calendar years before Judgment Day, or the end of the
world, Christ will return visibly to establish a visible kingdom on earth.   Simultaneously with His coming, they believe, there is to be a resurrection of the martyrs and other
saints, while the resurrection of the remainder of mankind
is not to take place till the end of the world.   The saints
will reign with Him on earth a thousand years, ruling over
the ungodly in particular and enjoying peace, prosperity,
and happiness.   This millennium they imagine to be a
golden age, a universal blooming-time and glory for the
Church, a Sabbath of peaceful and blissful security and
prosperity for the Church this side of Judgment Day.   All
this is an iridescent dream.   It does violence to the text and
contradicts clear statements of Christ and His apostles.

—— 1. The text does not state that Christ and His saints
will reign *visibly* on the earth.   The Chiliasts import this
into the text.

——2. Christ teaches that there shall be but one bodily
resurrection of both saints and sinners on the Last Day.
"The hour is coming in which *all* that are in the graves

shall hear His voice and shall come forth; they that have done good, unto the resurrection of life, and they that have done evil, unto the resurrection of damnation." John 5, 28. 29.

— 3. Christ and His apostles teach throughout that His Church on earth will never be without trouble and affliction so long as the earth shall stand. John 16, 33; Acts 14, 22, etc.

The words "a thousand years" must be taken in a figurative sense as denoting an indefinitely long period of time. The millennium must not be placed in the future. It began nearly 2,000 years ago, when Christ ascended into heaven, is here now, and will end "a little season" before His coming to Judgment.

LUTHER'S REFORMATION PREDICTED. — Chap. 14, 6—12 we have a prophecy of Luther's Reformation of the Church. Can you point out how the prophecy fits the great Reformer and his work?

SUMMARY OF CONTENTS. — *I. Prolog.* Chap. 1, 1—3. — *II. The Seven Messages to the Seven Churches.* Chap. 1, 4—3, 22. *III. The Fortunes of the Church on Earth.* Chaps. 4—20: Preliminary vision of heaven and the heavenly worship, chaps. 4 and 5; the seven seals, chaps. 6 and 7; the seven trumpets, chaps. 8—11; the connected visions of the woman, the dragon, the first and the second beast, and Babylon, chaps. 12—14; the seven vials of wrath, chaps. 15 and 16; the harlot and Babylon, chaps, 17—19; recapitulation, chap. 20. — *IV. Ultimate Victory and Glory of the Church.* Chap. 21, 1—22, 5. — *V. Epilog.* Chap. 22, 6—21.

How to Read the Bible in Three Years.

Comparatively few people read the whole Bible. More would probably read it in its entirety if a practical plan were submitted to them. The following plan might be called a continuous Bible calendar. It shows a Scripture-lesson for every day in the year for three consecutive years.

NOTE. — Such as purpose to read the whole Bible in one year must read three chapters every day.

JANUARY

January	Genesis Chapters	1 Chronicles Chapters	Matthew Chapters
1	1	1	1
2	2	2	2
3	3	3	3
4	4	4	4
5	5	5	5
6	6	6	6
7	7	7	7
8	8	8	8
9	9	9	9
10	10	10	10
11	11	11	11
12	12	12	12
13	13	13	13
14	14	14	14
15	15	15	15
16	16	16	16
17	17	17	17
18	18	18	18
19	19	19. 20	19
20	20	21	20
21	21	22	21
22	22	23	22
23	23	24	23
24	24	25	24
25	25	26	25
26	26	27	26
27	27	28	27
28	28	29	28
		2 Chronicles	Mark
29	29	1	1
30	30	2	2
31	31	3	3

FEBRUARY

February	Genesis Chapters	2 Chronicles Chapters	Mark Chapters
1	32	4	4
2	33	5	5
3	34	6	6
4	35	7	7
5	36	8	8
6	37	9	9
7	38	10	10
8	39	11	11
9	40	12	12
10	41	13	13
11	42	14	14
12	43	15	15
13	44	16	16
			Luke
14	45	17	1
15	46	18	2
16	47	19	3
17	48	20	4
18	49	21	5
19	50	22	6
	Exodus		
20	1	23	7
21	2	24	8
22	3	25	9
23	4	26, 1–15	10
24	5	26, 16–23	11
25	6	27	12
26	7	28	13
27	8	29	14
28	9	30	15
29	10	31	16

Thy Word is everlasting truth;
How pure is every page!
That holy Book shall guide our youth
And well support our age.

MARCH

March	Exodus Chapters	2 Chronicles Chapters	Luke Chapters
1	11	32	17
2	12	33	18
3	13	34	19
4	14	35	20
5	15	36	21
		Ezra	
6	16	1	22
7	17	2	23
8	18	3	24
			John
9	19	4	1
10	20	5	2
11	21	6	3
12	22	7	4
13	23	8	5
14	24	9	6
15	25	10	7
		Nehemiah	
16	26	1	8
17	27	2	9
18	28	3	10
19	29	4	11
20	30	5	12
21	31	6	13
22	32	7	14
23	33	8	15
24	34	9	16
25	35	10	17
26	36	11	18
27	37	12	19
28	38	13	20
		Esther	
29	39	1	21
			Acts
30	40	2	1
	Leviticus		
31	1	3	2

Father of Mercies, in Thy Word
What endless glory shines!
Forever be Thy name adored
For these celestial lines.

APRIL

April	Leviticus Chapters	Esther Chapters	Acts Chapters
1	2	4	3
2	3	5	4
3	4	6	5
4	5	7	6
5	6	8	7
6	7	9	8
7	8	10	9
		Job	
8	9	1	10
9	10	2	11
10	11	3	12
11	12	4	13
12	13	5	14
13	14	6	15
14	15	7	16
15	16	8	17
16	17	9	18
17	18	10	19
18	19	11	20
19	20	12	21
20	21	13	22
21	22	14	23
22	23	15	24
23	24	16	25
24	25	17	26
25	26	18	27
26	27	19	28
	Numbers		Psalms
27	1	20	1. 2
28	2	21	3–5
29	3	22	6–8
30	4	23	9. 10

The Law of the Lord is perfect,
  converting the soul;
The testimony of the Lord is sure,
  making wise the simple.
The statutes of the Lord are right,
  rejoicing the heart,
The commandment of the Lord is pure,
  enlightening the eyes. — Ps. 19, 7. 8.

MAY

May	Numbers Chapters	Job Chapters	Psalms Chapters
1	5	24	11–13
2	6	25	14–16
3	7	26	17
4	8	27	18
5	9	28	19–21
6	10	29	22
7	11	30	23–25
8	12	31	26–28
9	13	32	29. 30
10	14	33	31
11	15	34	32
12	16	35	33
13	17	36	34
14	18	37	35
15	19	38	36
16	20	39	37
17	21	40	38
18	22	41	39. 40
19	23	42	41–43
		Proverbs	
20	24	1	44
21	25	2	45
22	26	3	46–48
23	27	4	49
24	28	5	50
25	29	6	51. 52
26	30	7	53–55
27	31	8	56. 57
28	32	9	58. 59
29	33	10	60. 61
30	34	11	62. 63
31	35	12. 13	64. 65

I have not departed from Thy judgments,
For Thou hast taught me.
How sweet are Thy words to my taste!
Yea, sweeter than honey to my mouth!
Through Thy precepts I get understanding,
Therefore I hate every false way.
Thy Word is a lamp unto my feet
And a light unto my path. — *Ps. 119, 102 ff.*

JUNE

June	Numbers Chapters	Proverbs Chapters	Psalms Chapters
1	36	14	66. 67
	Deuteronomy		
2	1	15	68
3	2	16	69
4	3	17. 18	70. 71
5	4	19	72
6	5	20	73
7	6	21	74
8	7	22	75. 76
9	8	23	77
10	9	24	78
11	10	25	79. 80
12	11	26	81. 82
13	12	27	83. 84
14	13	28	85. 86
15	14	29	87. 88
16	15	30	89
17	16	31	90. 91
		Ecclesiastes	
18	17	1	92. 93
19	18	2	94. 95
20	19	3	96. 97
21	20	4	98. 99
22	21	5. 6	100. 101
23	22	7	102
24	23	8	103
25	24	9	104
26	25	10	105
27	26	11. 12	106
		Song of Solomon	
28	27	1. 2	107
29	28	3. 4	108. 109
30	29	5. 6	110—112

Thy testimonies are wonderful;
Therefore doth my soul keep them.
The entrance of Thy words giveth light;
It giveth understanding unto the simple.

Ps. 119, 129. 130.

JULY

July	Deuteronomy Chapters	Song of Solomon Chapters	Psalms Chapters
1	30	7	113. 114
2	31	8	115. 116
		Isaiah	
3	32	1	117. 118
4	33	2	119, 1—40
5	34	3	119, 41—80
	Joshua		
6	1	4	119, 81—128
7	2	5	119, 129—176
8	3	6	120—124
9	4	7	125—127
10	5	8	128—130
11	6	9	131—134
12	7	10	135. 136
13	8	11	137—139
14	9	12	140—142
15	10	13	143. 144
16	11	14	145—147
17	12	15	148—150
			Romans
18	13	16	1
19	14	17	2
20	15	18	3
21	16	19	4
22	17	20	5
23	18	21	6
24	19	22	7
25	20	23	8
26	21	24	9
27	22	25	10
28	23	26	11
29	24	27	12
	Judges		
30	1	28	13
31	2	29	14

I rejoice at Thy Word
As one that findeth great spoil.
I hate and abhor lying,
But Thy Law do I love. — *Ps. 119, 162 f.*

AUGUST

August	Judges Chapters	Isaiah Chapters	Romans Chapters
1	3	30	15
2	4	31	16
			1 Corinthians
3	5	32.	1
4	6	33	2
5	7	34	3
6	8	35	4
7	9	36	5
8	10	37	6
9	11	38	7
10	12	39	8
11	13	40	9
12	14	41	10
13	15	42	11
14	16	43	12
15	17	44	13
16	18	45	14
17	19	46	15
18	20	47	16
			2 Corinthians
19	21	48	1
	Ruth		
20	1	49	2
21	2	50	3
22	3	51	4
23	4	52	5
	1 Samuel		
24	1	53	6
25	2	54	7
26	3	55	8
27	4	56	9
28	5	57	10
29	6	58	11
30	7	59	12
31	8	60	13

Let my cry come near before Thee, O Lord;
Give me understanding according to Thy Word.
My lips shall utter praise
When Thou hast taught me Thy statutes.

Ps. 119, 169 f.

SEPTEMBER

September	1 Samuel Chapters	Isaiah Chapters	Galatians Chapters
1	9	61	1
2	10	62	2
3	11	63	3
4	12	64	4
5	13	65	5
6	14	66	6
		Jeremiah	Ephesians
7	15	1	1
8	16	2	2
9	17	3	3
10	18	4	4
11	19	5	5
12	20	6	6
			Philippians
13	21	7	1
14	22	8	2
15	23	9	3
16	24	10	4
			Colossians
17	25	11	1
18	26	12	2
19	27	13	3
20	28	14	4
			1 Thessalonians
21	29	15	1
22	30	16	2
23	31	17	3
	2 Samuel		
24	1	18	4
25	2	19	5
			2 Thessalonians
26	3	20	1
27	4	21	2
28	5	22	3
			1 Timothy
29	6	23	1
30	7	24	2

Thy Word doth move the inmost heart,
Thy Word doth perfect health impart,
Thy Word my soul with joy doth bless,
Thy Word brings peace and blessedness.

OCTOBER

October	2 Samuel Chapters	Jeremiah Chapters	1 Timothy Chapters
1	8	25	3
2	9	26	4
3	10	27	5
4	11	28	6
			2 Timothy
5	12	29	1
6	13	30	2
7	14	31	3
8	15	32	4
			Titus
9	16	33	1
10	17	34	2
11	18	35	3
12	19	36	Philemon
			Hebrews
13	20	37	1
14	21	38	2
15	22	39	3
16	23	40	4
17	24	41	5
	1 Kings		
18	1	42	6
19	2	43	7
20	3	44	8
21	4	45	9
22	5	46	10
23	6	47	11
24	7	48	12
25	8	49	13
			James
26	9	50	1
27	10	51	2
28	11	52	3
		Lamentations	
29	12	1	4
30	13	2	5
			1 Peter
31	14	3	1

Abide, O dear Redeemer,
Among us with Thy Word
And thus now and hereafter
True peace and joy afford.

NOVEMBER

November	1 Kings Chapters	Lamentations Chapters	1 Peter Chapters
1	15	4	2
2	16	5	3
		Ezekiel	
3	17	1	4
4	18	2	5
			2 Peter
5	19	3	1
6	20	4	2
7	21	5	3
			1 John
8	22	6	1
	2 Kings		
9	1	7	2
10	2	8	3
11	3	9	4
12	4	10	5
13	5	11	2 John
14	6	12	3 John
15	7	13	Jude
			Micah
16	8	14	1. 2
17	9	15	3. 4
18	10	16	5. 6
19	11	17	7
			Nahum
20	12	18	1. 2
21	13	19	3
			Habakkuk
22	14	20	1
23	15	21	2
24	16	22	3
			Zephaniah
25	17	23	1. 2
26	18	24	3
			Haggai
27	19	25	1. 2
			Zechariah
28	20	26	1
29	21	27	2. 3
30	22	28	4. 5

Open Thou mine eyes
That I may behold wondrous things out of Thy Law.
Ps. 119, 18.

DECEMBER

December	2 Kings Chapters	Ezekiel Chapters	Zechariah Chapters
1	23	29	6. 7
2	24	30	8
3	25	31	9
	Hosea		
4	1	32	10. 11
5	2	33	12. 13
6	3. 4	34	14
			Malachi
7	5	35	1
8	6	36	2
9	7	37	3. 4
			Revelation
10	8	38	1
11	9	39	2
12	10	40	3
13	11	41	4
14	12	42	5
15	13	43	6
16	14	44	7
	Joel		
17	1	45	8
18	2	46	9
19	3	47	10
	Amos		
20	1	48	11
		Daniel	
21	2	1	12
22	3	2	13
23	4	3	14
24	5	4	15
25	6	5	16
26	7	6	17
27	8	7. 8	18
28	9	9	19
	Obadiah		
29	1	10	20
	Jonah		
30	1. 2	11	21
31	3. 4	12	22

We have also a more sure word of prophecy, whereunto ye do well that ye take heed as unto a light that shineth in a dark place, until the day dawn and the Day-star arise in your hearts.

2 Pet. 1, 19.

INDEX.

[232]

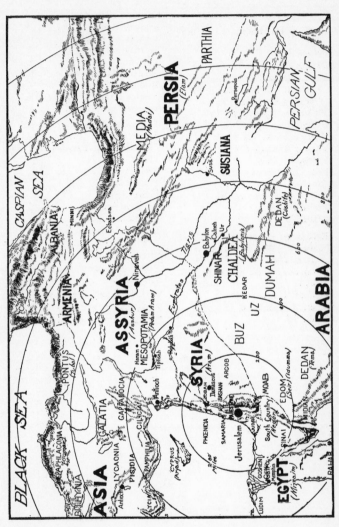

Map No. 1.

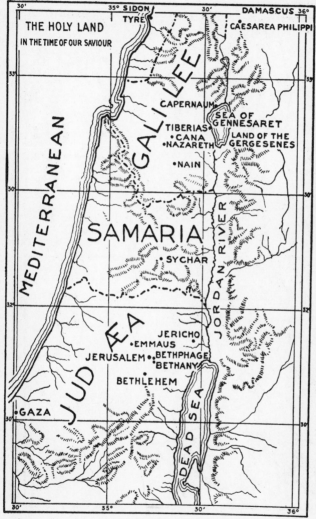

Map No. 2. Palestine in the Time of Christ.

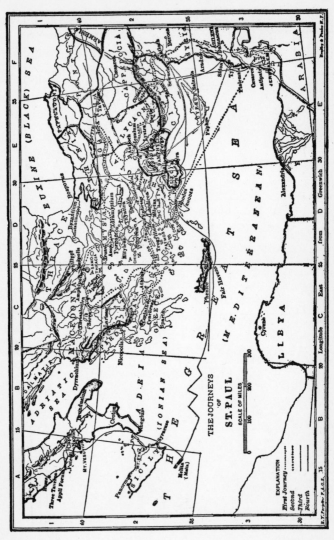

Map No. 3.